Bengal Famine

An Unpunished Genocide

Bengal Famine
An Unpunished Genocide

A Commentary on
SYAMA PRASAD MOOKERJEE'S
Panchasher Manwantar

Translated from Bengali & Edited by
Sudip Kar Purkayastha

Vitasta
LET KNOWLEDGE SPREAD

Published by
Renu Kaul Verma
Vitasta Publishing Pvt Ltd
2/15, Ansari Road, Daryaganj
New Delhi - 110 002
info@vitastapublishing.com

ISBN 978-93-90961-02-3

First Edition 2022

MRP ₹695

Edited by Papri Sri Raman
Cover by Somesh Kumar Mishra
Layout by Ram Kumar
Printed by Vikas Computer and Printers

Dedicated to Bengal and her countless children whose lives and dignity were destroyed by one of the worst crimes against humanity, a making of colonial-communal regimes, called the Bengal Famine of 1943-44

The Famine

When famine ravaged the city,
Lord Buddha asked his disciples,
one by one,
'Who amongst you would take on
the task of feeding the hungry?'
Merchant Ratnakar lowered his head.
With folded hands, he said softly:
'The hunger of this city is enormous.
I have not the resources.'
The Minister rose:
'I would have accepted the Lord's command
if giving my own blood would help.
There are no grains in my pantry.'
The landlord sighed.
'My golden fields are barren. I cannot even pay my taxes.'
Each turned to face another,
searching for answers.
In that silent chamber,
Upon that city in pain,
Buddha's warm glance shone on like an evening star.

Then spoke a young woman, an ascetic.
'I will take this on, my Lord', she said gently.
'Those who cry without grains are my children.
The task of distributing grains to this city is mine.'
The audience froze at her audacity.
'You are a beggar. Why such arrogance?
How can you take this on?
What do you have?'
She bowed and humbly held out her bowl of alms.
'Here – this is what I have.
I have nothing,
thus I will get all your blessings without reservation.
I will beg for grains from door to door, and
you will each give me what you have.
If you wish, my bowl will never empty.
I will save the city with the alms you shower upon me.
I will quell the hunger that pains my Lord.'

—A translation of Rabindranath Tagore's
Nagor Lokkhi by Sramana Mitra

Contents

Syama Prasad Mookerjee

A Life Sketch

Syama Prasad Mookerjee was born in a very well-known Calcutta family on 6 July 1901. He was the son of Jogamaya Devi and Sir Ashutosh Mookerjee. Sir Ashutosh was a Bengali nationalist, educator, physicist and mathematician, barrister, jurist who was not only a very respected judge of the Calcutta High Court but rose to be the Vice Chancellor of the University of Calcutta from 1906 to 1914 and again from 1921 to 1923.

Syama Prasad displayed exceptional academic brilliance as a student. He completed his graduation from the Presidency College, securing first class first rank (1921). He stood first class first again in doing a post-graduation from Calcutta University (1923) and repeated the same feat in the Bachelor of Law examination (1924). He furthered his legal education abroad and was called to the bar at Lincoln's Inn in 1927. He became the Vice Chancellor of Calcutta University in 1934, at the young age of 33 years and held the post till 1938. He was conferred D Litt in the same year by Calcutta University.

Meanwhile, Syama Prasad had entered the Bengal Legislative Council as a Congress candidate in 1929, representing Calcutta University. Following the Congress decision to boycott the Legislative Council, he resigned and got re-elected to the

Council as an independent candidate in 1930. In 1937, he was elected to the Bengal Legislative Assembly from the University constituency. In 1939, he participated in a conference of the All India Hindu Mahasabha, held in Calcutta. That can be seen as important from the viewpoint of his entry into mainstream politics. Next year he was made the president of the Bengal Provincial Hindu Mahasabha and also the executive president of the All India Hindu Mahasabha.

Syama Prasad was also affiliated with the Mahabodhi Society. He was a part of India's struggle to get back Buddhist relics, excavated in Sanchi by Captain Fred C Maisey and Alexander Cunningham in 1849. These were taken back to England and exhibited in museums. In 1939, the Government of British India asked the museums to hand over the relics to the Mahabodhi Society, Kolkata. Finally, after a great deal of negotiations, the relics arrived in Kolkata in 1949, and Prime Minister Nehru handed them over to Syama Prasad Mookerjee, who was then the president of the Mahabodhi Society.

In December 1941, Syama Prasad and Sarat Bose (brother of Netaji Subhas Bose) succeeded in installing the first secular, progressive coalition government in the province, giving people the much-needed respite from the communally surcharged environment that was building under the Muslim League-led ministry in the province since 1937. Syama Prasad served as finance minister in that ministry till November 1942 when he resigned to protest against repeated interventions by Governor Herbert in the ministry's functioning while a severe food crisis threatened to explode in Bengal, bringing a great famine to the fertile land.

During the 1943-44 famine, Syama Prasad waged a courageous battle against the League-British nexus and played a stellar role in providing relief to millions of famine victims in Bengal, cutting across caste and creed. His gallant struggle enhanced his stature in the whole country. In 1946 he was elected as a member of the Constituent Assembly. In early 1947, when the partition of India seemed inevitable and the League-British nexus worked to get the entire province of Bengal within Pakistan, it was Syama Prasad who led a mass movement and succeeded in forcing the authorities to keep the western part of Bengal within India. Syama Prasad can thus be considered as the major driving force behind creation of the present geographical entity known as the State of West Bengal

Syama Prasad served as the Industries and Supplies Minister in the Nehru cabinet during 1947-1950, when he mentored many ground-breaking initiatives. In April 1950, he resigned from the cabinet following serious differences with Prime Minister Nehru over the issue of protection of religious minorities in Pakistan. He founded Bharatiya Jana Sangh in October 1951, which heralded a powerful alternative political narrative before the people of India.

Syama Prasad vehemently opposed the Nehru government's Jammu & Kashmir policy. He attempted to enter J&K without permit on 11 May 1953, demanding scrapping of Article 370, following which he was arrested and detained in Kashmir. He died under mysterious circumstances in detention on 23 June 1953. His death was widely perceived as an outcome of political intrigue and created huge uproar in India. Though he died prematurely at the age of 52, his ideology has emerged as a powerful force in modern India.

Article 370 of the Indian Constitution gave special status to the State of Jammu and Kashmir from 1954 to 31 October 2019, conferring it with the power to have a separate constitution, a State flag and autonomy over the internal administration, unlike other States in India. It was a temporary arrangement that lasted more than half a century. On 5 August 2019, the Government of India issued a Presidential Order and abrogated it.

Chittatosh Mookerjee

Former Chief Justice of Calcutta High Court
and Bombay High Court
M.A., LL.B., D. Litt., (Hons, Causa)

126, Asutosh Mookerjee Road
Kolkata 700 025
Phone: +91 33 2455 7100
E-mail: ammibb@bsnl.in

MESSAGE

Dr. Sudip Kar Purkayastha deserves high praise for his book 'Bengal Famine - An Unpunished Genocide: A Commentary on *Panchasher Manwantar* by Syama Prasad Mookerjee'. The Bengal Famine of 1943-44 continues to be of abiding interest not only because it resulted in loss of millions of human lives but also because the same was caused by deliberate design and mendacity of men then in power in Great Britain and in Bengal Presidency.

The author has, on his own accord, translated Dr. Syama Prasad Mookerjee's Bengali book, *Panchasher Manwantar* (2nd edition), which contained, inter alia, his several speeches, statements, articles, and other writings and reports on famine relief works under his leadership. Dr. Kar Purkayastha has included in his book a brief but excellent appraisal of achievements of Dr. Syama Prasad Mookerjee.

The author has also undertaken considerable research of materials regarding Bengal Famine now available - they substantiate the author's view that the Bengal Famine was in fact a genocide which left a permanent scar on the Bengali society. I consider Dr. Kar Purkayastha's present work an important part of the literature on Bengal Famine 1943-44.

Chittatosh Mookerjee

(Chittatosh Mookerjee)

26th January 2021

Foreword

Dr Syama Prasad Mookerjee's contribution to India's national life is unparallel but unfortunately has largely been ignored or misrepresented.

The academia and intelligentsia who marginalised and suppressed Dr Mookerjee's legacy ensured that generations of Indians and Bengalis grew up without ever hearing of Dr Mookerjee's contribution to cementing India's integration and unity. Generations stayed unaware of his epic effort of launching a massive movement supported by the Hindus of Bengal including the leading thought-leaders of the state for demanding that a portion of Bengal be carved out and retained in the Indian Union. "We must have our own territory where we can live as free men, and build up our own culture, our own social and economic life in accordance with our best tradition,"[1]he said.

A section among the ideology-driven gate-keepers of Indian history have tried to portray the demand for the creation of West Bengal as a motivated move by 'caste Hindus, all belonging to the 'upper class', "*Bhadralok*" intelligentsia, both political and commercial, in order to safeguard their monopolies. But the truth is far removed from such a motivated assessment. In fact, prominent scheduled caste leaders of that era including Babu Jagjivan Ram, Pramatha Rajan Thakur, Radhanath Das, secretary of the Depressed Class League to name a few, actively supported Dr Mookerjee's call for the division of Bengal. That Jinnah was handed over a 'moth-eaten Pakistan' was largely because of Dr Mookerjee's political dexterity mobilisation.

The existence of a portion of Bengal in India is because of Dr Mookerjee's exertion and political sagacity and yet this portion of our history was deftly erased and forgotten.

The story of the Bengal Famine, especially how Dr Mookerjee addressed this gargantuan challenge, disseminated its truth throughout the country and exposed the complicity of the British administration, and the Muslim League government of Bengal in dragging the province through one of the greatest and most calamitous manmade disasters of genocidal proportions of the 20th century needs to be reiterated and widely narrated.

The Bengal famine has been examined in the past, but Dr Mookerjee's role in it has been minimised or distorted. His side of the story as someone involved in the herculean task for providing succor to the victims has been repeatedly brushed aside. It was he who had organised the largest non-official relief effort for the victims of the famine. His appeals elicited a huge response from business leaders and political, religious and social institutions from across the country. Responding to his call for support, a multi-course relief was provided, for days on end, to over a lakh victims of the famine.[2] For a generational reassessment of Dr Mookerjee's role, contribution and legacy, works such as these must have wider dissemination and must generate robust debate and contribute to a narrative course correction. The 75th anniversary of India's independence offers us that opportunity.

Sudip Kar Purkayastha's effort, therefore, needs to be highly commended and comes across as a very timely and much-needed intervention. It shall contribute hugely to the effort being made to re-situate Dr Mookerjee in the national narrative and consciousness. Coming as it does against the backdrop of the 75th year of India's Independence, it is a fitting tribute to one of the greatest patriots and statesmen of modern India.

Dr Anirban Ganguly
Director
Dr Syama Prasad Mookerjee Research Foundation
New Delhi
July 2021

Publisher's Note

> A million and a half of the poor of Bengal fell victim to circumstances for which they themselves were not responsible. Society, together with its organs, failed to protect its weaker members. Indeed there was a moral and social breakdown, as well as an administrative breakdown....
>
> *Famine Inquiry Commission Report on Bengal, p 107*

Famines were many in British India, especially in Bengal whose fertile land was used to grow cash crop in order to sustain the empire. In a period of 90 years from 1765 when the British East India Company took over the *Diwani* of Bengal to 1858, Bengal experienced twelve famines and four severe scarcities. The manner of deaths was terrible in every famine.

> Still fresh in memory's eye the scene I view,
> The shrivelled limbs, sunk eyes, and lifeless hue;
> Still hear the mother's shrieks and infant's moans,
> Cries of despair and agonising groans,
> In wild confusion dead and dying lie;
> Hark to the jackal's yell and vulture's cry,

The dog's fell howl, as midst the glare of day
They riot unmolested on their prey!
Dire scenes of horror, which no pen can trace,
Nor rolling years from memory's page efface.

This poem by John Shore was reproduced by Sir William Wilson Hunter in his famous book *Annals of Rural Bengal* (1868).

And did the plight of the people, especially the poor, change after ninety years of 'enlightened and civilised' British rule by its kings? the *Indian Annual Register* presents their psyche through this poignant Tagore poem:

...There they stand, heads bowed,
Mute; on their pale faces chronicled the sufferings
Of many centuries; on their shoulders they bear burdens
Which grow, carrying on, slowly, till life holds,
And then they pass them to the children for generations.
Fate they do not curse, nor complain, remembering the gods;
Men they do not blame, nor cherish any pity of love.
For themselves; only a few grains of food they glean,
And their tormented lives, somehow keep alive.
When even that meagre food someone robs,
And hurts their life in blind might's cruel oppression,
They know not to whose door they will turn for justice;
Calling on the God of the Poor, for once in their heaving sighs,
Silently they die.
Rabindranath Tagore, translated by Amiya Chakravarty.
[IAR, 1943 Vol 2, p 57]

Bengal that was once a key rice-producing region saw great decline in rice production in the 1940s as World War II began.

Import of Burmese rice that had sustained the population in Bengal also stopped with the Japanese invasion of Burma.

By 1942, the British had put into place a policy to prevent existing local resources from falling into Japanese hands in case of a land invasion. This policy was known as the 'Denial Scheme'. Surplus rice, an essential food crop, was confiscated in all coastal districts. This led to an almost overnight breakdown of then existing trade patterns in east India. The second part was to destroy serviceable boats in the coastal regions as well as in the inland waterways. Bengal's riverine land and deltaic areas depended on country boats (known as goyna boats) for almost everything. The large-scale destruction of these boats meant that families and livelihoods were wiped out. As sick, starving and ragged 'destitutes' from the countryside thronged Calcutta's streets, wailing for a cup of rice gruel (*phyan*), the city began to be called a metropolis of hunger.

This excerpt from the Woodhead Commission's Report on Bengal [p2] highlight how the Fifty's famine impacted social values: 'Families were broken up and moral sense lost. In that distress they often sank to sub-human levels and became helpless and hopeless automats guided only by an instinctive craving for food.'

Several faith-based organisations were involved in relief work at the time. The following poem by Nirupama Devi cited in the Indian Annual Register depicts what a terrible impact the famine had on the victims. She was in charge of relief work started by the Brahmo Samaj during the Fifty's Famine:

Humans die of hunger,
There is none to sorrow for them,
Except death there's no other to which they can look forward to;
These are the men and women

Who have no time to sorrow for their children who died untimely
But must the next moment start roaming from door to door,
Driven by hunger, driven unsatisfied,
For, none is there to give them food.
Quarrel for a morsel of food, fight to divide it,
Kick and beat (one another) for a morsel of food,
Conduct themselves as beasts do,
Parents strangle their children (driven by hunger)
Shame has lost all meaning for them,
Hunger as wide as the world,
Meanness as low:
Stricken by living death,
Alas! My Bharata, more dead than alive
[IAR, 1943, Vol 2, pp 58-9]

There are some features of famines which are universal, particularly those manmade ones. The poor are always at the receiving end and succumb to the exploitation by the rich, powerful and political intrigues. Terrible manmade famines across the world often witnessed hapless hungry poor lying on the roadside and dying in extreme solitude. It is no different, cutting across nations, as Aubrey De Vere depicts the scene in Ireland, in the poem, *The Year of Sorrow*:

On quaking moor, and mountain moss,
With eyes upstaring at the sky,
And arms extended like a cross,
The long-expectant sufferers lie....

In Bengal, the situation was far more scary and dehumanised. There were numerous instances where corpses were devoured by jackals, vultures and dogs and even dying persons were dragged away by these beasts before life was extinct. The Woodhead Commission Report revealed the scale and kind of devastation the Fifty's Famine caused. The report did not obviously elaborate on the kind of damages it wrought on the social fabric of Bengal. However, an indication of the damage is in the following excerpt from the start of its report, where the Commission observed:

> The Bengal Famine of 1943 stands out as a great calamity even in an age all too familiar with human suffering and death on a large scale. Between one and two million people died as a result of the famine and the outbreak of epidemic diseases associated with it. Many more who escaped death went hungry for many months, fell sick of disease and suffered in ways from the disintegration of normal life which the famine occasioned.

The role of the League ministry needs further investigation, the Indian Annual Register wrote:

> And the Ministry will live in the history of Bengal, in the memory of the people, as the one during whose regime there was a famine in which men, women and children died because food became unavailable, because it was selling at prices – rupees thirty to forty – which two crore of the people, one-third of the population, could not ever pay. Of these two crores more than fifty lakhs must have died by the end of 1943. The horror of this development is tragic enough. But its enormity was intensified as we watched the Nazimuddin Ministry accepting their high commission with promises of relief to the people, trying to keep them alive by these promises, trying to

put courage into them, and failing to fulfil these, failing to fight the forces of greed and corruption that were twisting life out of the millions of their fellow countrymen.

The IAR, after carefully considering pros and cons, was certain that the government in the province could have prevented the famine:

> But after considering all the circumstances, we cannot avoid the conclusion that it lay in the power of the Government of Bengal, by bold, resolute and well-conceived measures at the right time to have largely prevented the tragedy of the famine as it actually took place.

But why it did not do its bit is a question not sufficiently answered. Nor was it possible for analysts to answer this earlier as they were too close to that time and benefit of hindsight was not available to them. IAR wrote:

> We are too near these events to properly judge the failures of men in charge of high responsibilities....
> History, after the dust and heat of the present controversy will have subsided, after the bitterness of conflict for power and pelf has lost its venom, history will tell us why the Nazimuddin Ministry failed in its duty in one of the supreme crises in their Province's life. Till then we can only collect and keep in record the many influences, personal and impersonal, that beat down his Ministry, and disabled it in its frantic fight with famine. We are too near these events to properly judge the failures of men in charge of high responsibilities....
> [IAR, 1943 Vol 2, p 45]

It was, however, unmistakable that both, the League ministry in Bengal and the Government of British India, were keen in keeping Bengal under their thumb, down and out. Both used provision of Defence of India Rules aggressively to throttle voices of the media and the people. The situation did not seem to have changed much since 1770. The common poor masses could not gather courage to speak out against the combined might of the rulers. The timidity with which the poor were dying without upsetting the tranquillity of the ruling regimes had to be seen to be believed. IAR wrote:

> We have quoted from Sir William Hunter's *Annals of Rural Bengal* the reasons why the Court of Directors of East India Company could not understand the 'quiet' that prevailed in Bengal during the 1770 famine. They could not believe that men and women could die so quietly, and that in their millions. There has not been much of a change during the last 175 years in the people of India. And the present generation of British rulers must have felt as their predecessors had done when men and women and children could be dying in the streets of Calcutta without cursing anybody.
> [IAR, 1943 Vol 2, p 57]

Excerpts from a poem by Cyril Modak (*Modern Review*, March 1944) also give a glimpse of how rural Bengal was ravaged by the scourge of starvation:

> Village after village flying from the pillage
> Of the ghoulish hordes of Death,
> Flying torn asunder, flying from the plunder
> Of the ghoulish hordes of Death,
> Flying panic-stricken, flying, crying, lying

Hunger-stricken, choked for breath...
Skeletons now call
In Bengal!

Child and milkless mother, clasping helpless brother,
Bloodless, fleshless, nerveless lie,
Clasping bride and lover, clasping to recover
Breath enough to say 'Goodbye!'
Gasping hunger-stricken, clasping, grasping, gasping,
Choked with thirst and doomed to die,...
Skeletons now call
In Bengal!

Victims luckless, friendless, bearing torture endless,
Trapped by demons, gods and men,
Bearing famish'd anguish, daring thus to languish
In that blood-drunk jackals' den,
Tearing child from mother, daring, staring, tearing
Hunger-haunted, hapless men,...
Skeletons now call
In Bengal!

Post-Tagore, the *effect of hunger* was essayed by young Bengali poets who lived through the Great Bengal Famine. Poets like Sukanta Bhattacharya, Jibanananda Das, Premendra Mitra, Buddhadev Bose, Arun Mitra, Samar Sen, Biren Chattopadhyay, Manindro Roy, Subhash Mukhopadhyay, Golam Kuddus, Fahrrukh Ahmed and Dinesh Das painted the land's destitution in words. The teenage Sukanto in a work addressed to Tagore, said: O Great Life of Hunger, the world is prosaic, The Full Moon appears to be a scorched bread. O Great Life! No more of this Poetry, Now bring the hard, harsh

Prose, Let the poetic-tender-chime dissolve....' (*Chhinnapatra*, 1947; Translation by Osman Gani)

In another rebellious outburst, Sukanto writes:

My Spring goes by
Waiting in queues
For food
My sleepless nights
Are torn by
Vigilant sirens.

Birendra Chattopadhyay's poem, 'The Whiff of Intoxicating Rice' is surreal in its imagery:

The night sky
Smells of intoxicating rice
Even now, someone out there
Cooks rice, lays it out to eat.
And we are left sleepless
Praying, the night long,
Swathed in a whiff of intoxicating rice.

In another poem, Chattopadhyay talks of the city's sky, engulfed with a gigantic and metaphysical hunger:

As all other birds vanish,
Infinite crows gather all around....

Premendra Mitra's *Phyan* is one of the most telling poems of the times:

On the city streets
Roam strange creatures,

Human-like, yet, not quite human,
Cruel caricatures of humanity!
Yet they move and speak,
Like debris they pile up by the road,
Sit, foraging food, on piles of garbage
Weary
And cry out for phyan.

Among the visual artists whose art was shaped by the 1943 famine were Shomnath Hore and Zainul Abedin. A book called *Hungry Bengal* had pen and ink sketches of famine-stricken people crowding the streets of Calcutta and in deserted villages in Midnapore and it was quickly banned by the British Government and more than 5,000 copies were confiscated and burnt. The book and its sketches have been republished in 2011.*

---

* Input credit:https://coldnoon.com/journal/coldnoon-cities-mapping-the-metropolis-vol-i/a-metropolis-of-hunger-calcuttas-poetry-of-the-famine-1943/

Amartya Sen in his book, *Poverty and Famines*, has a chapter on the 'Great Bengal Famine' but he has not linked famine to cause and effect of hunger. The actions of both British regimes in London and Delhi as well as the League ministries violated every cannon of governance and defied common sense. The role of the British regime at both London and Delhi have been extensively studied by scholars, following de-classification of official papers of the British rule. Prof Madhusree Mukerjee's book is important in this connection.

It is in the context of this entirely man-made crisis that the book, *Panchasher Manwantar,* and Syama Prasad Mookerjee's interventions in famine relief have to be understood. Vitasta is proud to be able to present our readers with an important translation work on hunger and add to the body of existing literature on the subject.

Preface

Syama Prasad's contribution to the cause of India and Indian people has not been objectively assessed as yet. Its enormity on one hand and the tendency on the part of the left-dominated historians to downplay it partly explains the reason for this disregard.

Several of his political contemporaries – who had supported the demand of Pakistan, with some of them having advocated the case of an independent Bengal and opposed his struggle for West Bengal – later on sought refuge in that very province. They and their kindred probably did not want to acknowledge their debt to Syama Prasad, driven by their meanness or for the fear of exposing their own past actions of indiscretions.

For the past some years, research activities have been underway on his life and contribution, thanks to the initiative by the Government of India. Hopefully, these will fill the gap in the public domain about Syama Prasad's life, ideology and contribution.

Briefly speaking, he was a rare amalgam of several exalted qualities like merit and erudition, vision and statesmanship, courage and confidence, honesty and integrity, humanism and compassion, leadership and organising abilities, alongside a keen sense of justice and fair play. Simultaneously, he was vehemently against injustice, cowardice, hypocrisy and believed in taking these practices in politics head on. With all these attributes, he was a nationalist to the core and his life glittered with genuineness and truthfulness.

With equal felicity he worked for the cause of education and used politics for the welfare of his countrymen. Although he first represented the University Constituency at hardly 28 years of age in 1929, he entered into mainstream politics in 1940 under compulsion of circumstances. Bengal was then sinking in the abyss of communal politics under a Muslim League-led government. The State's secular fabric in general and the lives of the Hindus – the religious minority in the province – were coming under increasing strain.

Syama Prasad exhibited consummate political skill in joining hands with Sarat Bose, marshalling the spectrum of secular forces in the province and replacing the League ministry with an alternative broad-based secular cabinet in less than two years, following his entry into mainstream politics.

Never one to be daunted by any challenge, however formidable or diabolical, he came forward as a saviour of the distressed victims of the man-made Bengal famine in 1943.

To save the vulnerable people across castes and creed, he took head on the nexus of the British regime and the Muslim League ministry. The rulers had tried to keep Bengal under an iron curtain so that no help could reach from outside. This meant that starvation deaths would continue unabated. He defied the unholy administration's unethical plan, and tearing the iron curtain of silence asunder, reached out to the outside world, organised help and provided relief to lakhs of victims. IAR wrote:

> For reasons yet unexplained the Government did not favour this broadcasting of famine news either in India or outside. The Defence of India Rules were handy in gagging the expression of public feeling in this matter. And it required no little courage to defy this interdict. And when the history of this particular reluctance of the Government comes to be written the credit of weakening its rigours will go to Dr Mookherjee.
> [IAR, 1943 Vol 2, pp 59-60]

Syama Prasad's role can be appreciated better in this context. When bulk of the political spectrum had succumbed to the oppressive nexus of the British and the League, not only did he lead in organising private relief, he simultaneously led a crusade against the tyrant regimes, undaunted by the consequences.

He had written this book as a part of his overall crusade against the man-made famine in order to create and spread public awareness and mobilise the masses. It is probably the most authentic and firsthand account of the distress of people and the political machinations behind the famine. Fearlessly, he had raised his voice against the tyrant regimes at Calcutta, Delhi and London through speeches delivered at public meetings and also in the legislative forums. He used every kind of opportunity and platform to make the outside world aware of what was happening in Bengal with a view to bringing an end to the people's miseries.

The Indian Annual Report (1943 Volume 2) stated this fact succinctly: 'He it was whose voice rang throughout the country calling attention to the conditions of famine that threatened to decimate Bengal.'

Syama Prasad was a key architect of the only secular ministry in pre-independent Bengal. Though it succumbed to the British conspiracy in less than 18 months, he commanded trust and respect from both Hindus and Muslims. As a matter of fact, the Syama-Huq ministry, as it was popularly called, became a testimony of communal harmony. The manner in which he crusaded for the cause of famine victims added to his stature as a towering leader of Bengal. Before long, the rest of India came to recognise his leadership and benefitted from it.

Syama Prasad was an ardent advocate of united independent India. But, in the aftermath of the Congress accepting the proposal for partition and the British-League administration hatching a plot to attach the whole of Bengal to the proposed Pakistan, he had organised and led a mass movement to carve out West Bengal as part of India. His resolute fight on the issue also helped the struggle of the Hindus and Sikhs in Punjab, who too were victims of communal violence unleashed by Muslim League politics, in securing eastern Punjab as part of the Union of India.

In post-independence India, he set up an excellent example of extending both cooperation and constructive criticism to Jawaharlal Nehru's government. As part of the central cabinet, which he had joined at the instance of Mahatma Gandhi, he took several groundbreaking initiatives as the Minister of Industry and Supply of the country. At the same time, he was arguably the most powerful voice of opposition against questionable policies adopted by Pandit Nehru on issues relating to refugees from Pakistan, the Chinese occupation of Tibet in 1951 and India's J&K policy, especially the promulgation of Article 370 in the northern State.

He stood resolutely against the injustice to and persecution of religious minorities in Pakistan, and he was deeply anxious to protect the hapless refugees from the indifferent approaches that the central government held towards them. When the refugees of East Pakistan (East Bengal) were sacrificed like lambs to the communal regime of Pakistan through the Delhi Pact, he resigned from the Nehru cabinet.

On the issue of Jammu & Kashmir, he made repeated attempts to alert Pandit Nehru to the evil of keeping the State alienated from rest of India through the special provisions of Article 370. Finally, he made supreme sacrifice by laying down his life to sensitise the countrymen to the need for unification of J&K with India in full measure. This has to be seen as a part of his life's mission to establish the unity of this nation.

Later events in the life of the Indian republic have proved how prophetically right he was on each of these issues, be it J&K or China or refugees from Pakistan!

In the aftermath of independence, the party that came to rule the country sought to project its 'entitlement' to govern by claiming a monopoly over the freedom struggle. To make matters worse, a tendency of hero worship also began to cripple it, overriding genuine democratic practices. Unfortunately, there was no effective challenger in the Opposition to check this tendency.

In the circumstances, Syama Prasad threw a powerful ideological challenge to the extant political culture of hero worship, and non-assertion of democratic values in the ruling regime, asserting the 'Nation First' principle and suggesting that the right to rule should emanate from 'service to the nation'.

He set up a political party embodying this approach. Unlike most parties of the country which saw India as a nation born in 1947, which was to be developed on western lines – under capitalism or communism or a hybrid of the two – Syama Prasad's ideology envisaged India benefitting from her core civilisational values and ethos and arriving at the global stage as a leader among nations.

After decades of struggle in the democratic political system, his ideology seems to be getting increasing acceptance from the people of India and helping them rediscover some of India's civilisational legacy in national life. Besides what he had accomplished during his lifetime, the continuing impact of his ideology over the life of the nation sets him apart from other political leaders of high stature. This is a fact that remains less noticed.

If India finally emerges on the global stage as the world leader, the credit to a large extent will belong to Syama Prasad Mookerjee.

Syama Prasad's Book has Unmitigated Importance Even Today

Sudip Kar Purkayastha

There were several famines in different parts of India under the British rule. Of them, the one in 1770 AD in Bengal, which came to be called *Chhiyattarer Manwantar* or the 'Famine of the Seventy-six', in accordance with the corresponding Bengali calendar year of 1176, was legendary in terms of its viciousness. Since then, and spreading over the next century, famines and pestilences kept striking India at intervals. The occurrences abated in the twentieth century. But that sense of relief was torn asunder in 1943 AD, only a few years before India's independence, by a monstrous famine that cast an indelible slur on the British rule and challenged its claims to be a civilised nation.

Estimates vary on the death toll ranging between 15 to 50 lakh human lives.[1] It is incredible not only in terms of the scale of devastation, but also because such an immense population courted death almost silently, without waging a fight against the rulers, or even holding protest marches. Ironically their abode – the vast rural areas of Bengal – and the producers of food grains had suddenly been denuded of rice for reasons they were unable to comprehend!

Driven by extreme hunger, rural folks, in hundreds of thousands, sold their farm implements, land, roof thatches, homes and even their children, marched from villages to towns and cities in search of morsels of food, and numerous people got separated from their families. Arriving in Calcutta and various big towns they turned beggars, competed with beasts for left-over food in street dustbins, and slowly embraced death due to starvation or diseases.

The disposal of corpses had proved a staggering problem in Calcutta itself. The situation was horrific in *mofussil*[2] towns and more so in villages where dogs, jackals and vultures feasted on dead bodies. There were also several recorded instances of dogs dragging dying persons and devouring their limbs while they were still alive, but too emaciated to drive the invaders away!

Incredible though these narrations may sound, plethora of reports and photographs in contemporary leading dailies of

---

1 Lives were lost due to both starvation and epidemic or pestilence. However, the root cause was man made famine and that in turn facilitated the epidemic and greatly enhanced the scale of deaths. Segregated death statistics due to starvation, mal-nutrition, epidemic and non-epidemic diseases were unavailable, said the Indian Annual Report, 1944, Vol1, p 85 (hereafter IAR).

2 Mofussil (countable and uncountable, plural mofussils): Originally, the regions of India outside the three East India Company capitals of Bombay, Calcutta and Madras; hence, parts of a country outside an urban centre; the regions, rural areas. 18 century definition.

Bengal and descriptions in books, especially Kali Charan Ghosh's extensively referenced work, *Famines in Bengal 1770 – 1943,* bear evidence to the catastrophe that had unfolded in Bengal.

A question that naturally arises in every mind is how come only one of the British Indian provinces witnessed such colossal loss of human lives while other provinces or the princely States escaped such terrible fate?[3] The country was under the mighty British empire which was not at its infancy but shining with the glory of maturity. India, its 'crown jewel' in the words of Churchill, had all her parts well connected with each other. As to natural calamities impacting food crops that year, provinces and States like Bombay, Orissa, Travancore and Malabar were affected too but they escaped with no or bare minimum loss of lives. With regard to the war condition and inflation driving up prices of food grains and essential goods, all parts of the country were affected to varying extents. If that were the general state of affairs, why was Bengal in particular affected so badly?

Out of a long list, two prime reasons are offered conventionally. We have stated the first reason already which involved fury of nature. Natural calamities like cyclone and flood followed by pest attack took toll of the winter crop of

---

[3] In a famine-related discussion in the IAR, it was revealed that in Bijapur, Bombay Presidency, the famine relief work was systematically carried out with both the provincial government and the Servants of India Society doing their bits. The situation in Orissa was thought to be serious, but facts were not known due to Censorship. In Kerala, famine conditions existed even in 1942. There were famine and non-famine months. The challenge was addressed through quota system for distribution of available food grains across populations. Though this led to emaciation and death of 30,000 people, those were reportedly due to epidemic diseases in June-August 1943, not starvation. Kerala reportedly had 50 per cent shortfall in her food grains but by and large escaped a massive disaster. It is intriguing that Bengal, in comparison, had only 10 per cent production deficit but faced this holocaust. None of these cases could be compared to Bengal. [IAR 1944, Vol 1, p94].

1942 in Bengal's coastal areas. Second, following the Japanese occupation of Burma,[4] the rice import from that country had stopped. These two causes had affected the availability of rice in the province. But serious academic researches show that the total foodstuff availability in 1943, even after considering the above two reasons, was not so low as to warrant a famine.

In fact, in terms of availability of foodstuff, the year 1943 was better than 1941 and there was no famine in 1941. This point has been detailed further in the last chapter. To ward off any such uncomfortable but logical question and prevent deeper investigation into the real causes, the pro-establishment camp conceded some ground and agreed that besides the 'nature' and 'Burma' factors, there were also a list of acts of omission and commission that led to the crisis of foodgrains in Bengal. But, it claimed, those lapses were related to policy and administration. On that ground it went so far as to agree to call the famine 'manmade'– but insisted those were human lapses devoid of intention. A discussion on the real nature of these acts of men in power has been undertaken in the last chapter.

In 1943, some provinces including Punjab, Orissa (despite natural calamity striking its coastal areas), Bihar and Assam amongst others, were in a position to help Bengal with food grains. Even a neighbouring country, Nepal, was ready to help. Across the world, countries like Australia and Canada had volunteered to send assistance for the victims of the food crisis. The fact that those were either not used or refused, raise questions about the motive of His Majesty's and British India's governments.

Following the de-classification of papers of the British rule of the relevant period, to which we shall revert in the last chapter, there is hardly any doubt today that 'starving tens of

[4] Presently known as Myanmar

millions of people in Bengal' was a deliberate act. But why? One probable answer is the visceral hatred of the colonial regime for a province which treaded the path of armed freedom struggle against the British Raj for several decades. A grave provocation came in the midst of the World War II from nationalist leader Subhas Chandra Bose's great escape from Calcutta (on 17 January 1941) and his warm reception by Axis countries like Germany and Japan. The following para quoted from a paper by Asok Mitra[5] would help guess how that event and Japan's invasion of Burma (In January 1942 Japan invaded Burma and by 1 August 1943, declared it independent of the British and as the State of Burma) filled the British with vengefulness.

Mitra wrote:[6] 'My own hunch is that Herbert[7] probably took Netaji's flight as a slap on his face.' Mitra thought Subhas Chandra Bose seeking from and receiving assistance from Axis countries, 'must have stoked sentiments of hatred and revenge all along the line '.

Referring to the Japanese *kamikaze*[8] attack on two British warships in December 1941 and its invasion of Burma in 1942, Mitra observed how the act of reprisal in Bengal thereafter was 'not only motivated by utter disregard of Bengal's plight but by positive bloody-mindedness on the part of Herbert, abetted no doubt by Lord Linlithgow[9] and Amery'.[10] One of those acts was, of course, the ruthless adoption of denial policy

---

[5] Asok Mitra, an ICS officer, was at that time the deputy district collector of Bikrampur, Dacca, one of the worst famines-affected places and faced the challenge upfront.

[6] https://www.jstor.org/stable/4394343?seq=1#page_scan_tab_contents

[7] Sir John Arthur Herbert: He was Governor of Bengal during 1938-1943.

[8] Kamikaze: Suicide attacks, first demonstrated by the Japanese in WWII.

[9] He was the Viceroy of India from 18 April, 1936 till 1 October 1943, which included a crucial period of the Bengal famine.

[10] Leo Amery: He was Secretary of State for India and Burma during May 1940 to July 1945.

in Bengal which Herbert had copied from Soviet Russia's 'scorched earth' policy. While in Russia the common people voluntarily adopted that policy of self-sacrifice so as not to leave anything useful behind for the invading Nazis if it ever happened, Herbert forced it on Indian people, translating the act of supreme self-sacrifice as a 'totally contrary two-pronged weapon of perverse destruction'. His intention surely was, Mitra wrote, 'to rob the people of the will and the wherewithal to fight'.

The latest provocation to the British came from Midnapore, where responding to the 'Quit India' call by the Congress, freedom activists in Contai and Tamluk in that district overthrew the local governments and declared independence.[11] Herbert's wrath descended on the people of Midnapore in full fury. He took personal initiatives in unleashing brutal atrocities on the flood and cyclone-hit starving people of the district, bypassing the Syama Prasad-Fazlul Huq ministry (1941-42) through permanent officials. The British priority to ensure uninterrupted war supplies and crush every potential obstacle to that process gave him justification to wreak vengeance. In the process, if such a rebellious province like Bengal could be starved to death, why not?

However, it needs to be borne in mind that the British regime, despite all its brute power, would not have succeeded in making such a famine happen, unless it got an accomplice in the provincial government. As a matter of fact, the secular, progressive coalition ministry of Syama Prasad and Fazlul Huq determinedly opposed the British policies of 'denial',

[11] Incidentally, the freedom fighters were able to maintain the local independence till some time in 1944.

'evacuation' and 'boat control'.[12] Syama Prasad also stoutly opposed Herbert over his policy of oppression of the people of Midnapore and quit the ministry in protest. Even thereafter, at his strong insistence, the Huq ministry agreed in the assembly to carry out an investigation into the atrocities on people of Midnapore, which was a direct affront to Governor Herbert. That probably would have made him think that this ministry would not toe his line blindly merely for the sake of continuing in office. This explains why he used unethical means to oust that ministry and bring in a new one led by Sir Nazimuddin of the Muslim League.

From the correspondence between high British officials it is clear that Herbert was desperate at that juncture to have an 'indigenous ministry' in place in the province that would shield the British Raj from the moral guilt of starving people. It may be argued that had the Muslim League not stepped in at that time, the British could not have been so reckless with regard to its basic duty of feeding people, at least to save their face in the comity of nations.

Even if the League had insisted on an 'all party' government, there would have been pressure on the British to provide food to the starved population. Why did the League sacrifice the interests of a vast number of poor people, which also included Muslims, has not been understood, and that has so far prevented a complete understanding of the causes of the Bengal famine. A logical answer to this question is provided in the next few paragraphs.

---

[12] Interestingly, the foolhardiness of such a policy did not escape the eyes of D F Karaka, the Calcutta correspondent of *Bombay Chronicle,* who saw how the destruction of boats, barges, carts etc. and discouraging farmers in East Bengal from storing rice was compounding the calamity and wrecking Bengal. He succinctly said the authorities ought to have realised that 'one could not deny to a possible invading army in the future, unless one also denied to oneself, in the present'. MR LXXIV No 5 Whole No 443 November 1943 p 324.

Since 1937, the politics of Bengal was getting increasingly more communalised. The root cause was the Indian National Congress refusing to respond to the offer from the Fazlul Huq-led Krishak Praja Party to form a secular coalition government. This was both politically advantageous in the all-India context and an opportunity for the Congress to save Bengal from communal politics.

The Congress had emerged as the single largest party in Bengal in the first election, held under the Government of India Act 1935. However, the Congress' refusal pushed Huq towards the League, helping the latter to establish a vice-like grip over the politics of the province. It may not be far from the truth to say that this was a blunder that contributed significantly to the partition of both the province and the country.

Barring one patch during December 1941 to mid April 1943, the politics of Bengal was increasingly vitiated by Muslim League. It was only during this brief period of about 16 months that a new secular coalition ministry, fashioned by Sarat Bose (Subhas's brother) and Syama Prasad with Fazlul Huq as its head governed Bengal. Fazlul Huq was persuaded by Mookerjee and Bose to resign as the head of the League-led ministry and take over as the leader of the new coalition. A day before the ministry was to take oath, the Governor got Sarat Bose, who was to play a pivotal role in the cabinet, arrested on alleged links with the Japanese consulate.

Following this grave setback, the core responsibility to work out the experiment fell on Syama Prasad's broad shoulders. This new ministry functioned on secular agenda and helped foster the spirit of communal harmony between Hindus and Muslims. Syama Prasad served as finance minister in that cabinet for nearly 11 months before he resigned, protesting against repeated intervention by Governor Herbert in the working of the provincial ministry.

The Syama-Huq ministry, as this secular ministry was called affectionately by many, was the eye sore of the League and considered an obstacle to the goal of Pakistan (yet to be formed). The fact that the same Huq, who had introduced the Pakistan Resolution in Lahore in March 1940, was heading it was the cause of greater irritation to the League, worthy of retribution. It must also be noted here that the loyalty of the Muslim population of Bengal was divided at that time between the Fazlul Huq-led Krishak Praja Party (which was more popular, with sizeable Muslim peasant population, especially the poor) and the Muslim League (claiming allegiance of the wealthy and landlords).

The priorities before the Muslim League were to quickly gain power to rule, and the advancement of the goal of Pakistan. To secure these goals, the League seemed to be ready to do any bidding of the Governor. The loss of lives of poor Muslims by starvation was probably a collateral damage!

Reverting to the famine, it appeared that right since regaining office in April 1943, the League-led coalition ministry and the British Governor (representing the Raj in the province) worked in harmony. The British priority lay in exporting rice from Bengal to overseas, and its procurement for military consumption. Besides, the Raj endorsed large-scale procurement of rice by government departments, corporations and owners of large factories for future needs of employees and workforce. The latter was aimed at ensuring food for the capital city of Calcutta and its adjoining industrial areas, which in turn was connected to production of war supplies. The League's priorities, on the other hand, were communalisation of politics, consolidation of the party's hold in the province and advancement towards the goal of Pakistan. Corruption and nepotism were corollaries and lubricators.

The main stance of the League ministry was that there was no food shortage in Bengal and the problem was one of maldistribution and hoarding. That gave the British the moral justification to avoid the duty to feed people and continue with the policies of exports, large-scale procurement and not availing offers of help from outside India. Even though hundreds of thousands of poor and low middle-income people were dying of hunger, the League ministry remained a passive spectator. The British did not intervene, citing the ethical high ground of non-intervention in 'provincial autonomy'.

If the life cycle of this famine is studied carefully, one can see that the starvation deaths began to spiral from May 1943 and showed the first signs of abating in October 1943, after Wavell[13] took over as new Viceroy. Majority of deaths till October could be directly attributed to starvation. However, starvation had so emaciated a very large population that it made them victims of epidemic that came in the aftermath of the famine. As a matter of fact, the epidemics too caused large numbers of deaths. On the whole, famine and pestilence, both arising out of acts of omission and commission by the League ministry and the British Raj ended up taking lives of a few million people.

---

[13] Viscount Wavell: He was the Governor General and Viceroy of India from 1 October 1943 to 21 February 1947. Before that he was the commander-in-chief of the British troops in Southeast Asia from July 1941 to 1943, which gave him some exposure to India. He succeeded Lord Linlithgow and under his tenure, the famine of Bengal began to improve. He was followed by Mounbatten who oversaw the partition process.

The reader can track the sequence of events during the famine and epidemics, stretching up to 1944, through the speeches and writings of Syama Prasad Mookerjee. The acts of apathy, indiscretion, high-handedness and heartlessness of the governments at three levels in Calcutta, Delhi and London during the famine are manifested in them. The pattern of interactions by the ruling party members and ministers with Syama Prasad during the course of his speeches in the Legislative Assembly of Bengal offer interesting insight into the attitude of ruling party members including ministers.

Syama Prasad was one of the key politicians of Bengal with an all-India stature, having deep insight into the politics of the province. Driven by humanism, compassion, nationalism, honesty and courage, he relentlessly struggled against the combination of British and League politicians to protect poor masses across caste and creed throughout the famine.

As finance minister in the Huq-led government, he had tried sincerely to tackle the challenges with whatever means available, and did not hesitate to resign when the governor repeatedly obstructed the working of the cabinet. However, even after his resignation, he never stopped tendering well-meaning advice to the ruling regimes in the province and centre, to alleviate the severity of the famine.

At the time of writing his book on the Bengal famine, Syama Prasad did not have inside information about the functioning of the British regime at London, and its *protégés* at Delhi and Calcutta, as are available to us these days. Still, the cruel and barbarous attitude towards the suffering millions on the part of all three governments eventually created grave apprehension in his mind that it was brought about by the three governments and they were responsible for driving millions of people to death in Bengal.' He expressed such doubts more clearly in a later edition of the book. He had also demanded that a Royal Commission be appointed to enquire into the real reasons for the grave tragedy.

The Woodhead Report

It is true that the Government of India had appointed an Inquiry Commission headed by Sir John Woodhead to look at what had caused the famine. Amery, the Secretary of State for India and Burma, played a role in choosing Sir Woodhead, in whom he had confidence. Predictably, Woodhead's report laboured to protect the case of His Majesty's Government. In a reasoned critique of this report, contained in a later edition of his book, Syama Prasad found many gaping holes in its findings.

He was certain that the real culprits had not been identified by the Commission deliberately. Still, people could make out from the report, in whatever form it was, that there was a mass extermination in Bengal and they had, as such, the right to demand a public trial for the guilty men. Syama Prasad was unequivocal in saying that whenever there will be chances to scrutinise the entire government records, people will realise that there was absolutely no justification for the Bengal famine of 1943. On the contrary, in-depth scrutiny will reveal that the famine was *engineered* by the British regime, the Government of India and the Muslim League Government acting in a nexus.

We are of the opinion that the full truth still remains buried from the gaze of the world. If it is resurrected even today, the guilty can be tried at the bar of time!

More importantly, like every man-made famine, Bengal famine of 1943 has unique lessons for entire humanity. That remains to be learnt for the future good of mankind.

English Rendition of Syama Prasad's Bengali Book

Finally, a brief description of the present work:

It is essentially an English 'translation' of Syama Prasad Mookerjee's book, *Panchasher Manwantar,* written in Bengali. The year 1943 corresponded to the year 1350 as per Bengali calendar, which Syama Prasad used to name his book. This famine has been known by this name in Bengal.

The present translation is based on the 2nd edition of Syama Prasad's work. The selected contents from it have been re-organised and presented under five broad categories: speeches, articles, letters, statements and reports relating to relief activities by organisations he was involved with. The items under the first four categories have been incorporated in a strict time sequence to help the reader get a better understanding of the life cycle of the famine and the political dynamics around it.

As regards the fifth i.e., the report relating to relief work presented under Appendix I & II, it needs to be stated that considerable relief activities were carried out thereafter, also encompassing wide-ranging areas such as free kitchen, free ration, cheap ration, cheap canteen, milk distribution, orphanage, hospital, dispensaries, clinics, distribution of medicine, and even centres for disposal of dead bodies. Besides, there were arrangements for economic rehabilitation and education of destitute persons. According to a report of the Bengal Provincial Hindu Mahasabha Relief Committee (June 1944),[14] it directly maintained 227 Mahasabha Relief Centres in 24 districts, serving over 1.07 lakh people on an average, every day. The Mahasabha also helped 31 other organisations in their relief work.

---

[14] *Rashtrasangram O Panchasher Manwantar* p 116 (hereafter Rashtrasangram).

As regards the speeches he delivered in the Bengal Legislative Assembly, Syama Prasad had furnished only their abridged versions in Bengali in his book. This was probably in view of the strict censorship prevailing at that time. These speeches are invaluable from the perspective of 'timing' and 'contents', to get a deeper insight into the political dynamics behind the famine. In the present book, all three speeches in their full and original form i.e., in English as delivered by Syama Prasad have been reproduced.

The first speech was made in July 1943 when the starvation deaths had begun to spiral. The second one was delivered in October 1943 while the famine was at its peak, devouring lakhs of lives. Syama Prasad delivered the third speech in April 1944. By then, the British had decided to put a brake on their repressive polcies in India, particularly Bengal, and initiated suitable alleviating measures, but the actions of the incumbent Muslim League Government were still betraying both inefficiency and communal bias, even in the matter of providing relief to the victims.

Before each speech, article and statement, the translator-editor has added brief descriptions of the extant situation in the province to contextualise them. The book has three chapters by the translator-editor. The first, i.e., the present chapter argues why Syama Prasad's book has unmitigated importance even today.

The second intervention comes as the penultimate chapter and it is a compilation of Syama Prasad's observations on the Woodhead Commission's Report and his renewed conviction that this famine was brought about by the British and the League, and it amounted to killing of people on a massive scale.

The third intervention constitutes the concluding chapter. It makes a critical assessment of Syama Prasad's view about the true causes and nature of the famine in the light of the political dynamics of Bengal in greater details and takes into account other relevant issues.

It seeks to decipher the nature of alliance between the British and the League, both in the context of the famine and wider politics in the province. This work conducts a brief comparison of the Bengal famine (1943-44) with another horrendous famine in Ukraine (1932-33), in this connection, both manmade and political in nature.

The last chapter additionally points to an aspect of this Bengal Famine which has largely remained ignored. It argues that the famine not only took away millions of lives but also shattered the social fabric and cultural moorings of Bengal. It refers to websites, newspapers, journals, periodicals and books including the *Famines in Bengal 1770-1943*, by Kali Charan Ghosh, which is a must-read for every researcher on famines in general and Bengal Famine 1943 in particular.

There are footnotes about personalities whose names have appeared in the main body of the book without any details. The footnotes also provide meanings of some Bengali words or terms used in Syama Prasad's Bengali book for the benefit of readers who are not familiar with the Bengali language. While translating, in some places a word or two was added to bring out the implied meaning of the complete sentence. These are identifiable in square brackets.

To international researchers this book commends itself as a rare source to understand the dynamics of provincial politics of that time as told by a much-respected statesman politician from Bengal.

Anandamath*

After the ornaments were divided, one robber said, 'What shall we do with gold and silver? Let someone take a piece of ornament and give me a morsel of rice instead. I am dying of hunger. Today I am living only on tree leaves.' Once he said thus, all others raised similar cries: 'Give me rice. Give me rice. Life is about to end in hunger. I don't want gold or silver.' The leader of the robbers attempted to calm them down, but none would listen. Gradually the voices grew louder, abuses flew, blows were about to be exchanged. Overcome by anger, they hurled their share of ornaments at the leader. He beat up one or two of them. Then all pounced upon the leader and started hitting him. The leader was wearied and emaciated due to starvation. After taking one or two hits he fell to the ground and gave up his life. Then one amongst the hungry, angry, agitated and out-of-mind robbers said: 'We have eaten flesh of jackals and dogs. Dying of hunger. Come brothers, let us today eat this fellow.' Saying thus, the emaciated, dark, ghost-like figures laughed aloud and began to clasp and dance in the darkness. One of them got ready to light a fire to burn the body of their leader.

* This is a famous novel written by Bankim Chandra Chattapadhyay which was published in 1882 and gave a vivid description of the famine of 1770 AD, the worst of all famines in Bengal.

Syama Prasad at the time of publication of the First Edition of the Book in 1943

Submission

Panchasher Manwantar is being published at the intense urging of a few enthusiastic relief workers.

This book was not written in a calm environment with a detached outlook. I have had to deliver many lectures on the famine in the legislative assembly and other places. I have also issued some statements in course of performing my duties. Their essence [in Bengali] have been incorporated in this book. Even a few weeks ago, it was beyond my imagination that what I had said or written from the menacing environs of crematoriums while hearing the loud wailings of distressed humanity would come out in the form of a book!

Since I have had to speak about the same thing in different places, there are several repetitions. Much of what I had said in my lectures could not be printed due to the compulsions imposed by the foreign rule over the country. For that reason, it is possible to find lack of coherence in the expression of emotions here or there. In a few cases, the spontaneity of language has probably become a casualty of translation [from English to Bengali].

Still some heart-rending truths have surfaced in the telling. Having come in contact with thousands and thousands of [my] miserable countrymen in the course of my work, I have realised these truths. Notwithstanding the shortcomings, collecting and collating them at one place will help in appreciating our helpless condition. It is for this very reason that I did not come in the way of the enthusiastic workers [in publishing this book].

There is one more reason. It is absolutely necessary to collect the entire [range of] information relating to the famine. Many mysteries will be uncovered as a result. The people of the country can become as much vigilant as possible so that such misfortune cannot strike [us] once again. Our purpose will be served if *Panchasher Manwantar* succeeds in awakening the inquisitiveness in those who have energy and time.

The [ruling] party that is patronised by the government has relentlessly engaged in distorted interpretation of our work. [Our] Endeavours in rendering help to the distressed humanity have been attributed to political motive. [Even] To respond to such mentality that indulged in slander during the worst of times, and which, despite revealing its incompetence time and again never felt ashamed, amounts to honouring it. We embarked upon the task [of relief] with extremely limited resources as compared to the enormity of the distress. The magnitude of the relief measures ought to have been a hundred times bigger than what we could [mobilise] by straining all our energies. But one thing has been achieved. Efforts were made [by the ruling regime] to hide mountainous misdeeds and inefficiency. We nullified that. People have died. But the panicked cries of the dying could not be gagged within the confines of the province. These have reached [the] rest of the country and also lands across the seas.

I am helpless if some people have been hurt by my lectures or writings. [But] We cannot forgive those, whatever be the argument, whose impetuosity inflicted such boundless miseries on the people of my country. What punishment have we been able to impose on them by mere words of mouth? History will laden them with infamy for eternity.

Simultaneous with witnessing miseries and distress of the people accompanied by human meanness, we have also been amazed by the boundless magnanimity of people. We had appealed to our countrymen for help. [Sadly] Those on seats of power were, in fact, indirectly hindering the relief efforts by trying to make light of the crisis and attributing 'motives' [to us]. Despite this, help has come in abundance from within and outside of India. The provincial differences as well as communal meanness have been swept away by the mighty current of eagerness to save people in distress.

We have been overwhelmed by the irrefutable faith and stream of love on the part of thousands of donors. I am intimately involved with the Bengal Relief Committee and Bengal Provincial Hindu Mahasabha Relief Committee. A brief description of what these two [organisations] have done has been provided in the appendix. Hundreds of volunteers have worked day and night to render service. Let [our] opponents raise eyebrows, the people of the country have once again demonstrated the spirit of unity and service beyond measure.

But putting up plates of rice before the mouths of the distressed is neither the only, nor the most important, task. The homes and households of people have perished in the famine. The methods of livelihood and economic foundations have tumbled. The Bengalis are about to become a race of beggars relying on others' charity. The condition of the middle class or weaker sections is [the] most heart-rending. Our greatest duty is to retrieve the dignity of lakhs of our countrymen, especially the above two classes and to re-establish them in social life.

What miserable scenes did we witness month after month in the middle of the twentieth century with [our] own eyes? The future generations may not like to believe that such a thing had really happened. It is harvest time now – [winter] crops are filling homes. Unless mismanagement and corruption take hold, good days will probably return. But lakhs and lakhs of quiet households which once brimmed with joy have been wiped out without a trace; innocent hungry men and women died on the sidewalk bit by bit. The spectre of destruction [of these helpless multitude] shall haunt us as long as we live.

Shri Shyamaprasad Mukhopadhya[1]
77, Ashutosh Mukherjee Road
Kolkata 2
1 Paush, 1350 Bangabda[2]

1 Syama Prasad wrote his name this way in Bangla.

2 This is the corresponding Bengali date that appeared in Syama Prasad's book.

The Fifty's Famine

***Editor's note:** In this opening article, Syama Prasad surveyed important famines in the country under British rule right since its beginning, reviewed their backgrounds and identified the lessons they left for posterity for preventing future famines. In the process, he compared the current famine with previous ones and showed how the lessons from the past could have been utilised to address the challenges posed by 1943's famine.*

Bengalis have not been able to forget the dreadful memory of the 'Famine of Seventy-six'.[1] The 'Fifty's Famine'[2] will also stigmatise the history of Bengal for eternity.

---

[1] Refers to the Famine of 1770 AD corresponding to Bengali calendar year of 1176.

[2] In the year 1943 AD, another terrible famine struck Bengal. Unfortunately, it has been known more as man-made than a natural catastrophe. The famine and the attendant pestilence claimed over 3 million human lives. The English year 1943 corresponded to Bengali calendar year 1350. The famine derived its name, Panchasher Manwantar or The Fifty's Famine, according to the Bengali calendar.

On 12th of August 1765 AD, Clive[3] had procured the *dewani*[4] of Bengal, Bihar and Orissa on behalf of the East India Company. The state of affairs in the country at that time was a form of anarchy: many rulers and myriad rules of governance. Exploitation was in progress already in full measure. On top of that, drought and loss of crop had struck [the land] due to scarcity of rain. The famine of 1770 AD was their inevitable consequence. The country had turned into a graveyard. [Still] There could be some excuses for the 'famine of the seventy-six', as the British rule, the glory of which the English routinely trumpet across the world, had not found sufficient time to strengthen its roots within a period of only five years.

But no such excuse can hold good in the year 1943. The mighty white rule has been running [the land] over two centuries. The twentieth century has brought abundance of facilities and conveniences to mankind. By the charity of Science [today India's] ties have been established with the entire world. [But] We have seen with [our] own eyes month after month, and we continue to see the spectre of innumerable children dying in the laps of their mothers and humans fighting with animals to eat 'waste food' from the dustbins.

The civil supplies minister of Bengal advanced twelve reasons for the 'Famine of Fifty', which are:

---

3 Robert Clive laid foundation of the British empire in India by winning the battle of Plassey against Nawab Siraj-ud-daulah. He was also the first Governor of the Bengal Presidency.

4. It was a 'right' the British East India Company secured from the Mughal emperor in respect of Bengal, Bihar and Orissa to collect revenues and levy civil cess on the population in these provinces in lieu of paying a fixed amount annually to the Mughal emperor.

- The quantum of *aus*[5] crops during the year 1942 was unsatisfactory;
- The yield of *aman*[6] crops during the year 1942-43 was also low;
- The production in Medinipur and 24 Pargana districts was less due to damage by cyclone;
- The crop perished due to pest attack;
- The policy of boat removal has disrupted the transportation;
- The [rice] production has suffered due to removal of population from the coastal areas;
- The refugees coming from Burma and Arakan have crowded [in Bengal];
- The number of workers coming from other provinces to the industrial centres [here] have risen substantially;
- The [food] deficit could not be met as the rice import from Burma has stopped;
- Due to construction of many airports in many areas, cultivation could not be carried out;
- The foodstuff consumption rose as there has been significant rise in the armed forces population;
- The quantum of import from other provinces has been less;

[Significantly] During a debate held in the [British] Parliament on 4th November 1943 concerning the state of things in Bharat [India], inflation was held as one of the chief reasons

---

[5] One variety of rice catering to the consumption need of Bengal. Known as autumn or pre-kharif crop, it is sown in summer along with the pre-monsoon shower and harvested in autumn. It is usually rough in quality.

[6] An important variety of rice catering to the largest rice-consumption need of the people of Bengal. It is sown during rainy reason and harvested in winter. Known as winter crop as it is harvested in winter.

for the Famine of the Fifty. It finds no mention in the list of the twelve causes offered by the minister of civil supplies. Clearly, he has suppressed the real issue and hyped the minor causes. The government has issued a huge volume of paper currency to pay for the war supplies. The government employees, the vendors of war supplies and the makers of war equipment received this paper currency in abundance and began to merrily spend to buy all sorts of goods. [A] Majority of the population had already sold their stock of food grains for petty amounts, which they thought was relatively high at that time. The new money supply never reached their hands. Consequently, the prices of goods soared way above their capacity to buy. Lakhs and lakhs started dying of starvation. The responsibility for this money-supply induced inflation squarely rests upon the Government of India and the British administrative regime. The minister of civil supplies would have earned respect had he shown the guts to speak out the truth.

In course of the debate, Mr Pethick Lawrence[7] had said some genuine things: 'Innumerable people do not have means to buy bare minimum food grains necessary for [their] survival. Inflation is the main reason for such excessive rise in prices. None but the Government of India is responsible for this [state of affairs]'. Mr Leo Amery[8] too kind of endorsed this [view] albeit hesitatingly: 'The problem has been both inflation and inadequacy of food grains. The fact is the public did not have enough money to buy. If that were the case, the situation would not have been so miserable.'

---

7 A British politician and parliamentarian who rose to become the Secretary of State for India during 1945 to 1947.

8 A British politician who was Secretary of State for India and Burma from 1940 to 1945.

One thing must be kept in mind. Just having money does not suffice. Many a people survived on daily earnings. Their 'means' could not keep pace with the continuously rising price levels. Large numbers of such people, destitute and foodless, succumbed to death. Yet no effective steps were taken to halt the runaway inflation. It was only after the situation went out of control that the bosses were alerted.

The issue of 'wastage' too is absent in the 'list' of the minister of supplies. There has been lots of posturing against the farmers, the middle-class, the shopkeepers and such others up till now. Mr Amery's party has maintained that these very people brought about this famine by hoarding food grains. By such lines [of accusation] the attention of people has been distracted from the real reasons. The government is the biggest buyer in the market. Together with factory owners and capitalists, it also happens to be the largest hoarder of food grains. Who would account for the colossal wastage of the food grains that were hoarded? Massive quantities of food perished in the 'war-related' warehouses along the Burma border. After the true account of the enormous wastage of wheat, flour, grams and grist from the storage[s] of the Government of India is received, many mysteries surrounding the present famine will get exposed. That there was huge wastage even from the nominal storage held as reserve for the victims of enemy attack (courtesy ARPB),[9] has now become public knowledge.

The famine did not arrive in the span of a 'day'. From the list of twelve reasons furnished by the minister of supplies, one can make out that the terrible famine has devoured Bengal bit by bit. The Central Government betrayed deplorable apathy to tackle it. Companies after companies of soldiers from various

---

[9] Relating to Air Raid Protection.

countries streamed into and filled Bengal, thousands of war prisoners were brought in and the burden of many of them was imposed on the province; numerous people from Burma sought refuge here and factory workers beyond count from other provinces also congregated here. The Central Government still seemed to be thinking that Bengal would keep feeding such an enormous population and there was no need for additional arrangements.

The food allocation of soldiers is considerably more than the common man's. Not only rice but also fruits, vegetables, eggs, fish and meat are bought for them in large quantities. As those stuff became both expensive and scarce, rice came under greater pressure. On top of that the government kept warehousing to ensure one million tons of food grain remain ever ready, for the soldiers' consumption. The owner of big factories, flush with funds out of war supplies, began to procure food grains for future use by their labourers and employees. The government indirectly helped them [in such procurement]. None spared a thought for the common man!

Apprehending enemy invasion, paddy was removed from a few districts. But how could the hunger of local people be made to vanish by removing the food grains? They began to loiter [in the streets] in search of food. Price of rice suddenly shot up as boats were drowned and by regulating their movements panic spread amongst people. In such [a] situation, efforts ought to have been made to keep the people's confidence intact. [Instead] the government hastened to indulge in all kinds of deeds that made people gradually lose confidence in them. Famine spread across the whole land.

In Bankimchandra's novel, *Anandamath*, the picture of the Famine of the Seventy-six shines. There is no literary excess in that description. A Famine Commission was set up in 1778. The description of famine in *Anandamath* is an *ad verbum* Bengali translation of some parts of that report. If we compare today's situation with that in the *Anandamath*, it can be understood that history has [been] repeated.

Several famines occurred after 1776 too.[10] Out of them, during the famine of 1873-74, nearly two crore [20 million] people were facing starvation. But appropriate measures were adopted rapidly. Thus, number of deaths were nominal. That was the one single occasion when the government put up a creditable performance. But the measures of 1873-74 have been completely ignored this time. Rather, the imprudence and mismanagement that had turned the situation horrendous in 1770, 1783 and 1866 AD was again in sight during the Fifty's Famine. Of course, there was no threat of external invasion then. Except that, entire circumstances [then and now] are strangely similar.

As soon as the famine of 1770 began, the authorities immediately hatched a plan to buy and hoard six months' of supply [of food grain] for the soldiers. In October cries of hunger arose across the land. Company officials bought all the available food grain for the sepoys in November, [even] from those who produced [a meagre] one or two *kahan*.[11] In the month of November itself, the Collector General feared that the population will be wiped out.

Is not the situation in 1943 similar? I quote the words of the government: 'Food were bought in abundance on behalf of the army to meet the steadily rising needs of the forces defending the country. Besides, foodstuff had also

---

[10] Like in 1783, 1866, 1873-74, 1875-76, 1884-85, 1891-92, 1897, 1900 etc.

[11] Unit of measurement that was in use in Bengal in British India to quantify rice.

to be purchased as a preventive measure against state of emergency.'

In those days, [that is before 1877, the East India] Company did not succeed in buying rice from the British officials [stationed at] of Allahabad and Faizabad.[12] On the present occasion too, the Bengal Government faced difficulties in purchasing rice from other provinces, especially those ruled by the Viceroy.

It was suspected that rampant trading of food grain took place during the Famine of Seventy-six for personal gains. The servants of the Company had created [such] a situation that rice became unavailable in the market. There were loud cries [from the people]. Protests began to be raised. Even directors of the Company profusely condemned the misdeeds and abysmal greed of the company employees. But that did not help.

Same things are happening in 1943 too. It was only after raising a hue and cry, [that] the minister of civil supplies admitted on 15 September that the government had made some profit by selling the rice procured from other provinces but [sought to mitigate the gravity of the issue saying] that happened only in the initial stage etc.

Even [in] those days [1770] fiats were issued against buying and hoarding of foodstuff in large quantities. People were dying for want of rice, still export was being made without restriction. According to George Thompson,[13] 'If only export

---

[13] It was the native officials of the Company who were entrusted with the task of taking care of famine victims in Bengal, but they were refused cooperation by the British officials of the company stationed at Allahabad and Faizabad as they were more concerned about feeding the Company's army and decided to hoard the rice.

[13] Sir George Thomson was a renowned British orator and philanthropist. He visited India during 1842-43 to 1856-57.

alone was suspended during the famine, the available rice would have somehow met the need. People would not have starved to death.' It is not known when had such export started. History says that after lots of efforts, the export was eventually stopped on 14 Nov 1770.

This time too, lots of noise was made against export [of food grains]. [But] The authorities did not bother to listen. After considerable delay, [such] export was partially halted from 23rd July, but it did not stop fully. Even now [in 1944, at the time of first publication of this book] exports can be made to other countries for select purposes and according to the government estimate, this does not exceed 1,000 tons per month.[Significantly] The [role of] export also does not find any mention in the list that the minister of [civil] supplies held out as reasons for famine.

Bengal could not handle the shock of the 1770 [famine] easily. Scarcity had continued to linger. In 1783, the famine re-appeared. Then the authorities showed better sense. They completely stopped exports through waterways. A committee was formed and given absolute power [to take harsh decisions]. Directions were issued to the effect that if any businessman secretly hoarded food grains and refused to sell it at reasonable price in the market, not only would he attract severe punishment, but his goods would also be confiscated and distributed amongst the poor.

Similar directions were issued during the Fifty's Famine. Result? Thousands of people [evidently] suffered the consequences at the cost of their lives. Government orders were freely and almost openly flouted. The government too went on modifying its own orders – one after another.

During the 1783 famine, another remarkable proposal was mooted – to build a durable warehouse to store food grains for Bengal and Bihar. Accordingly, a huge granary of pucca masonry was constructed on which was written: 'For the perpetual prevention of famines in India.' But that granary has remained ever empty and not a handful of paddies was ever placed into it.

Likewise, in the Fifty's Famine, the food grains committee has recommended construction of a central warehouse. It remains to be seen whether it will be of pucca construction and how much grain will be stored in it!

Another famine that occurred in 1866 has generally been known as 'the Orissa famine'. The whole of Orissa was overwhelmed by that all-devouring famine. Its waves had also splashed against Bengal's districts of Medinipur,[14] Bankura, Burdwan,[15] Nadia, Hooghly and Murshidabad. The conditions in Orissa under the grip of that famine and those in Bengal today are exactly the same. From one end of the land to the other, innumerable people have been succumbing to death for want of rice. Dogs and jackals are clawing and tearing human corpses. Of course, the minister of supplies has been wanting to say that not all regions of Bengal are affected. But truth could not be suppressed by bluffing. In the 1866 famine nearly ten lakh [about one million] people had perished. If the true account of 1943 ever comes out, the loss of population during this time will surpass all previous famines.

In 1865, after watching partial failure of crops, the Collectors of various districts wanted to investigate the situation on the ground. Proposals were made to exempt [people from] some taxes as well. But the commissioners did not support it.

---

[14] Also spelt as Midnapore in some places.

[15] Also spelt as Bardhaman in some places.

Even the revenue board had directly dismissed the proposal. In a detailed report the board informed the Government of Bengal that though the crop production could be somewhat less, there was no reason to worry. The available crops would suffice to feed the population. May be, the carry-over stock for the next year would be less, but there was absolutely no possibility for a famine.

[The] Situation in 1943 is the same. After Burma went out of hand [conceded to Japan] there was talk that Bengal may face dearth of rice by the end of the year. This topic was raised by one highly-paid official of the Indian government. Only that much! On 30 April 1943, a newspaper carried a report that in the course of post-mortem of a famine victim, grass was found inside his stomach. Faced with extreme hunger, that helpless man had eaten grass but could not digest it. But exactly one week after that, on 7 May, the minister of supplies [Huseyn Shaheed] Suhrawardy said: 'The solution for the crisis is imminent.' Next day, on 8 May he said: 'As a matter of fact, there are adequate food grains in Bengal.' On 13 May, Major General Wood, the then top boss of the food department, resorted to detailed calculation and demonstrated that Bengal has no scarcity. On 15 May, honourable Azizul Huq, [a] Member of the Central Government, speaking in Krishnanagar [in Nadia district] said: 'There is no shortage of rice in Bengal yet.' Even on the thirtieth, Suhrawardy Sahib did not say it openly that 'there is inadequate foodstuff in Bengal or that adequate import has not been happening.'

In 1866, the then Lieutenant Governor of Bengal, Sir Cecil Beadon's Government had said that there was no genuine shortage of rice in the country. Abundant food grains rested in the hands of the businessmen and they were hoarding it with the hope of making undue profits. Likewise, in 1943, the Bengal Government said: 'The rise in prices has been disproportionate to the quantum of food grains that are available. The problem will disappear if only the hoarded goods can be brought out into the market.'

In 1866, demands were raised for importing rice in the month of March itself. Around that time, people had begun to abandon their homestead and loiter hither and thither [in search of food]. Foodstuff was being looted in places. But the government could not perceive the looming crisis. On 28 March, Sir John Arthur Cotton[16] had asked the government to be vigilant in order to prevent famine. In the month of April, arrangements were made in Calcutta to feed the starving people by raising subscriptions. But the revenue board was still in doubt whether there was genuine shortage of food. Gradually, rice became completely unavailable. Rice could not be obtained even for soldiers, government employees and prisoners in jails.Then, the Lieutenant Governor issued order for import of rice from outside. Due to such inefficiency of the government, nearly ten lakh people had succumbed to death during that [1866] famine. For this, the famine commission heavily blamed the revenue board. On 11 August 1867, the revenue board while admitting umpteen lapses on its part said: 'The misfortune occurred because of not starting the work in time, and also because the measures fell far short of the need. There were novices amongst the officials who could not recognise the signs of famine even after looking at the omens. Things turned so bad because of the

[16] Sir Arthur Thomas Cotton was a famous British general and an irrigation engineer. He has been known for doing commendable work in harnessing river waters in south India, especially the mighty Godavari, to help people in the famine and cyclone ravaged districts.

excessive delay in initiating [administrative] steps [so] that later on, food was not available even by spending money.'

The revenue board admitted that if suitable measures were initiated soon after getting Mr Ravenshaw's[17] telegram, innumerable lives could have been saved.

The situation is exactly same during the famine of 1943. Lots of untoward things have happened because responsibilities were entrusted to novices. A person who got an assignment was transferred to another department before he could gain some experience. Both, the Bengal and the Central Governments, have reshuffled employees related to matters of food [supply] with a rapidity that outpaced the motion pictures. From October 1939 to September 1942, the Central Government held six conferences to regulate prices. In the month of December 1942, the food department was created. A food advisory council had come into being in April 1942. In April 1943, a regional food commissioner was appointed. Four [persons] became 'food members' in succession at an average interval of two months. This was the case with regard to the Central Government. As regards Bengal, all of us have witnessed in how many different ways the canvas kept changing before our eyes.

The situation in 1943 became exactly as miserable as in 1866 due to government insouciance. Rice was not available even by throwing money. Several institutions collected subscriptions and arranged to feed [starving] people. The government came to think that if few thousands of such persons were fed, the public would reconcile [with food shortage], and it would not have to break its head over the matter. But the fact that

[17] Sir Thomas Edward Ravenshaw was an educationist par excellence. He was commissioner of revenue and circuit at Cuttack and credited with nearly 30 years of distinguished service in India.

the people had left [their] homes, were out on the streets and rushing to towns to fill their stomach escaped the notice of the authorities.

But that very situation was most dangerous. If food could have been reached to the villages, the rural households could have remained somewhat intact. They could even have earned something, and the desire to become self-supporting as early as possible would have remained awake in them. Famine drives people from villages to cities. [Consequently] One who used to be a householder loses self-respect and turns a beggar in the street. In this regard Sir Richard Temple[18] had said in the famine commission of 1878: 'The most horrific thing about famine manifests when people abandon homes and start loitering in search of food. Consequently, they tend to become morally degraded. Such movements should be stopped by arranging delivery of help in [a] disciplined manner in villages. There will be one centre each for a few villages. If rapid help is rushed in time, that will stop such wanderings.'

In 1866 too, people had abandoned their homes. Like in 1943, people used to lie on streets awaiting death. Large numbers died after getting drenched in the rain in the month of August. Skeletal people used to congregate on *Langarkhanas*[19] in droves. They did not have proper shelters. The government noticed that outsiders were spoiling public health in the cities. Then the Langarkhanas were closed almost by force, and the destitute persons were evicted from the towns. After seventy

[18] Sir Richard Temple succeeded Sir George Campbell as the Lieutenant Governor of Bengal Presidency and played an important role in handling the famine of 1873-74 in a competent manner.

[19] The word 'Langar' means 'free food'. A langarkhana is a centre from where the poor is served free food. These centres which were in the nature of relief centres operated out of humanitarian ideals.

years, we are seeing the repetition of those very events. Then fifteen to sixteen thousand people had gathered in Calcutta. In 1943, the number is one lakh [almost a hundred thousand] as per the government estimate.

Cooked food items used to be served even then and objections were raised against it. According to George Kirkwood, the relief commissioner of Cuttack, giving help in such form led to moral degeneration in the recipient. It is true that people cannot misuse this help by secretly selling the cooked food. But another aspect needs to be pondered over too. Taking such help [cooked food] hurts self-respect of many families, [and by refusing to avail this assistance] they silently advance to death. The same problem appeared in 1943 as well. Was any special arrangement made by the government to save those who were unable to go to the Langarkhanas?

In 1873-74, the government became aware of the famine at its very start. That helped prevent large-scale deaths. Before people left [their] villages, arrangements were made rapidly to reach them with help and they got chances to take up work before their physical strength ebbed. Again, to decide on whether or not a candidate qualified for help, the evidence of local people happened to be most authentic. If centres were opened in cities, such evidence would not have become available. Many unworthy persons would have grabbed the aid while majority of the destitute would not have managed to reach these relief centres. The junior Viceroy, Sir George Campbell,[20] had been especially enterprising to avoid such [a] situation. His opinion was that rendering help in disciplined

---

[20] Campbell was the Lieutenant Governor of Bengal during the 1873-74 famine while Lord Northbrook was the Viceroy. Campbell is credited for handling the famine ably.

ways would be impossible unless the people stayed put at [their] own homes, and were identified in terms of villages and by individual names. One relief centre was opened for every fifty or hundred villages. Entire Bengal was divided accordingly. In every such centre, a large granary was opened from which food was sent to the village granary. One responsible official used to inspect the operation every week. Such endeavours in 1873-74 to tackle famine may be said to be a model from all points of view. The same was completely ignored during the famine of 1943.

But, amidst such good arrangements at that time, rice was still being exported. George Campbell had strongly protested against this. On 12 October 1873, having warned the Government of India about the impending danger, he had urged: (1) begin the relief work forthwith; (2) arrange rice import from outside; and (3) stop exporting rice from India altogether. [But] The Viceroy did not agree to stop the rice export. He let the Secretary of State know about his objections: what would happen to Indian coolies who went to Mauritius, West Indies, Ceylon and other countries (mostly to work in European estates) in the event rice export was stopped? The echo of it has been heard in 1943 as well. We have been made to worry about Indian coolies in Ceylon and Indian soldiers in the Mediterranean countries. [But] We adopted none of the good measures that were adopted in 1873-74. Instead, the policy of rice export of that time alone has been maintained!

**In the compilation of this article, help was taken from the material collected by Shrijut Kali Charan Ghosh.

** Kali Charan Ghosh was a Bengali scholar whose book, *Famines in Bengal, 1770-1943,* is considered as one of the most celebrated works on the Bengal famines. This book gave a special coverage of the Fifty's Famine. Hereafter, references to this book are made by his surname i.e., Ghosh.

Speech at Town Hall

Calcutta, 6 June 1943

Editor's note: *Bengal Governor Sir John Arthur Herbert had coerced a popular, stable, secular coalition government led by Fazlul Huq out of office in March 1943, and instead of an all-party ministry installed the Muslim League-led ministry in power with Nazimuddin as the premier in the last week of April 1943. Over the next seven weeks i.e., till 6 June, the new ministry demonstrated that it had neither the capacity nor inclination to solve the food crisis.*

To the great anxiety of people, it seemed that governments at Delhi and London were acting in tandem with the government in Calcutta. Right since its inception, the League ministry took the line that Bengal had no food shortage. On 13 May, Major General Wood, Secretary of the Food Department, Government of India, also endorsed that view and said only 550,000 tons of rice and other cereals from the Central Government ought to suffice the need of the province. In London L S Amery, the Secretary of State for India, began to leverage the 'no shortage' theory to justify its inaction.

On the ground, the increasing unavailability of rice in the province was tearing apart the veil of comfort. The wholesale price of rice soared to new heights.[1] *The buying agents of the government, hoarders and dishonest traders played a key role in the unfolding of the crisis.*

Against this backdrop, the League ministry now promulgated the Bengal Food Grains Control Order and launched a 'food drive' essentially directed at the rural areas of Bengal. The drive excluded from its purview Calcutta and Howrah, the two most important places of hoarding. Further, the formula to calculate the permissible quantity of rice each family could hold was insensitive and ignored the consumption needs of children and other valid needs.

There were widescale reservations about the 'food drive' as it began to cause panic among the common people while not addressing the major hoarders.

For people of Bengal, another ominous thing was the hidden political agenda of the League ministry. Its proposal to form branches of the Muslim League at every Union board level and food committees corresponding to two thanas[2] *across the province demonstrated a tendency to advance its party interests more than a genuine concern for resolving the food crisis. Further, the initiatives for organising the Pakistan Conference amidst the situation of acute food crisis raised questions about the ministry's intention.*

Syama Prasad delivered this speech at the Town Hall, Calcutta on 6 June 1943. It was included in his book viz., Panchasher Manwantar in the chapter titled 'Collections'. The following is an English translation of his lecture.

---

1 The wholesale price of rice went up from Rs 22 per *maund* on 22.4.1943 to Rs 34 per *maund* in Calcutta: Ghosh, p 41. *Maund* was a unit of measurement of weight used in some Asian countries, especially in India. It equals roughly 37 kilogrammes.

2 A police station is called 'Thana' in Bengal and various other parts of India.

The [Muslim League] ministry has been in power for months. Still, they could not present a holistic policy to the public towards [a] solution of the food problem. This is lamentable. Quite contrary to facts, by repeatedly saying that there is no real dearth of food grains in Bengal, they have done great damage. It is the primary duty of the government to provide common people with bare minimum food. It is abject misfortune of Bengal and India that the food policy of the government is never determined keeping in view the interests of lakhs of its people. Many Indians survive on half stomach throughout the year even during peacetime. By paying excessive importance to the needs of those involved with war affairs, the interests of civilian residents have been neglected. It was the unreasonable statements made by ministers of Bengal that enabled Mr Amery [to] say in Parliament that the food crisis occurred due to hoarding of food grains. The blame was thus shifted from the shoulder of the government on to the common people. I do not deny that some quantity of food grains has been stored. But the upcoming food drive will not be conducted against big hoarders and profiteers who have flourished under government patronage and shattered the market by buying food grains at excessive prices. The drive will run in the rural areas in search of [the elusive] stored food grains.

It is certainly desirable to ascertain the quantity of the food grain that is available. But before the investigation is done, starting with a bias that there is abundant stock in the villages or that one particular class of people are squeezing the poor as has been publicised in the government communique, is absolutely unjust. [What is] 'Stocking' has been defined but [while framing the parameters] no consideration has been given to the 'need' for education, medical treatment and religious matters that are indispensable for every family. If two or one thousand maunds of food grains are recovered here and there, that can bring no solution to the problem. I do not think any significant quantity of grain will be found. This [exercise] will only add to the irritation of the people. Let such census be undertaken by trustworthy people. It will be unfair to take away small quantities of food grains stored by the [ordinary] householders before the census is complete, and it is fully proven that the goods have been stored with the purpose of profiteering.

The present ministry is tied through loyalty to Mr Jinnah[3] and [the goal of] Pakistan. Even as the war and grave food crisis rage, they are organising Pakistan conferences in different parts of Bengal. But it is an irony of fate that these very people have to run around other provinces that are outside their imaginary Pakistan, seeking help for food. After having understood the economic futility of the [proposed] Pakistan, will the Muslim League ministry refrain from its divisive activities and deeds that cause disunity in the present moment of crisis?

In the Eastern Zone, restrictions have been lifted upon trading [in food grains]. But the adjoining provinces have grown scared that famine-struck Bengal will suck away their food grains by offering very high prices, [in which case] the famine will spread to them as well. Still there is no doubt that some measure of support may come from those areas. But the ministry has not so far been able to make any firm assessment about this.

The people of rural areas where the 'food drive' will be conducted have been facing shortage and suffering themselves.

---

[3] Muhammad Ali Jinnah was a barrister, politician and the founder of Pakistan. Jinnah served as the leader of the All-India Muslim League from 1913 until Pakistan's independence on 14 August 1947, and then as Pakistan's first Governor-General until his death.

At the same time, big hoarders and profiteers have been allowed to buy rice from all parts of the province at any price without any restriction. [Prima facie] Such a method has been devised to secure the welfare of the poor households and to make each region self-dependent. But it is beyond our intelligence to comprehend how can these [goals] be achieved?

In the recent weeks, rice has been bought in places outside Bengal. It is necessary to obtain complete accounts of these [purchases]. Through whom and at what prices have the rice been acquired? What measures have the government adopted to ensure that the vendors cannot make illegitimate profit by selling this rice? We want answers to these [questions]. Has the government paid higher rates to the businessmen who bought rice at lower price in places outside Bengal? It is the clear duty of the government to secure complete control over the rice brought from outside and to ensure that the [procured] rice is sold across the distressed areas at justified prices through the shops under its control.

It is universally desirable that the 'grow more food' movement spreads all across. [But] from various areas reports are coming that people have eaten away the seeds [meant for the next crop] and seeds have thus become unavailable. The government should take immediate steps so that such pathetic things are not allowed to happen. The government has been campaigning, persuading people to eat substitute foodstuff instead of rice. Therefore, the government will have to guarantee supply of those substitutes. Else, such campaigns will be meaningless. People have been asked to eat *atta*[4] in lieu of rice. It means that the import of wheat has to be raised many times. The Central Government has offered twenty-two

[4] Wheat flour, not a natural crop in Bengal and the rest of East India.

lakh tons of wheat to Bengal. To get rid of the present crisis, Bengal needs at least another ten lakh tons of wheat. Clear answers are needed from the government, whether the specified quantity of wheat will eventually reach Bengal and further, whether the additional supply will be made available? If need be, arrangements will have to be made to bring wheat from across the seas. Even during the normal times, the crops raised in the country are insufficient to meet our requirements. By supplying [these crops] for war needs and to countries across the seas we have become more emptied now.

The British defeat in Burma is one of the reasons for our misery. Rice has not been coming from Burma. Some other special arrangement will have to be made [to meet this shortfall]. The Allied powers need to consider the food crisis in Bengal as a component of the war strategy. It is necessary for the rulers to remember that the misfortune of Bengal will not be conducive to gain the war objectives of the Allied powers. The [Bengal] ministry has [actually] been aggravating the crisis by announcing that there is no scarcity of food grains in the province and that the crisis owes to excessive stocking by common people. It's high time they stop such acts of intentional self-deceptions.

I am specifically reminding the ministry about one thing. They are determined to carry on the 'food drive'. Let such drive not be carried out to serve any political or party interests. Recently, a circular has been issued by the Bengal Provincial Muslim League to form branches of the Muslim League in each Union.[5] Arrangements are also being made to appoint a food committee covering every two thanas. We cannot say whether this drive has any connection with the aforesaid endeavours of

[5] 'Union' referred to a small group of villages situated in closely adjacent areas.

the Muslim League. The people of the land will have to be ever vigilant, so that the food committees are truly representative and cannot create any party-centric conflicts or communal unrest. The ministry did not think it necessary to secure the opinions of various parties and organisations on this plan. It will be impossible for those who, even in time of crisis such as the present occasion, think only about party interests and party loyalty, to unify people at large and inspire them about the [present] food policy [of the government].

No solution can be achieved about the food crisis unless the interests of the people and the government are unified. We must be given the certain assurance that the correct information shall not be hidden from us. If need be, the policy and the operational details of the government will have to be made available to the public. Without a [proper policy of] supply and distribution, there is no way we can get rid of the crisis. We shall unitedly present a demand for a political and economic policy framework towards that [end].

Bengal's Crisis

14 July 1943
Speech at Bengal Legislative Assembly

Editor's note: *The despotic manner in which the League ministry was handling a grave crisis got exposed from the outcome of the 'food drive'. By threatening ordinary householders with penal measures, if excess store of rice were detected, and gagging the press under Defence of India Rules, the ministry spread panic in the masses. This was accompanied by irresponsible and contradictory statements. On 30 June 1943 Suhrawardy, the civil supplies minister, had expressed satisfaction about food stock but on July 2 he said that deficit was observed everywhere. The panicked common men had sold away their meagre holding and those were lapped up by agents of the government and other dishonest businessmen. As a result, rice found their way to Calcutta and urban centres, denuding villages and greatly aggravating the food grains crisis. Unholy alliances between the ministry and select business houses were in evidence.*

Meanwhile, tidings of acute distress were reaching Calcutta from different parts of Bengal. Hungry people from villages began to wander to nearby towns on a large scale. In June 1943, about

600 people reportedly flooded Jalpaiguri from different parts of Murshidabad and adjoining districts. Next month hundreds of starving people converged on Bhola town of Barishal district. The destitute thronged Calcutta.... In July there were cases of starvation deaths on the streets of the city. The condition of Chittagong in the south east of the province was reported to be miserable, making the district magistrate send wire for rice supply. But the League ministry seemed unconcerned.

It did not forcefully pursue the 'quota' that the Central Government had committed to the province. Against this backdrop Syama Prasad, in a speech delivered at the Bengal Legislative Assembly in connection with a special motion on food, sought to evoke the sense of responsibility that a government must have towards the people. This speech constitutes an important document relating to the famine. Through his lecture and repartees, the attitudes of some political parties such as the Muslim League, the European Group and others on the issue of government policy on 'famine' is vividly painted, before the reader.

In his book, the author gave the essence of the specch in Bengali under the heading 'Banglar Sankat', translated as 'Bengal's Crisis'. Here the original speech in full is reproduced.[1] *Few footnotes have been added by the editor to help understand a term, word, sentence, person etc.*

Syama Prasad Mookerjee: Mr Speaker, Sir, for two days we have debated on the present food situation in the province. It goes without saying that we stand face to face before a national crisis. An attempt has been made on behalf of some of the

---

[1] Source: Assembly Proceeding Official Record, Bengal Legislative Assembly, Sixteenth session, 1943. The speech is reproduced as delivered in 1943, except for a few editorial interventions to improve readability.

spokesmen of [the] Government to suggest that the present situation is due to a legacy left by the past ministry. Sir, I do not propose to enter upon a detailed discussion of the good and weak points of the past ministry. One thing stands out prominently before our eyes; the past ministry did attempt to solve the food situation but where it did not succeed, it did not keep the reasons back from the Legislature or the public of Bengal. There were certain policies which were forced on the province more on account of the decision of the Government of India than of the provincial ministry, more on account of the obstructive and interfering conduct of the Governor than of the ministry, relating, for example, to the denial policy, to large scale exports and the purchase of rice by or on behalf of the Government of India.

Those were panicky weeks and months when the authorities thought that Japan, after conquering Burma, would invade Bengal, and the main thing that could prevent Japan from occupying this province would be the removal and destruction of leaky country boats and other conveyances and of stores of rice from the coastal districts of Bengal. Sir, the then Chief Minister made it abundantly clear that on account of the obstructive attitude taken up by the Governor and some of the permanent officials, it was impossible for the then ministry to carry into effect the policy that it advocated.

Today, as my friend Mr Suhrawardy has pointed out, the Department of Civil Supplies can boast of Indian officers of repute, although that very same attempt made by the past ministry was vetoed by the Governor who was not prepared to hand over key positions in this department, acting in his individual judgement, except to European members of the Indian Civil Service or non-official Europeans. I have nothing to say against them, but the fact remains that the policy which they tried to introduce and give effect to failed. The officers are still there; some of them have been promoted; some of them are suffering from nervous breakdown, but no one is here taking into account the horrid state to which they had reduced the province.

A Judge of the High Court was hurriedly brought from the Bench to preside over the Department of Civil Supplies and he did not know how quickly to go back to his old place again. But, Sir, the point before the House today is, I submit, not what the past ministry did or did not do, because it is out of office today, and the main onslaught on the past ministry during the March session was due to its alleged failure to control the food situation. The point before the House today is, what has the present ministry done and whether – considering the situation dispassionately, the House will agree that given the opportunities that the present ministry has had from the beginning of its office – it has justified the steps that it has taken and has really served the larger interests of the province.

Now, Sir, I come to the statements which the Hon'ble Minister for Civil Supplies made since the beginning of his new office. There was one thing which the past ministry did and that was to declare that Bengal did suffer from shortage of food-grains. That was one definite contribution to the credit of the past ministry and it also made the Government of India agree that the situation facing the province was a serious one due to shortage of foodstuffs. That was in March.

In April Mr Suhrawardy took office as Minister of Civil Supplies. I have scrutinised the numerous statements couched in beautiful language which were issued by him or on behalf of the new ministry and God knows why this attempt was made by him to play a colossal hoax on the unfortunate people of Bengal, namely, to declare that there was really no shortage of foodstuffs, no shortage of rice in Bengal and all that had happened was that there was maldistribution and small hoarders, private consumers and agriculturists were responsible for the present deplorable state of affairs.

Now, Sir, in one of the statements issued by Mr Suhrawardy it was said that the worst feature of the last ministry's food policy was its insistence on shortage. That was on 17 May. Then again, he said, 'There is in fact a sufficiency of food-grains for the people of Bengal.' I ask specially the members who are sitting opposite, anxious to give their support to the ministry, to demand an explanation from Mr Suhrawardy. What were the data before him which justified him to make that remark that there was in fact a sufficiency of food-grains for the people of Bengal? Not satisfied with his bare statement, he proceeded to remark,'Full statistical details, which will clearly demonstrate that there is a sufficiency, will shortly be published.' Where are those statistics? Have these statistics been collected or are they being manufactured?

Then again, Sir, he says in a statement which was issued on behalf of the government, both in Bengali and English:

আবেদন ও সতর্কবাণী

An Appeal and a Warning

দরিদ্র জনসাধারণকে আর উৎপীড়ণ করা চলিবেনা

You must not grind the faces of the poor.

Who is that 'you'? Is that Mr Suhrawardy standing before a mirror and addressing himself or was he seriously addressing the people of Bengal?

সত্যই কি বাংলাদেশে খাদ্যশস্যের অভাব ঘটিয়াছে? না নিশ্চয়ই না।[2]

'Is there a real shortage of food in Bengal? No, most certainly no', says Mr Suhrawardy in spite of the soaring prices and in spite of the untold sufferings of millions of the poor!

---

2 Meaning: No, certainly not.

Then he says, 'তবে আসল ব্যাপারটা কি? এ বছরের শেষ পর্য্যন্ত আমাদের অভাব মিটাইবার জন্য যথেষ্ট পরিমানে খাদ্যশস্য আমাদের ছিল এবং তাহা ছাড়া অন্যান্য দেশ হইতে ও আজ পর্য্যন্ত প্রচুর পরিমানে খাদ্যশস্য আমদানি হইতেছে। আড়ৎদার, ব্যবসায়ী, অবস্থাপন্ন কৃষক এবং আরো অনেকে আতঙ্কবশতঃ অথবা জনসাধারণকে নির্মমভাবে শোষণ করিবার আশায় প্রচুর খাদ্যশষ্য গোপনে জমা করিয়াছেন এবং এখনো করিতেছেন।[3]'

That was the statement, which was issued, that was one of the official documents issued by the present ministry of Bengal: there was no shortage; there was ample foodstuff and it was the people themselves who were responsible for causing suffering. And it was not the big hoarders, big stockists and big profiteers like A, B, C and X, Y & Z whose stocks were searched and unearthed, but it was the ordinary people, the private consumers and agriculturists who were alleged to have been grinding the faces of the poor and a crusade was directed against them. Now, it is curious that simultaneously with this announcement made by the new ministry of Bengal, which had the special blessing of the Governor of this province and a section of permanent officials, His Master's Voice spoke out in the House of Commons. There Mr Amery declared, 'Yes, there is some trouble in India and in Bengal but there is no shortage of food-stuffs in the country; there is only hoarding and maldistribution and the government is looking after this aspect of the problem'.

The false picture painted by a so-called responsible ministry just enabled the representative of His Majesty's Government to get up in the House of Commons and to announce to the world that the serious situation that threatened Bengal, which

---

[3] Meaning: What is the real issue then? We had adequate food grains to meet our needs till the end of this year. Further, adequate food grains are being imported to meet any shortfall till the end of this year. Stockists, businessmen, affluent farmers have secretly accumulated huge quantities of food grains either driven by panic or to mercilessly squeeze the masses and they are still doing so.

was near the eastern war frontier, was not due to the pursuit of any wrong policy by the Government, either in Delhi or in Calcutta but due to the foolish and obstructive attitude taken up by the people themselves.

Now, Sir, what happened next?

Mr Suhrawardy declared that there was plenty of foodstuffs in Bengal. All that had to be done was to find out the foodstuffs even from under *taktaposhes.*[4] After a tired and busy night, he seriously made a speech declaring that, if necessary, he would himself go under the taktaposh of every householder and bring out the rice. I know that many householders got nervous. If Mr Suhrawardy really starts entering into households and going under the taktaposh at night or even during daytime, Heaven protect those householders from the after-effects of the ministerial attacks. Could there have been, I ask, a sillier approach to a problem vitally affecting the lives of millions of people?

Now, another reason put forward by Mr Suhrawardy was that the problem was mainly psychological.

I do not know when Mr Suhrawardy became a student of abnormal psychology. His place would then be Ranchi and not Calcutta because that was the place where persons suffering under delusion and anxious to study abnormal psychology were properly dealt with. He says that the problem is psychological. And how is that to be tackled? People are merely to be told, 'Don't get panicky. I am here sitting as the Civil Supplies Minister and telling you there is plenty of foodstuff. We have statistics which we do not intend to publish. Everything will be alright. Don't get panicky.' Even if he, as spokesman of Government, is to try some sort of appeal, reassuring [the] public mind is he capable

[4] Takhtaposh: A simple four-legged wooden bedstead which is used by common householders in Bengal.

of getting the people [a]round him psychologically, by simply a wave of the magic wand from Writer's Building?

There was no question of his taking advice from different parties. He talked of psychology. He talked loosely of appeal for cooperation. But he never cared for popular support; he never honestly sought the cooperation of all parties. He was swayed by party politics himself. The party leaders were sent for on 17 May. It is no secret. The demand was made by all, including the admiring group of the European Party, that the whole scheme of the government must be placed in the hands of the leaders before any opinion could be expressed. A solemn assurance was given by the Civil Supplies Minister and the Chief Minister that copies of the scheme which the government had in view would be placed before the party leaders.

What happened then?

Days and weeks passed. Then suddenly, only a few days before the actual famous food drive with an incompetent and ill-equipped coachman was to be started in Bengal, the party leaders were hurriedly summoned in the Bengal Legislative Assembly House. We had been meanwhile to some district towns and there we were given copies of the scheme by others who had already received them, cut and dried, circulated throughout the province with instructions that it should be given effect to from the 8 or 9 June. This camouflage of consultation between the Minister and the party leaders took place about a few days before the actual food drive was to have started. That was the sort of cooperation which the new ministry wanted to depend upon, to make a psychological approach to the problem.

Now, Sir, what about the details of the food drive?

I am not going to trouble the House with the details of the scheme. There is none who will object or who can object to the proposal that a census of stocks should be taken in the province. In fact, that should have been done long ago and was actually decided upon by the last ministry. It is no secret that this decision was upset [revoked] by no other person than His Excellency the Governor himself, who said that it was not necessary because there were more urgent and important things to be done, relating to the removal of rice and boats from the coastal parts of Bengal, lest the Japs should come and take advantage of these great resources of the province.

Now, Sir, so far as taking statistics is concerned, no one can have any objection to that. But the scheme was much more than mere stock-taking. I got a copy of a Bengali pamphlet only this morning, coming from a distant part of Bengal which is the real basis of the great scheme for which originality has been claimed by Mr Suhrawardy.

It appears that before the new ministry came into office, a circular was issued by the Palli Unnayan Bibhag – I believe, the Village Reconstruction Department – under the signature of Mr Ishaque which was practically the basis of the scheme which the new ministry, after devoting hours and days of thought, was supposed to have discovered for the benefit of the people of Bengal.

There is one main difference in the scheme which Mr Suhrawardy has placed before the people. While calculating the surplus stock, Mr Suhrawardy directed that children below four years of age of poor families were not expected to take any rice and should be excluded. Well, he did not even know that they could not live on other food like Horlick's milk and other delicious children's food ordinarily available for richer people. Mr Ishaque, the Director of Rural Reconstruction, had the goodness of including even children who were aged below four. But Mr Suhrawardy came and the great reform he made was practically to suggest that children might be starved!

Kiran Sankar Roy:[5] Because he has no children.

Syama Prasad Mookerjee: I do not know that, but this omission showed up his mentality and methods.

Then, Sir, what was the result of the food drive?

The food drive went on. We stated from the beginning that the food drive was not going to lead to anything but simply to criminal waste of most valuable time. An order was issued under the Defence of India Rules that no newspaper would be allowed to comment on the food drive unless the editorials were placed before the Home Department for previous scrutiny. That was a taste of the new regime of the 'liberator of freedom', to quote Mr Siddiqi.[6] If people wanted to criticise and point out what is fundamentally wrong with the scheme – they were to be gagged and no article was to be published without pre-censoring by the Home Department. The scheme was devised to cause a tremendous stir.

What was exactly the scheme, we asked the government officers and Mr Suhrawardy at the conference we attended. What did the ministry actually intend to do? There was no guarantee to make up deficits. In one place, the ministry stated that it wanted village self-sufficiency, it wanted local self-sufficiency; it did not want that any surplus rice should be removed from any area unless the needs of that area were

---

[5] Kiran Sankar Ray was an important Congress leader in the Bengal Legislative Assembly. After partition, he was leader of Congress opposition in Pakistan Assembly. Later he moved to India. He was the Home Minister of the West Bengal government for about a year, until he died untimely.

[6] AR Siddiqi was elected to the Bengal Legislative Assembly from the Muslim Chamber of Commerce.

first met. In the same breath we found that rich traders and profiteers were allowed a free movement in all parts of the province, and out of the panic of application of Defence of India Rules and forcible seizure, the rice which came out was purchased at fancy prices by these profiteers and traders who were moving round Bengal like so many vultures and mainly removed the stocks to Calcutta areas.

What has been the result?

The result was that whatever rice was or might be available was taken away from rural areas. Practically the entire rural area was denuded. And except on paper there was no attempt to make up deficits. Mr Suhrawardy, in one of his statements stated: 'it was significant that this drive has already resulted in a sharp drop in prices.' Two or three such statements appeared and then the statements also vanished as rice began to disappear and the prices started rising up. He has been discreetly silent about prices during the last fortnight. We have not yet received reports from all parts of Bengal, but I take upon myself the responsibility for stating that in about eight districts from which we received information, the price of rice has already gone up from 3 to 5 rupees per maund more than what it was on or about the 25th of June 1943. At Siliguri it is +Rs 4-8; at Rangpur +Rs 4; at Manikganj +Rs 4; at Mymensingh +Rs 4; at Netrokona +Rs 6; at Jessore +Rs 5-8; at Khulna +Rs 5; at Satkhira +Rs 5; at Dinajpur Rs 5; and so on. That is the net result of the food drive.

And why were Calcutta and Howrah excluded?

If you were really sincere and genuine, if you wanted that there should be a full stock-taking, you should have started with Calcutta and Howrah. Why did you not take the stocks of those wealthy profiteers like Messrs Ispahani & co,[7] who, according to the Minister himself, can today forego a profit of 40 lakhs for the benefit of the poor people of this province. There may be Shaw Wallace & Co., there may be other people. Why did you exclude these particular firms? What was the reason? The reason was that there were certain firms which cannot be easily touched; the reason was that there were certain quarters near which the mighty Mr Suhrawardy dared not go, because they were the people on whom the ministry had to depend for its existence. So, they had to be left out, and this so-called drive had to be undertaken against poor consumers and agriculturists.

Of course, any stock-taking in Calcutta now would be meaningless, as stated in a leaflet circulated by one of the supporters of Mr Suhrawardy criticising his activities that – even if a drive was now undertaken in Calcutta, one cannot get at the truth because rice would be removed from this particular area to other parts meanwhile.

Now, Sir, so far as the deficit is concerned, Mr Suhrawardy has given us no information, for he says collection of statistics is not yet completed. The statistics will never be published for they would show colossal figures of deficit in every area. He says that he has received information that a surplus, which would amount to six to seven million maunds, has been secured. The figure is illusory as it does not take the deficits into account. But is he really correct about the figures? Six to

---

7 The Ispahani family are a Perso-Bengali business family in Bangladesh and Pakistan which owns and manages the Ispahani Group. Originally hailing from Isfahan, Iran, the family have been settled in the Indian subcontinent for more than a century. The company now has corporate offices in Chittagong, Dhaka and Khulna where it employs over 20,000 people in many sectors such as tea, textile, real estate, crisps, poultry, shipping and internet services. They were active in Calcutta before Independence.

seven million maunds means 60 to 70 lakhs of maunds. When Mr Suhrawardy will give his reply I hope he will please check the statement he has made because it is contrary to a statement which, though not an authorised one, was published a few days ago in a Calcutta newspaper to the effect that the stock would be about eight to nine *lakhs* and not *millions* of maunds. Sir, there is some difference between 80 lakhs and 8 lakhs. Even if it is 80 lakhs, as Mr David Hendry[8] has pointed out, it would mean food for fifteen days only to the people of Bengal, on the supposition there was no deficit, which again was far from the truth.

What then? I would ask Mr Suhrawardy to answer this question, what next? Before he launched upon this programme we warned him about a possible failure of the drive to discover big stocks sufficient to serve the people. We said, 'You are evading your responsibility, you are throwing the entire responsibility on the people themselves. If you fail here, what next?' He said, 'I do not know'.

H S Suhrawardy: I did never say that.

Syama Prasad Mookerjee: You did say: 'I do not know'. If you want to withdraw the statement now, you are quite welcome.

H S Suhrawardy: I said I did not know what next to do.

Syama Prasad Mookerjee: Sir, he admits he said that he did not know what next to do. Does he mean to say that a responsible Minister should have launched upon this drive without making himself certain as to the steps he has to take next in case the drive fails, as it has indeed actually failed? Sir, is this the way in which he discharges his responsibility?

(**Suhrawardy** mutters something.)

---

8 David Hendry was the leader of the European Party in the Bengal Legislative Assembly.

It is no use his coming here and speaking in a tone which befits the residents of the Zoological Gardens. If the position he took up was that he did not know what he was going to do next in case the drive failed, I would say he shirked his responsibility and is not fit to hold his office.

Sir, let me come to the constructive part of the ministry's activities – the great free trade zone in North-Eastern India. That was a great triumph, Mr Suhrawardy said. Sir Nazimuddin[9] expanded himself when he said, 'We have got free trade in Eastern India'. Today that free trade is going to disappear without bringing any rice to Bengal or conferring any benefit to the people at large, except the contribution of Mr Suhrawardy to make Mr Ispahani the sole purchaser for Bengal Government on mysterious terms to which I shall refer presently! I say, Sir, that the ministry bungled from the beginning by failing to take proper advantage of the free trade scheme on account of its haste, its indecision, its anxiety to patronise particular firms and persons. It thus lost a great chance to serve the province. Sir, what should have been the duty of the Civil Supply Department?

H S Suhrawardy: Nonsense!

Syama Prasad Mookerjee: Nonsense is an epithet which applies to the Civil Supply Minister because he is today entirely devoid of sense, and if that means nonsense, he is nonsense personified.

Now, Sir, so far as Bihar or Orissa was concerned, what did Mr. Suhrawardy do?

---

[9] Khwaja Nazimuddin held the office of Prime Minister of Bengal from 1943 to 1945. He was leader of the Muslim League, and an important Bengali leader in Pakistan. After partition he was the first chief minister of East Pakistan. He became Governor General of Pakistan after Jinnah's death and also served as Prime Minister of Pakistan between October 1951 and April 1953.

It is no use his trying to shout in irritating tempter inside the Chamber. He has got to give replies. I am giving him facts and let him reply by stating facts. What did Mr Suhrawardy do with regard to Orissa and Bihar? Why did he not negotiate with the Government in those provinces? He sent wealthy traders and other private individuals with full liberty to purchase rice. What was the result? The price of rice there varied from Rs 6, Rs 8 and Rs 10 to Rs 15 and Rs 18. Immediately the prices started jumping up. Here were people with plenty of money in their pocket coming from Bengal, offering to purchase rice at any price. The result was that like a blaze of fire, famine conditions spread from Bengal to Orissa and Bihar, with this difference perhaps between the Orissa ministry and the present Bengal ministry that the Orissa minister had the courage to admit that conditions were serious and in one district alone, during a fortnight, 70 people died of starvation on account of famine conditions prevailing in Balasore and here on the other hand, facts are suppressed and government responsibility is constantly evaded.

That was the procedure adopted and that was how you lost the cooperation and sympathy of neighbouring provinces. You let loose wealthy traders and individuals who wanted to profit by easy purchases in different parts of Orissa and Bihar. The government of Orissa revolted; the Government of Bihar revolted. Then Mr Suhrawardy tried to negotiate with them. I say, Sir, it was the clear duty of the Bengal ministry to do it at the very first stage and that is the charge which I bring forward against it. Why did Mr Suhrawardy hesitate first to go to Orissa and Bihar? Was it because he, a protagonist of the Pakistan scheme, did not care to ask favours from Orissa and Bihar as they formed part of the future Hindusthan?

Alas, the economic structure of Pakisthan (sic) is collapsing and Bengal, the future home of Pakisthan (sic), has to be provided for through the generosity of adjoining Hindu provinces. Mr. Suhrawardy has to apply to the Central Government for help. Without a Central Government you cannot, after all, control the affairs of Bengal and India. He has to apply and run to Orissa and Bihar; and he told us,'We may have to go to Nepal'. I said, why not go to Burma; you will get rice quickly from there and the problem may be solved, if you are allowed to return home! But let me ask in all seriousness, why did not Mr Suhrawardy approach the Bihar Government and Orissa ministry and try to come to some settlement. Why did he not go and say to each, 'Can you spare, say five or ten lakhs of maunds of rice for Bengal? We are starving'. The question of price could have been fixed round the table between the Bengal, Orissa and Bihar Governments without allowing traders, and profiteers and middlemen to play havoc with prices. The Ministry could have approached the problem from that point of view, but it did not.

I next come, Sir, to the question of appointment of Ispahanis as the sole purchaser on behalf of the Government of Bengal. I can at once say that I have nothing personal against Mr Ispahani, much less do I know all the partners in the firm. It is not a personal issue; it is a question of principle. It was nothing short of a scandal that the ministry should have appointed a particular firm as the sole agent, and what is more, advanced about two crores of rupees to that firm without a single scrap of document. Can Mr Suhrawardy produce a single contract entered upon between Ispahanis and the Government of Bengal?

Where is the direction taken from the Bengal Legislative Assembly? It is a mockery. We are sitting here as the

Bengal Legislative Assembly trying to decide the fate of the province. The budget was attempted to be brought in a hole-and-corner fashion. The budget has gone back, but even the budget that was presented for our consideration last week did not include this figure of rupees two crores or more, which has already been advanced without authority to Messrs Ispahani and Company. It is clearly an unauthorised and illegal expenditure from public funds the like of which it is difficult to find, unless you go back to the tantalising and mysterious surroundings of Pretoria Street, about which we heard a lot and the rest may be narrated by Mr Suhrawardy himself.

Now, Sir, no terms and conditions have yet been finally agreed upon between Ispahanis and the Government of Bengal. I make this statement and let the government contradict it if it dares to. Up till now there has been no written agreement between the government of Bengal and Ispahanis. No tenders were invited. The terms have not been offered to others. Ispahanis have refused to pay any security as demanded by the government of Bengal. Will government dare say 'no'? Is it not a scandal of the first magnitude that at this perilous time, two crores of rupees or more, of public money is to be handed over to a firm, a partner of which is a pillar of the party to which Mr Suhrawardy belongs? It is said the purpose is to serve the millions of Bengal's unfortunate children. Why, I ask you – and this has to be answered by Mr Suhrawardy – why was this extraordinary procedure adopted?

What was the necessity? Why were not tenders called? Mr Suhrawardy says that the Chambers of Commerce were consulted. Such a brazen-faced falsehood was never uttered on the floor of the House. It has already been stated on behalf of the Bengal National Chamber of Commerce that that Chamber was not consulted. The representative of the Marwari Chamber of Commerce yesterday got up and said that that Chamber was not consulted. I have the authority of the Indian Chamber of Commerce to say that that Chamber was not also consulted. Then why this deliberate attempt to delude the legislature and the public of Bengal?

Why were not tenders called? You talk of foregoing of profit. What is this profit of Rs 40 lakhs? What does it mean? I do not know what it means. Mr Suhrawardy might be able to explain, but I suppose the position is like this. I am taking certain figures hypothetically. Ispahanis may have in their possession five lakhs maunds of rice which at market rate today in Calcutta may be sold at Rs 30 per maund. Supposing Ispahanis come forward and say,'We will sell this rice to you at Rs 22 per maund'. It means for every maund, the Ispahanis are supposed to give up a profit of Rs 8 and if it is 5 lakhs of maunds, the total makes Rs 40 lakhs. But the point is, at what price did the Ispahanis purchase originally?

Should not there be an enquiry as regards the purchase value of this rice – whether it was Rs 10 or Rs 12 or Rs 15? By allowing the Ispahanis already to make a profit of Rs 7 or 8 per maund, you have filled their pocket with a profit of 28 to 32 lakhs of rupees. Who is the profiteer, I ask? What is the policy of the present Government of Bengal in giving protection to favoured profiteers and allow them to prosper and thrive on the miseries of the people of the province?

I would appeal to the Muslim members who are sitting on the other side to consider the situation dispassionately and not treat this as a party question. It is not a question of Muslim League or Congress or this party or that.

Abdul Motaleb Malik:[10] We learnt from you.

Syama Prasad Mookerjee: You did not learn from us.

And if you did, why should you copy what is bad and pernicious. It is true that the Ispahanis got a *benamdar* contract[11] during the office of the previous ministry but it is known that was done under the orders of the governor of Bengal by the Joint Secretary. This has been mentioned by Mr Fazlul Huq here on the floor of the House and the facts have yet to be challenged. May I ask in all seriousness how are these transactions going on now? I am told there is a suggestion that Ispahanis will not purchase rice on their own account so long as they serve as government agent, but that is a term which Ispahanis want to modify, a term to which they have not yet agreed. They have suggested that they should be given the permission to purchase on their own account with the approval of the Director of Civil Supplies. These important terms have yet to be settled and meanwhile crores of rupees are being handed over from the public exchequer to a favoured member of the Muslim League Party.

Sir, for far less serious allegations Mr Hendry and his party became furious and withheld their support to the past ministry. There have been no allegations like these against the past ministry. What are they going to do now? They are sitting here like tame lambs and they will be taken like dumb driven cattle to the lobby along with Mr Suhrawardy. A certificate has been given to the Ministry by Mr Hendry and like a petulant child

---

[10] Abdul Motaleb Malik was a leader of Muslim League. He became a minister in independent Pakistan and also held several important positions. He was briefly the last civilian governor of East Pakistan. After Bangladesh became independent, he was confined for waging war against it.

[11] A contract entered into by a party in a name other than his or her own. Here, the beneficial owner of the interest under the contract is different from the nominal owner.

he has asked for a certificate from the ministry too! 'I scratch your back and you scratch mine'.

(**A voice from the Government Benches**: They scratched your back also.)

Syama Prasad Mookerjee: Sir, I am glad that my honourable friend said that. Yes, they tried to scratch our back, but when they found that it was something different from what they liked it to be and we were not prepared to scratch theirs, the European Party turned to the side of the Opposition in March last and put the present ministry in office.

Now, Sir, the House would like to know from Mr Suhrawardy today why Mr McInnes[12] resigned.

Nalinaksha Sanyal:[13] He was prevailed upon to resign.

Syama Prasad Mookerjee: Mr McInnes left his office in disgust. Does Mr Suhrawardy dare deny that? I say, Sir, that Mr McInnes went away because he was disgusted with the manner in which the Minister was administering the Department of Civil Supplies. Did he not say that if the affairs of this department were to be controlled in thc interest of or according to the wishes of one particular firm which was itself so closely involved, it is much better that government should deal with that firm directly and not through a dummy Post Office? Sir, I shall not deal with this point any further except to say one word.

(At this stage **Abdur Rahman Siddiqi** muttered something while sitting.)

---

[12] A A McInnes was appointed as Food Grains Control Officer in January 1943 by the Governor without taking Fazlul Huq, the chief minister, into confidence, attracting protest by the latter.

[13] Dr Nalinaksha Sanyal was chief whip of the Congress Party in the Bengal Legislative Assembly. He was a vocal critic of British rule and also the policy of the provincial government during the famine. In independent India, he held several important positions in the government and represented the country in international bodies.

Sir, I am glad that Mr Siddiqi has interrupted me and his conscience has been aroused. Mr Siddiqi declared the other day that he was an independent member so far as questions of constitutional practice were concerned. He need not be impatient. I shall now give him a problem of constitutional practice. If you will please refer to page 34 Chapter I of *May's Parliamentary Practice*, there is a convention which is supported by law that no member of the House of Commons who is a Government contractor has the right to vote or even has the right to continue as a member of the House of Commons. I cannot, Sir, actually raise a point of order, because I know that this is not based on convention but on a definite statute passed by the British Parliament. Now, Sir, Mr Siddiqi is famous for his knowledge of constitutional practice and convention in England, in Turkey, in Spain, in France, in Belgium, in Honolulu and everywhere else. Will he now have the courage to admit that having regard to this very salutary principle, Mr Ispahani and any other government contractor should cease to be a member of the Bengal Legislative Assembly?

H S Suhrawardy: There were contractors during your ministry.

Syama Prasad Mookerjee: Who are they?

H S Suhrawardy: Look round and see them.

Syama Prasad Mookerjee: If there were MLAs who were government contractors, they should have been similarly dealt with and they deserved no sympathy. One of the reasons why Mr Suhrawardy condemned the previous Minister in charge of the Commerce and Labour Department was his undue patronage and favouritism, and now if Mr Suhrawardy says that his self-satisfaction lies in thinking that he is following in the glorious footsteps of the last ministry in this respect, perhaps with compound interest, the consolation will be his and of the party to which he belongs. But let hypocrisy then stand unmasked before the public of Bengal.

The next point is with regard to the system of distribution. Here I shall be very brief. With regard to the system of distribution, government says that controlled shops have failed and it proposes to open government shops to the extent of 800. Sir, I do not hold a brief for controlled shops. I know that controlled shops have failed in many cases for two broad reasons: (1) want of supply, and (2) corruption in some cases. My point is that if controlled shops individually have failed on account of corruption, get rid of them. No one will come and find fault for any such action. But why do away entirely with the ordinary channels of trade which is inconsistent with the policy pursued by any government with regard to distribution?

I am not saying [this] with regard to purchase. That I shall come to later. With regard to distribution, why should a proposal be made that all ordinary channels of trade are to be dispensed with and government shops are to be opened? What are these shops? To whom will they be offered? At what price? On what consideration and for what areas? Now, Sir, the last ministry decided that unless a man was in trade for at least three years, he would not be entitled to a controlled shop. That was a salutary check. Why has that order been ignored? Is it a hindrance in the way of distributing patronage on communal and political considerations?

What about the 'Grow More Food' campaign?

What are the constructive proposals of government? Food will not grow on paper and mere propaganda is an eyewash. Every day we are getting letters from all parts of Bengal that there is a tremendous dearth of agricultural seeds and unless government takes proper steps now, the next aman crop of the year will be failure. What will be the result? With the province practically denuded of rice and with the prospect of the next main crop failing; can you even visualise the dire consequences which will follow?

I do not know whether the ministry is receiving information, but there has been an extraordinary loss of cattle suffering from particular diseases in different parts of the province. Cattle purchase for military requirements has also proceeded on an enormous scale. One member of the Assembly who recently came from his native home said that out of 14 bullocks which he had, 13 had died of small-pox and only one has been left alive and that is the general picture from different parts of the province.

What are the constructive proposals of government with regard to various aspects of the 'Grow More Food' campaign? Again, has the ministry considered the dangerous consequences on public health due to spread of diseases and epidemics in the coming months which may well fall as the last fatal blow on the already shattered health and vitality of millions of Bengal's unfortunate children? What steps, I ask, have been taken to prevent deaths due to starvation and disease?

Now, Sir, what is the remedy? The remedy is, government must declare a famine and apply generously the normal provisions for meeting famine conditions. government must undertake full responsibility for feeding the people of the province and not indulge in a cheap doctrine of self-help or of forcible loans of rice, that barely exists, repayable by village committees when able, without any guarantee from government. You must take the responsibility for feeding the people or get out; and let your masters, who have created this state of affair in the province, the British government which is the real ruling power, let the British government take the responsibility for feeding the people of Bengal and maintaining peace and order.

So far as the main problem is concerned, there must be a full and complete control over prices and supplies. As Mr Hendry put it, there are three ways of doing it: government may make all purchases; the traders may purchase; or both government and traders may purchase. It is the government's coming to the market which has upset the situation completely. The situation will never be overcome unless government takes full control. The traders cannot be given an unfettered jurisdiction because it means depleting the province and unfair and inequitable distribution. It is government which can take full control of supplies and prices and distribution leading to rationing.

Rationing means guarantee of supply. Without supply rationing is meaningless. What government is doing is worse than rationing. Government is practically starving the people. There is no supply, and government does not say that it will introduce rationing and take responsibility for the supply. People are prepared to suffer and sacrifice, provided justice and equity govern the principles of supply and distribution, affecting all classes of people.

What sort of government can take charge of this great responsibility? Not certainly an illegitimate offspring of intrigue, fraud and un-constitutionalism, or a combination of betrayers and strong partisans. At this supreme crisis in the history of the province, it is not possible for any party Government to take full control of supply and prices and undertake the responsibility for feeding six crores of people of Bengal. That is a sheer impossibility. If the Muslim League is in opposition and if this side forms the cabinet, even then that government cannot solve the problem.

Indeed, we have got to forget party differences. The ministry must enjoy the confidence of all sections of the people. If you are genuinely sincere in your attempt to help, there must be a national approach to the problem – not the sort of approach, prompted entirely by party and political considerations – and there should be a Cabinet consisting of representatives of all parties and groups who are willing to work together.

Rasiklal Biswas: Including yourself?[14]

Syama Prasad Mookerjee: Not myself for I refuse to be a cat's paw. Mr Rasiklal Biswas knows it very well, just as everyone knows, his own anxiety to go higher and higher up the ladder by fresh acts of betrayal and treachery. But there will be enough competent people who may be willing to shoulder responsibility. Party spirit must die out in the face of this common national calamity.

H S Suhrawardy: Hear, hear.

Syama Prasad Mookerjee: And that party spirit will die out not by the shouts of 'hear hear' by a Minister who is actuated only by party and communal considerations, but by all agreeing to come to a settlement in such a manner as is conducive to the welfare of the province and not to any particular party which thrives on British patronage.

H S Suhrawardy: Hear, hear (again).

Syama Prasad Mookerjee: Now, Sir, I would like to conclude, if I may, with a short reference to history. I shall not quote Bankimchandra, lest it be said he held biased views. Historians, British historians, have reiterated that cycles of famine and pestilence in the history of Bengal have come with strange precision and certainty. Hunter refers to the amazing

[14] Rasiklal Biswas was a member of the Bengal Legislative Assembly elected from Jessore constituency.

circumstances under which the kingdom of Gour fell a victim to pestilence, just when the Moghul Empire was spreading its arms round Bengal. In one year, that great and beautiful city which was the pride not only of Bengal but the whole of India, vanished, and as Hunter put it in his inimitable language, it became a hunting ground of tigers and monkeys.

Then the Moghul Empire came, ruled and disappeared. After some centuries, came the famous famine of 1770 in Bengal known in Bengali as ছিয়াত্তরের মন্বন্তর (famine of seventy-six) and that again just after the battle of Plassey, when the British were trying to establish suzerainty over Bengal. That was the second cycle.

Now, Sir, today we are face to face with another famine and grave economic crisis. Whether the second cycle will continue to have a further lease of life or to the misfortune of Bengal, a third cycle of foreign domination is in sight, Heaven alone knows! Reports of death, suffering and misery are pouring in from all parts of Bengal. Much as [the] government may try to suppress them or minimise their gravity by sweet-worded communiques issued by a pliable ministry, the finger of fate points irresistibly towards a strange and awful repetition of history. Let us ponder here for a moment, when history is going to repeat itself, as regards the situation in Bengal when the great famine of 1770 took place. Now this is what Hunter says. I would beg members to apply their minds to this picture and ask the British authorities how they mean to discharge their obligation in 1943.

(Interruption by **Mr Abdur Rahman Siddiqi**.)

I know it hurts Mr Siddiqi.

Abdur Rahman Siddiqi: It does.

Syama Prasad Mookerjee: There may be others in the House who are more merciful and who may have more tender feelings for the people of this unfortunate Bengal. If Mr Siddiqi coming from distant Sind is yet to be satisfied with the pile he has made from Bengal and has yet to rouse himself to have pity for the people of this province, I can only take pity on him. Now, Sir, here Hunter[15] gives a picture of the famine of 1770:

> All through the stifling summer of 1770, the people went on dying. The husbandmen sold their cattle; they sold their implements of agriculture; they devoured their seed-grain; they sold their sons and daughters till at length no buyer of children could be found. They ate the leaves of trees and the grass of the field; and in June, 1770, the Resident of the Durbar affirmed that the living were feeding on the dead. Day and night a torrent of famished and disease-stricken wretches poured into the great city.... Streets were blocked up with promiscuous heaps of the dying and the dead. Interment could not do its work quick enough; even dogs and jackals, the public scavenger of the east, became unable to accomplish their revolting work and the multitude of mangled and festering corpses at length threatened the existence of the citizens.

Now, Sir, a similar picture was given by no less a person than Macaulay[16] in his *Life of Lord Clive:*

> Tender and delicate women whose veils had never been lifted before the public gaze came forth from the inner chambers

---

[15] Sir William Wilson Hunter was the author of the famous book, *The Annals of Rural Bengal,* a celebrated work based on famines in India, especially the grand famine of 1770 AD.

[16] Thomas Babington Macaulay was a noted British historian, essayist, reviewer and politician who played a key role in introducing English and western concepts to education in India.

> in which Eastern jealousy had kept watching over their beauty, threw themselves on the earth before the passers-by and with loud wailings implored a handful of rice for their children. The Hooghly everyday rolled down thousands of corpses close to the porticoes and gardens of the English conquerors. The very streets of Calcutta were blocked up by the dying and the dead. The lean and feeble survivors had not energy enough to bear the bodies of their kindred to the funeral pile or to the holy river or even to scare away the jackals and vultures who fed on human remains in the face of day.

Sir, it is not stories but actual reports that we are getting from different parts of Bengal – today I received half-a-dozen letters from different parts of the province – that seems similar to what I have described are being enacted already. Sir, the question which I would like to put to the House is: What is the solution of this great calamity? Where will our parties be, where shall we be, if life in Bengal comes to an abrupt end, not on account of any ravages of nature as had happened on previous occasions but on account of a wrong policy pursued by the authorities responsible for the administration of this province and country? For nearly two centuries the people have been bled to death, exploitation has gone on unchecked. During the last four years for the so-called purposes of the war, the interests of the common people have been ruthlessly sacrificed and they have today almost reached death's door.

Now, Sir, this is what Macaulay says, giving his reasons for the serious state of affairs in Bengal in 1770: 'No doubt nature did its work, but over and above nature there were the effects of misgovernance of English administration just before 1770.' And these are the actual words of Macaulay:

> Every servant of British factory was armed with all the powers of his master; and his master was armed with all the powers of the Company. Enormous fortunes were thus rapidly accumulated at Calcutta whilst thirty millions of human beings were reduced to the extremity of wretchedness.

Could anyone paint better the sordid picture of the foundation of the great trusteeship of British rule in India?

> 'They had been accustomed to live under tyranny, but never under a tyranny like this. They found the little finger of the Company thicker than the loins of Surajah Dowla.[17] Under their old masters, they had at least one recourse; when the evil became insupportable, the people rose and pulled down the Government, but the English Government was not to be so shaken off. That Government, oppressive as the most oppressive form of barbarian despotism, was strong with all the strength of civilization. It resembled the Government of evil genii rather than the government of human tyrants.

This is the picture of how English rule started in India nearly two centuries ago. Today we are in 1943. Are we in any better position today to serve our own people and country and save them from the hands of organised exploiters and adventurers?

My appeal to you is this. Today everyone knows that the ultimate responsibility for this state of affairs rests on the

---

[17] Usually spelt as Siraj-ud-daulah, he was Nawab and ruler of Bengal. He was defeated by Lord Clive of East India Company in the battle of Plassey in 1757 and executed.

British administrators in India. They wanted first to provide for their troops. They wanted to cater for those who were directly or indirectly concerned in war efforts, forgetting their great responsibility to the people of the country who must be fed and kept alive. We in Bengal, Mr David Hendry reminds us, are on the border of the Eastern War Zone. How will this war be won? If Bengal is famished, if Bengal is ruined, can the war be won? Will peace and morale ever remain intact?

Is it Bengal's fault that we are suffering like this? Whose fault is it that Burma fell? Whose fault is it that Singapore fell? It was not the fault of Bengal. Why then should the people of Bengal suffer? We have got to get from the government of India and the British government supplies, immediate supplies of foodstuffs for the people of Bengal.

(**A voice from the European Group**: Why don't you go to Tojo,[18] who is your pal?)

That is the way in which we are to expect a reply from the European Group. Does my friend seriously suggest that we should look to Tojo for supply of rice and food and not to British government? Will he advise Mr Amery to say so publicly in the House of Commons? There could be no more ignoble end of British rule in India than such an abject admission of failure. He says that Tojo is our pal. It has yet to be decided by the verdict of history as to who are our pals. If after 170 years of British association with India, Bengal is going to be starved and famished like this, you are not certainly our pal. That much I can say. Whether Tojo is our pal or not, it remains to be seen and I shall say no more just now.

---

[18] Hideki Tojo was the prime minister of Japan during World War 2 from Oct 1941 to July 1944.

So far as the obligations of the Government of India are concerned, you just look into the figures. The wheat quota of Bengal for 1943 – Mr Suhrawardy will correct me if I give wrong figures – was 224,000 tons. The normal quota in peace time is about 2 ½ lakhs of tons. So, there is no additional wheat given to Bengal, on account of the present serious emergency. But how much of this has come in 1943 from the Government of India? Only about 50,000 tons: in other words, 25 per cent of our quota. Mr Suhrawardy said that Bengal would live on other alternative substitutes such as jowar, maize and bajra. What was the quota for 1943? Two lakhs of tons. And how much has actually arrived? About 10,000 tons.

What is the use of Mr Suhrawardy getting up and making soothing speeches and false promises? What is the use of the Government of India issuing misleading communiques from time to time, if ships cannot bring wheat from Australia and if food-grains cannot be brought to Bengal from other parts of India. Every Indian member of the Bengal Legislative Assembly should rise to a man. There should be a government, strong and representative, whom the India government or the British government or the real masters of the Bengal government will not be able to flout.

A message should be sent to the Prime Minister of England that in view of the serious position that threatens Bengal, it is disastrous to the interests of the Allied Powers themselves not to supply necessary foodstuffs to Bengal: it should be regarded as a war measure and there should be no more tinkering with it. If the higher authorities fail, the ministry should abandon all responsibility and come out of office. Let us then see how peace and administration can continue with the help of the Governor and his coterie of officials. If Mr Suhrawardy can only effect this….

H S Suhrawardy: I agree with him.

Syama Prasad Mookerjee: He agrees sometimes with all points, I know there is a dawn of returning sense in Mr Suhrawardy. If he really agrees, then let him forsake party loyalty and domination; let us all combine and put forward our demand on behalf of the people of Bengal irrespective of race, community or colour and stand by them in this hour of supreme crisis. (Cheers)

Statement After Visiting Flood-hit Areas

24 August 1943

Editor's note: *The famine was in full cry by this time. Starvation was taking toll on a large population. Meanwhile, on the night of 16-17 July, the Damodar river*[1] *breached its left embankment a few kms away from Burdwan, inundating a vast stretch of land up to Kalna. This aggravated the impact of the ongoing famine. Adding to its follies, the ministry planned to buy the aus paddy from the farmers. In the vast rural belt denuded of rice, the cultivators were looking at its impending harvest as their own lifeline. As the news about the government plan broke out, there was pervasive anxiety and fear in the rural belt.*

---

1 An important river which originates from Palamau in Chotanagpur in Jharkhand State and later traverses through various districts of West Bengal before joining the Bay of Bengal. It has been known for causing annual floods in its catchment areas. Districts like Bardwan, Hooghly, Howrah and Midnapur have been particularly vulnerable to the flooding of this river.

Deeply concerned about the situation, Syama Prasad issued the following statement after visiting the flood-affected areas, to impart some measure of sensitivity in the government. Though deeply moved by the distress of people, he remained pragmatic. He suggested a list of 'dos and don'ts' that would help mitigate suffering of the masses. Thus, he gave advise on how the government and people could join hands in ensuring a better yield of the winter crop i.e., aman paddy – the mainstay of Bengal's food, in the coming months.

As regards providing relief to famine victims, he had by then already begun to take concrete initiatives together with Badridas Goenka, Dr B C Roy and others. He reminded the government that it had to come forward and do much more to save lives.

Finally, he warned that the League ministry's tendency to shield the British regime was aggravating the suffering of the people of Bengal. In this context, the attitude of the League ministers was exposed to the people through their statements and speeches. For example, Suhrawardy, the civil supplies minister, while addressing a public meeting in Calcutta on 2 August 1943 advised people to eat less and get adjusted to substitute foods. The fact on the ground was that the famine victims did not eat less, they did not eat at all. The talk of substitute food was nothing but a fairytale to them.

Syama Prasad Mookerjee issued the statement on 24 August 1943. It was included in his book viz., Panchasher Manwantar in the chapter titled 'Collections'. The following is its English translation.

Text of the Statement

I have just returned after a four-day tour of few of the flood and famine-affected areas of Burdwan and Nadia [districts]. The picture that I have seen and the tidings of destruction, misery and starvation that reached me are very frightening. Whatever relief measure the government has initiated is trifling compared to the need. Different non-governmental organisations have been trying to alleviate people's sufferings, but their capacity is limited. What makes the matter far graver is that they have not been able to procure food grains. How will the hunger of people be met if food grains are not available? Innumerable men and women have been starving, many have died, and people have been selling and abandoning their children and dependents. Spectre of helplessness pervades all over.

People have become so emaciated due to starvation or measly [amount of] food that Bengal is staring at total destruction unless remedial measures are initiated without delay. People without shelters have been turning into beggars. For yet another class of people no [relief] measures have been initiated [at all] – they belong to the poor middle class. [Being] unable to line up at the Langarkhanas for food, [and] also unable to beg, there is only one road that is open before them – to embrace death bit by bit by starvation.

Non-governmental relief committees have been set up in different parts of the province. I have returned after visiting many of them. Let them work in cooperation with all others, keeping in view especially two things. First, they must keep a vigil on the ongoing relief efforts by the government so that these are completely carried out in the interests of the common people. Second, as far as possible, money and goods are to be mobilised from the local people. The relief measures have to be made extensive by pooling together the local resources.

I have repeatedly said that it is the government which has to take the full responsibility to provide food to the people. The public will render all kinds of cooperation to the best of their capacity. What the government has been doing is scanty. There is no plan behind many of its initiatives. Demands will have to be presented on behalf of the common people so that the government conducts its policies in the following manners:

1. Even now rice is being purchased and removed from districts where there is severe crisis of food. The government has not yet published the results of the food inventory taken in last June. During the food drive, rice has moved away from deficit areas to other places. Even after the devastating flood in Burdwan, rice was removed from that district in thousands of mounds. Similar reports have come from Nabadwip and Krishnanagar too. Rich merchants and military contractors are buying and removing rice and paddy even from areas where people have been dying due to starvation. Many heart-rending complaints have reached me concerning these.

   It has been announced that the government will buy out the surplus 'aus' paddy from the open market. This has led to indescribable panic and discontentment in the public. If this announcement is implemented, an ambience of destruction and chaos will engulf Bengal and there will be no hope left to come out of the crisis. All along, we have been saying that should the government consider it necessary to buy food grains, it can do so but only after assuming full responsibility to feed all sections of people. We are in dark about the government's account of area-wise deficit or surplus quantities [of food grains]. I am warning the ministry that if they [still] stubbornly stick to their desperate policy of [such] 'buying', the situation will become extremely dangerous. Men and women have reached the outermost limit of distress in the flood-affected areas. Sending out rice from those areas will have to be stopped forthwith.

2. The Langarkhanas opened by the government in West Bengal are few in numbers. We demand that for Burdwan and Medinipur [districts], one or more Langarkhana must be opened in each village. In other distressed areas too, at least one Langarkhana must be opened in every Union. In those areas non-governmental relief system is being organised. The proposed governmental arrangements will supplement that.
3. No arrangement has been made to rebuild the huts of the homeless men and women. The quantum of assistance being extended is meagre compared to the need.
4. The non-governmental relief organisations are not receiving supplies of rice at low prices from the government on a regular basis. At the least, let each of them receive this minimum support. In fact, what they are doing is the duty of the government.
5. Many middle-class families have been starving. There is no arrangement to render them help. Relief measures are a must to save them. [In this regard] The government shall provide food grains at cheap price to the non-governmental organsations who have started working [towards famine relief].
6. There is urgent need for medical help. Extensive treatment facilities are necessary for malaria and

stomach-related illnesses. There is no arrangement for distribution of cloth either. Innumerable people, including women, are without clothes. They are at sea not knowing how to protect their dignity.

7. Agricultural loans are being given. But people are in the dark about where to buy the seeds. It is necessary that without delay, the people know about the government plan in this matter. In Burdwan district alone, the 'aman' crop yield over three lakh acres of land has perished due to flood. Immediate arrangement will have to be made for re-cultivation in these lands. Water will recede by the end of October. Arrangements must be made so that adequate quantities of seeds are available at that time for cultivating wheat, barley, gram and *kalai*.[2] The land [here] is very fertile and particularly suitable for cultivation of wheat. Abundant food grains can be raised in this vast area.

   If appropriate arrangements are not made immediately, Burdwan will have to face far more dangerous situation after six months. Wherever I went, I have held discussions about this matter with eminent persons in the localities. All of them have expressed anxiety about the farmers facing difficulties in procuring seeds. [Before returning] I have made arrangements with some non-governmental organisations in this matter and they will be especially proactive. It is my earnest submission to the government that it chalks out plans for seed collection and distribution and let the distressed people know about it without any further delay.

---

[2] One kind of pulse.

The real problem [at this juncture] is to secure enough food grains for lakhs of starving people by importing them very rapidly. The government has failed to stand by the side of the common people. Here I do not wish to engage in hair-splitting of responsibilities among the present ministry, the permanent government officials and the government of India for the present predicament. A situation of acute shortage of rice has arisen. It is necessary to distribute whatever stock of rice is available equally amongst all sections of people. Let the government [also] forthwith stop exporting rice from areas facing shortage. Unless they take the responsibility to feed people, they must not buy rice at all.

The crisis that has appeared in Bengal is assuming dangerous proportions with every passing day. Let men and women of the country mobilise resources, howsoever meagre, to save the distressed populace. Let public opinion be aroused. Demands are to be raised fearlessly so that the government is compelled to discharge its duty to the people. Let the governments here and in England realise that starving Bengal can become a potential threat to their own interests. This situation has to be tackled immediately by importing rice from other parts of India, and especially abroad.

We have been observing lamentable conflict of interests between the people of the country and its rulers with regard to the governance of the country. The present crisis can only be resolved if the government unifies these interests and comes forward with courage and strong resolve for the sake of public welfare. The present ministry has demonstrated its failure in protecting the interests of the common people. The 'real' rulers remain behind the curtain. They would have been exposed to public eye if only the [Bengal] ministry had tendered its resignation with dignity! Those who are the real representatives of the British government must be made to come to the open forum and explain to the common people of this starving country. I want to ask the residents of Great Britain what steps would they have taken against their own government if they were made to go through even fractions of the sufferings that we have been undergoing over past several months?

Open Letter

7 September 1943

Editor's note: *As people in thousands were dying of starvation, Sir John Herbert, widely held responsible for the tragedy and deaf to the suggestions by the opposition political parties, fell ill. He was relieved of his charge on third of September and Thomas Rutherford, the then Governor of Bihar, assumed governorship of Bengal as additional charge on sixth September. On the very next day, Syama Prasad wrote this detailed letter. Being a person with a positive frame of mind, he assumed that the new incumbent would be interested to address the acute food crisis with a spirit of openness, good will and sincerity. The famine was getting worse by the day. In the month of August, reports of people selling their own children in Burdwan and Nadia districts were doing the rounds. No time could be wasted in finding faults with whatever happened in the past. The only way forward was to take a series of corrective and positive actions immediately.*

But the League ministry, obsessed with communal politics, was still acting in an irresponsible manner.

Without any clue as to how to ensure supply of food grains to the public, it fixed ceiling on wholesale price of rice in Calcutta on 28 August 1943. It also issued warning to the contractors without any plan to chastise the violators. That made food stuff disappear from the open market. As a matter of fact, the government, itself engaged in grain trade through agents, encouraged favouritism and corruption, and therefore had little moral authority over the dishonest businessmen. Black market was thriving but Suhrawardy was pretending as if he had no clue about it. On the whole, the League ministry, instead of giving hope and confidence, pushed masses to the abyss of despair.

Syama Prasad pointed out to the new incumbent that the key challenge for the government was to establish complete control over both price and supply of food grains with urgency. The challenges were complex and multi-faceted. Syama Prasad offered him a list of constructive suggestions to overcome the adversities. He highlighted the need for mobilising all resources including enlisting the cooperation of large numbers of political prisoners. Simultaneously, he pointed out to the new Governor the danger that was being posed to the relief efforts by the communal agenda of the ministry. He made a special mention about the bureaucracy in Bengal. The cunning and anti-people psyche of the permanent officials in particular, were a legacy of John Herbert. He warned the acting Governor that unless he consciously avoided the trap that the bureaucracy cast wide across the province, he would be hard put to make any difference to the situation.

Syama Prasad incorporated the Bengali version of this letter in his book with the title 'Khola Chithi' meaning 'Open Letter'. The following is the English translation of the letter.

Dear Sir Thomas Rutherford,

You have come as the ruler of Bengal at a time of grave crisis and when the situation is absolutely abnormal. I ventured to write you this open letter, hoping that you have come with an unbiased mind and a genuine eagerness to render service to the natives of this province, while they are in the midst of extreme distress. At the outset you need to earn the trust of the public. You have to observe all events by yourself objectively and hear the whole range of opinions, however diverse they are. Kindly do not consider yourself as the spokesperson of the bureaucracy or a passive spectator of what the ministers are doing.

The foremost requirement today is to mobilise the entire resources of the province and the strength of its people, across parties, both official and unofficial, towards the ideal of service to masses. It is not my objective to criticise the mistakes committed in the past. Still, we need to keep in mind that much which is a bare necessity to ensure that no repetition of the same happens. I am urging your immediate and direct attention to the following issues:

1. The government will have to assume complete responsibility for the supply of food grains and other essential goods so that the people do not lose their lives or health due to scarcity and starvation. Up till now excessive emphasis has been laid only on War and to keep intact the whole gamut of arrangements relating to war efforts. The present distress has arisen mainly because of that. Right from the start the government has not been informed of its responsibility to keep an eye on the welfare of the common people. It is the primary responsibility of the state to keep its civil population alive. At the same time, it is also indispensable to maintain peace and security within the province during

war time. Let there be no carelessness in such matter in future.

2. Arrangements will have to be made to receive supplies from other parts of India on a regular basis. The government of India has recently reduced the allocation of food grains for Bengal. That will have to be increased. Over the last six months we have been saying this – that arrangements must be made to import food grains into Bengal from outside India, especially from Australia. Bengal wants to know why such arrangements have not been made even today. If it is found that the imported food grains are not adequate to meet the requirements, then efforts should be made to receive rice for Bengal in the same way that Greece got food grains through the intermediation of international red cross last year.
3. After the restrictions on trade were withdrawn, the method Bengal government adopted to buy rice from adjoining provinces has been utterly defective. Without inviting tender, one favourite business house connected to the Muslim League was selected for that purpose. Till date, Rupees four crore and fifty lakhs have been given to that house. [But]No promise was extracted from it that it would sell the rice at the lowest possible price to the Bengal government, nor any measure was adopted to protect the interest of the people of the land. We are urging you to get the matter investigated by an impartial bench. There are justified reasons for us to believe that such procurements are not being carried out in proper ways and by keeping in view the interests of the people of Bengal. If an impartial probe is held, we would be able to demonstrate how the present ministry meted out injustice to Bengal and only became eager to

distribute favour within the party structure, keeping at bay the welfare of the countrymen.

4. We have been specially aggrieved by the measure the government adopted to procure food grains from within Bengal. You need to be aware of the opinion of the common people about the much-publicised 'food drive' undertaken last June. The outcome of that drive has not been published even today. We are demanding that the same be done forthwith. We have no ways to know which are the 'deficit areas' nor where lies the 'surplus' according to the government census.

   Utmost damage has been done to Bengal by allowing business houses and big wholesalers to buy rice from various areas without any restriction. As a result, whatever grains were stored in villages were removed [forthwith]. It was, in fact, the policy of the government that encouraged such reckless purchases. This has led to extensive distress. The government clamped price control [on sale of rice but] without making proper arrangements for supply. Before imposing the control, big stockists and buyers were given more than a week's time to travel across various parts of the land to buy up the rice and the paddy. The rise of black market and speculations [in food grains] have been the inevitable consequences of this [policy]. Distress and price rise appeared wherever the government bought rice from. We do not dispute that the government has no ways but to buy [grains]in order to be able to meet the shortage in [rice] deficit areas. But when the government arrives at the market to buy food grains, it must as well be prepared to take the responsibility for their justified distribution amongst the masses. The present purchase policy of the government calls for radical amends. If it is not revised before the harvest of the aman crop in the month of December, there shall be no way we can protect ourselves [from the impending ruin].

5. We also urge you to inquire into the system of distribution. We deem this as especially flawed. According to a proclamation recently issued by the government, the local officials will select the distribution agents. The communal identity will form part of the set of criteria to select them. If the government is guided by party or communal considerations while chalking out the policy of distribution that will lead to dangerous consequences. [Again], We are not aware of the quantity that the government has bought or seized for emergency requirements. Meticulous investigation into the system of distribution of the grains thus procured is imperative. What is the quantity of stock [now] held by the war department in the province and what are the quantities hoarded by the railways and big businesses? Can parts of it not be released for the civilian population on the promise that the government of India will meet the deficit, if any?
6. There is no doubt about the fact there is scarcity of food in Bengal at present. The manner in which the responsible ministers have wasted time over the last few months by proclaiming that there is no food shortage and thus cheated the people has been painful indeed. Be that as it may, the foremost duty at this hour is to assess the requirements of the province till the aman crop is harvested and implement a just and judicious system of distribution. When the supply is limited, the only way to deal with [the situation] is to introduce rationing.

People are ready for sufferance and self-sacrifice but all, across the board, will have to forego selfish interests. A well-regulated distribution system will be its edifice.

7. I do not intend to dwell upon the dire distress the residents of Bengal are presently going through. Whatever we are witnessing in Calcutta is heartrending itself. The tidings arriving from various parts of Bengal are more frightening. The condition of one [particular] class of people has become extremely miserable – they belong to the low middle class. Neither are they able to collect food at the Langarkhanas, nor can they accept the charity of the government. Verily they are the backbone of Bengal's political and social life. Dangerous consequences will follow if they are squeezed and emaciated. Non-governmental organisations are trying their best to alleviate their sufferings. The help and sympathy that we received from various parts of India has touched our hearts. It is the duty of the government to render full-throated support to these non-governmental initiatives. However, non-governmental efforts can do little of what it takes to tackle [such] a humongous crisis. The government must assume the final responsibility. In its working, the government must enlist help from every section of people. The present cabinet of Bengal is representative of one particular party. Their appeal will not succeed in fetching help and cooperation of people across the board.

   There is no doubt that the present ministry does not enjoy the trust of a large section of the inhabitants. They have utterly failed in protecting the interests of the common people. I do not intend to raise any party-specific question in this letter, but I must urge you to keep one thing in mind. The food crisis has not arisen due to natural calamity alone. The mistakes by the politically biased administrative regime are responsible for it too. A government which is trusted by the entire population and which can comprehensively control both supply and price situation alone can tackle the problem.

The high authorities in whom the real power has been conferred by the Defence of India Rules must similarly vest their full confidence in such a government. If it is not feasible to constitute such a representative national government or if it is not possible to place trust in such a government then, you have to be the alternative and assume complete responsibility as the representative of the British government. You will come before the people of Bengal with your own plan and programme. The British government still claims itself as the Lord of the Indians. So, let the rulers themselves come forward to discharge the primary duties [expected] of a civilised government.

8. Finally, I would like to say with firmness that lakhs of people have reached the extremities of destitution, and the number of deaths have already become frightening. If the survivors' lives are to be saved, the supply of food without delay is a certain necessity. But procurement of food [for them] is not the only problem. We have to adopt special measures so that the Bengalis do not turn to becoming a race of beggars. A team of people, competent and farsighted, will have to work [towards this goal] with the fullest cooperation from the government.

Long term plan needs to be devised to protect Bengal from economic decay and destruction. In our anxiety to meet the requirements of the military we must not forget the long-term implications of this issue. The government's 'grow more food' movement has lapsed into a huge failure. It is absolutely necessary to re-organise and strengthen the [concerned] department. I am giving only one example. In the Bardhaman district alonc, four lakh acres of land has been inundated by the flood of the Damodar [river]. Aman paddy could be grown over this entire stretch of land. Few weeks ago, upon returning from this flood-ravaged area, I had said in a statement [how] it was essential to distribute seeds [there] without any delay so that barley, wheat and kalai could be sown in that vast land simultaneous with the retreat of water by the end of October. The local farmers had piteously begged us for this kind of help. But the government has not [yet] taken any effective steps in this regard. This is only one example. Many more can be cited should that become necessary.

9. I do not want to discuss other problems in detail in this letter. There are many more challenges like: rescuing children and women, arranging residence for the shelter-less, protecting the educational institutions, arranging treatment for thousands of malaria-afflicted people, especially in the Medinipur district. They are on the death bed.
10. There is a particular need at present to create a conducive environment inside the country. For that purpose, the political system is indispensable too. We urge you to have courage and release all the political prisoners. They have a strong desire to serve the country

in this crisis-ridden time. Should they become free they will have an opportunity for this. From my personal knowledge I can say that there will be unprecedented improvement in the economic and political situation of Bengal if such measures were initiated. Many others and us hold the clear opinion that there cannot be any permanent solution to our problems unless India becomes independent with regard to her economic and political policies. Like the men and women of your own country who take pride in holding the opinion that no one should tolerate the over lordship of other countries, we too hold exactly the same view, whether it be in the east or in the west. [However] We are not oblivious of the dangers of the present reality; the people of Bengal will have to be saved at any cost. Bengal will cease to exist if they die of poverty and starvation.

11. Duties are very formidable. A solution can come about if only the interests of the government and people are merged in full measures. Time has come today to end the discordance by bringing in sincerity and goodwill. Even the best of rulers can get entrapped in the bureaucratic web of the administration that has gripped India presently. We do not know how you will carry out your activities nor how you are planning to discharge the rigorous duties. But I would like to conclude saying that, if you have the courage and far sight to properly call upon the people of Bengal, all will assemble extending their hands of cooperation for the resolution of the present crisis.

Who is Responsible?

17 September 1943
Speech at Bengal Legislative Assembly

Editor's note: *Around this time, epidemics also began to secure a toehold in the land. Deadly diseases like cholera, malaria and other illnesses were taking hold of the starvation-hit emaciated masses at will. The victims were deprived of medical help as well. People were dying in tens of thousands under the joint assault of hunger and epidemic. Disposal of mounting dead bodies became difficult for the surviving relatives and friends. Terrifying reports were pouring into Calcutta from different parts of the province. For example, on 11 September, an appeal by the District Relief Committee of Noakhali published in Associated Press stated that every day men, women and children were dying in great numbers, some on roads and at other public places, and disposal of dead bodies had become a problem for the survivors.*[1]

The speech is reproduced as delivered in 1943, except for a few editorial interventions to improve readability.

[1] Ghosh, p 106

Disturbing reports were coming through news agencies from various other parts of Bengal. As a matter of fact, disposal of dead bodies was becoming a grave problem in various places. Sometimes dead bodies were thrown into rivers instead of being properly buried or cremated.[2] *Such reports were coming from many places like Madaripur, Manickganj, Munshiganj etc. In his speech Syama Prasad specifically mentioned a town in Midnapore (Medinipur), where jackals and dogs were devouring dead bodies openly.*

The desperate condition of Bengal was summed up by J P Srivastava – the Food Member in the Viceroy's Executive Council, during a press conference in Lahore on 8 September 1943. Noting that there was acute shortage of foodstuffs in Bengal and that the next three months would be critical for people of the province, he said: 'The only way to tide over the situation is to get whatever grain one can have either by seizing, borrowing or stealing from other parts of India. This is the only method to save the starving millions of Bengal.'[3] *On 10 September, Sir Jagadish Prasad, ex-member of the Viceroy's Executive Council, urged high officials in Delhi to visit Bengal and see for themselves how that hapless province was facing one of the worst famines in living memory.*

But the League ministry seemed to be unconcerned. Though by this time some rice and wheat had begun to reach Bengal from Orissa, Punjab and other places, these were not reaching the distressed population. Both, the government and Ispahanis, were busy reaping profits by trading in these food grains. On 14 September, the Food Member of the Punjab government brought a serious allegation that 'either the Bengal government or the middlemen, stockists and millers were making profits from

---

[2] Ibid, p 105

[3] IAR Vol 2, 1943, p 15

wheat and wheat products, otherwise the prices in Bengal should be at parity with the Punjab prices'.[4] *Worse even, the Central Government was making obscene profit at the cost of the lives of poor people.*

In this connection a statement reportedly made by Suhrawardy that 'no one who has money need starve' epitomised the attitude of the League ministry towards the vast poor masses of Bengal. The government plan of buying aus rice had already consigned people into a fresh spell of agony. Corruption and dishonesty pervaded the distribution. People were dying in places where heaps of food grains were lying in warehouses. The ministry's concern seemed to be Calcutta and greater Calcutta, at the cost of the vast rural areas.

Syama Prasad expressed the fear that unless the situation was handled with urgency, Bengal ran the risk of turning into a province of beggars. He was working hard in his own way by mobilising non-official help and trying to restore people to economic life. Though he did not mention expressly, it appeared his call to rest of India to help Bengal was beginning to bear fruit. Non-official help started coming into the province from all over India.[5] *Obviously, the scale of such help was way below the need of such a large province, but they were ending the dreadful isolation of Bengal.*

Through this speech, Syama Prasad moved a resolution condemning the incumbent Bengal ministry for its failure to discharge the elementary responsibility of any civilised government to save human lives and provide its people essential commodities for their bare existence. Taking part in House deliberations on the

---

4 https://archive.org/stream/dli.bengal.10689.17960/10689.17960_djvu.txt

5 Modern Review wrote in September 1943 that the manner in which other provinces hastened to do what they can in order to alleviate the sufferings of the hunger-tortured masses in Bengal was 'gratifying in the extreme'. It went on to say: 'Our faith in the hearts of our countrymen has been fully justified.': Modern Review (hereafter MR) LXXIV No 3 Whole No 441 Sep 1943: p173.

'Food situation', he moved the following resolution, accompanied by a speech in English in the Bengal Legislative Assembly on 17 September 1943. In his book he gave the essence of it in Bengali with a heading viz., 'Dayee Ke', which in English means 'Who Is Responsible?' The original speech in full[6] *is reproduced here. Few footnotes have been added to explain a term or introduce a person.*

Syama Prasad Mookerjee: Sir, I beg to move that,

'This Assembly is of opinion that the statement of the Civil Supplies Minister on the food situation is utterly disappointing and unsatisfactory. The policy pursed by the ministry with regard to procurement and distribution of food grains and also in the matter of increasing production within the province has been completely unplanned and ineffective and has been responsible for a gradual deterioration of the situation leading to appalling famine conditions now prevalent in all parts of the province. Its latest action in promulgating price-control of rice without making suitable provision for supplies has intensely aggravated the misery of the people. The Ministry has failed to discharge the elementary responsibility of any civilised government by its failure to save human lives and to procure for the people essential commodities for their bare existence.'

Sir, since the Assembly last discussed the food situation it has dangerously deteriorated and today it presents problems of a far-reaching character, affecting the lives and welfare of millions of Bengal's populations. The statement of the Civil Supplies Minister, as I have just now stated, is utterly unsatisfactory: It is empty-worded and visionless. Judged by actual results the food policy of [the] government has miserably failed.

---

[6] Source: Assembly Proceeding Official Record, Bengal Legislative Assembly, Seventeenth session, 1943.

I shall not refer to the personal abuses that Mr Suhrawardy heaped upon me and others who are trying to alleviate human sufferings. Such attacks should be treated with the contempt they deserve. They are indeed the outcome of masterly incompetence and impudence. Mr Suhrawardy has looked at men and things through the prism of his own mind and career, which I leave to others to depict in true colours. Today, Sir, we stand face to face before an unprecedented condition of misery and destitution throughout the length and breadth of this province. Time will not permit me to discuss detailed cases of sufferings which I leave to others, specially coming from the countryside. Let me, however, emphasise that the death roll mainly due to starvation and diseases following such starvation is rapidly increasing.

Reports of suicide, desertion of families and children, of dead bodies lying uncared for are pouring in from different parts of Bengal. For days and weeks, people were allowed to die on the streets of Calcutta, and they were refused admission into hospitals although ARP beds were lying vacant. This is one of the major scandals of the present government. Now [the] government has partially opened the door of hospitals in Calcutta, but this is yet to be done in the mofussil centres in all parts of the province. Only last week I was in Midnapur. In my presence there was the case of a person who came to have his food at a free kitchen and the very sight of food resulted in such a state of excitement that before the food could reach his mouth, he lay there unconscious and never woke again. People complained that there were beds lying vacant in the hospital, but men were allowed to die and lie sick in the streets of Midnapore. I made an enquiry of responsible officers. We were told that 40 beds in the Midnapore hospital must be kept reserved for ARP purposes. Even the Collector had not the authority temporarily to place these beds at the disposal of those persons who stood in need of immediate help until the government passed orders to that effect.

Now Sir, in Contai, jackals and dogs have been freely feeding themselves on dead bodies and such animals were ordered to be shot.That was an instance which was brought to our notice by men residing in Contai town and the description of it is something which does not bear repetition. The sight of the destitute and starving people in Calcutta is, heart-rending as it is, nothing compared to what is happening in mofussil towns and the villages. I have myself seen innumerable specimens of human skeletons in rags – men, women and children, irrespective of caste or community, slowly proceeding to the door of death due to want of food. While the suffering of the poorest classes, the landless, the homeless and the penniless, has been immense, people belonging to middle class families with fixed income or with reduced income barely sufficient in ordinary times to keep their body and soul together are today undergoing a tragic process of slow and painful extinction.

They have been the backbone of our social and political life. They have been doing the essential services of the nation in the true sense of the expression and have to be saved if Bengal is to live at all. One shudders to think what the extent of death roll will be in Bengal during the next few weeks and months. Many who may be spared the cold hand of death will be devitalised in a manner which will put them outside the role of useful citizenship. The extracts that I read out from Hunter's *Rural Bengal* and Macaulay's *Life of Lord Clive* during the last session of the Assembly, depicting the scenes of ruin and havoc in Bengal in or about 1770, will correctly apply today to the surroundings of Bengali life and society in

1943 after 170 years of glorious British rule in this country. I earnestly call upon Mr Conran-Smith, the Home Secretary to the Government of India, to pay us a kindly visit to this province and then seek to criticise men on the spot for the so-called over-dramatisation of Bengal's woeful tale. In this crisis, non-official help and sympathy have come from all parts of India, including offers of men, money, shelter and food grains. True it is that this cannot touch even the fringe of the colossal problem that awaits solution, but this nation-wide sympathy for Bengal has broken all provincial barriers and brings into prominence the reality of Indian unity and integrity. This sympathy puts courage and fortitude in the hearts of the suffering millions. It has roused public opinion and has made the government realise its responsibility. It has focused the attention of all India and even countries outside on Bengal's desperate situation.

While I have always maintained that every section of the public, nay every individual, must deem it his duty to do everything possible to come to the rescue of the sufferer, no matter how limited such scope may be, the main responsibility for feeding the people, for providing supplies, for creating a state of affairs which will lead to the saving of human lives must rest on the government of the country. It is not my intention today to review in minute detail the policy hitherto pursued by [the] government, but, maintaining as the Opposition does that the government has failed and failed miserably, the probable causes of such failure must be dispassionately examined. Such examination is to be made not in a narrow spirit of mere fault-finding but in order to secure a change of policy in administration either by agreement or by force of public opinion. Detailed discussion on these various points will take place in the course of the consideration of the Budget.

My first charge against the government is that this policy of procurement from within and without has been open to grave objections. The ministry started with its reckless propaganda that there was no shortage of food grains in Bengal and that hoarding was primarily responsible for the misery of the people. Today the Minister stands disillusioned, and he admits that there is acute shortage of food grains. Meanwhile, he has wasted valuable time and pursued a policy based on wrong data during the last five months. The food drive [under]taken in June resulted practically in driving food out of the rural areas of Bengal. The results of the statistics are yet unpublished; in fact, [the] government dare not publish them. We demand, Sir, that we should know the figures for each district and subdivision in order to determine which, according to the government, is a deficit area and which is a surplus area.

One of the gravest errors committed by the Ministry was to have permitted stockists and traders to purchase rice at any available price during and after the food drive. We want to know what stocks were purchased, where they have been removed and where they have gone? There has been no real attempt to send adequate supplies to deficit areas. In some places, stocks have been seized and sealed and even now they are lying hoarded under the orders of the government, although in those very places people are actually dying of starvation.

The scheme of purchase of aus paddy, practically from all parts of the province, has been a criminal blunder which has placed the rural areas in a state of utter helplessness. An amazing part of the government's policy has been to encourage purchase and removal of rice even from actually distressed areas like Burdwan and Midnapore. Only this morning a gentleman came from Kalna who reported that at least 5,000 maunds of rice were purchased from the Kalna area by Ispahanis as agents of government during the last few days. As you know, Kalna is an area where acute distress prevails today on account of the floods and on account of the low economic condition prevailing in that area.

Regarding supplies from outside Bengal, the original quota allotted to this province by the Government of India was revised in July last. I do not know how many members of the party now supporting the government are aware of this fact: why did the Bengal ministry agree to such a reduction? It is a question which the opposition will ask; it is a question which the ministerialist party should ask of the ministers they are supporting. Why did the ministry agree to the reduction of the quota originally allotted to Bengal by the Government of India? We were told in a conference that the ministry had no option because the Government of India was adamant. I ask, why did not the ministry resist the reduction, and when Bengal was unjustly treated, why did it not resign rather than surrender?

H S Suhrawardy: When and in what conference?

Syama Prasad Mookerjee: Mr Suhrawardy asks, when and in what conference? The last conference in which the quota was reduced: the Hon'ble Minister himself agreed to the reduction and Sir Jwala Prasad Srivastava said that the Bengal ministry agreed to such a reduction.

H S Suhrawardy: I say, No.

Syama Prasad Mookerjee: The reduction had been made and the Food Member of the Government of India had said that the reduction had been made with the concurrence of the Government of Bengal.

H S Suhrawardy: The Food Member did not know… it was done in spite of our protests.

Syama Prasad Mookerjee: The Hon'ble Minister says that the reduction was made in spite of the protests of the Bengal Ministry. Even if the latter statement is correct, Bengal wants to know why did the Bengal Ministry at all agree to such a reduction? Why did they not say, 'we would resign rather than submit to any reduction of the quota which has been allotted to the province of Bengal?' (Loud noise from the Coalition benches.)

Now, Sir, we want a clear statement as regards the stocks that have come into the province from outside. Do they fulfil the quota allotted to this province? From the Punjab Minister's statement made two days after Mr Suhrawardy's return from Lahore, and he had expressed satisfaction that everything was well at Lahore – it appears that the Bengal government has been making a profit of 40 lakh rupees by selling wheat to the hungry and starving people of Bengal at a rate which is much higher than the rate at which it was purchasing in the Punjab. Why this profiteering on the part of the Bengal government at the cost of millions of Bengal's starving and dying people?

Now, Sir, the Civil Supply Minister has abused me, because I demanded an enquiry regarding the appointment of Ispahanis as sole agents of the Bengal government. We shall discuss this matter in detail during the budget discussion. I am asking the ministry today to lay before the House a statement giving full information on the following points:

1. The total payments or advances made to Ispahanis and the dates and amount of such payments;
2. A copy of the agreement between the government and the Ispahanis;
3. The dates on which, the places from where, the persons or agents through whom, the quantity and the prices at which purchases have been made by the Ispahanis from outside Bengal on behalf of the Bengal government.

More than four-and-a-half crore of rupees, not from Mr Suhrawardy's bank account but from the public funds, have been paid to the Ispahanis and Bengal has the right to know, especially because of the political connection between the firm and the ministry, whether every pice[7] of this colossal sum is properly accounted for. Information has been supplied to us from unimpeachable quarters that the prices at which the Ispahanis are supposed to have sold rice to the Bengal government are in many instances much higher than the prices prevailing in the markets from where such purchases were made. Sir, this does call for a strict investigation: it is no question of abuse and counter-abuse. I hope for the reputation of the ministry, if any is still left, the information I have asked for will be laid on the table before the discussion on grants commences on Monday. We are asking for certain information as regards matters which certainly will come within the purview of public interest. This alone will disclose the scandalous manner in which the transaction has taken place.

Another action taken by the ministry has been to promulgate price control of rice without arranging for supplies. Government is supposed to have taken census throughout the province, and it knows and ought to know where stocks are lying today. If today supplies have dried up, price control is utterly meaningless. Price control has its value if supplies are available. But if they have gone under-ground and if the government cannot trace them, their stock-taking was an utter farce and their incompetence is a colossal reality. Even today rice is being purchased by government agents both at controlled rates and at higher prices. I make this statement because we have got the information from the mufassal today that rice is

---

[7] Paisa, a pre-Independence coin, called pice in English.

being purchased at prices higher than controlled rates from areas which have been openly declared as denuded areas. Local officers admit that acute distress prevails but no food grains are available, and therefore no relief can be given. We have received half a dozen telegrams from different officers in different parts of the province which say that relief is urgently called for but no food grains are available.

A F Stark[8]: Telegrams to you?

Syama Prasad Mookerjee: Telegrams to the Bengal Relief Committee.

Nalinaksha Sanyal: The telegrams are not directed to Mr Stark in any way!

Syama Prasad Mookerjee: Sir, reports are pouring in from all parts of Bengal, disclosing a most alarming state of things following complete disappearance of rice from the market, leading to wholesale starvation. If this is not remedied immediately, the situation will go entirely out of control and the province will be thrown into irremediable misery and suffering. Wherever government has started making purchases without undertaking simultaneous responsibility for providing supplies, if and when necessary, it has led to chaos and confusion.

Sir, it is not rice alone that has to be considered. People suffer from want of almost every essential commodity on the supply of which their very existence depends. Take for instance sugar. Now, sugar is under hundred per cent control of [the] government, but the prevailing market price is much higher than the control price, and why? Sugar is controlled by the Government of India at the centre. The quota which is allotted to Bengal is determined by Delhi? The quota comes to Bengal only to those licensed importers who are selected by the

---

[8] A F Stark was a member of the European Group in Bengal Legislative Assembly.

Government of Bengal. These licensed importers, in their turn, can give delivery only to licensees to whom licenses are issued by the government of Bengal. There is no other third party coming just from the market or from anywhere else who can interfere at any stage. Why has the control still failed? What is the reason?

The reason, I make bold to say, is that selection of some of these provincial importers has been made on grounds other than anything to do with the interests of the people-party grounds, political grounds and so forth. The selection of the licensees also has been made on similar considerations. I am not saying that all the licensees are of that type, but selection of certain persons, both amongst the big importers and also among smaller traders through whom the ordinary consumer will receive sugar, has been made in accordance with a plan which has nothing to do with the interests of the people. Now, here is price control introduced, plan executed by the government, the public has got nothing to do with it; the government has control over the source of supply and still there is black market, still there is profiteering, still sugar is not available in the market.

Now, Sir, the other day, a trader produced before me an original copy of an order issued by the government of India asking for supply of mustard oil. The controlled price of mustard oil is Rs 37 or Rs 38 per maund. The government of Bengal here, of course, is in good company. The Government of India asks for a supply of mustard oil at Rs 50 per maund.

H S Suhrawardy: That is the price.

Syama Prasad Mookerjee: Is that the price fixed by the government of Bengal?

H S Suhrawardy: Yes.

Syama Prasad Mookerjee: Now, Mr Suhrawardy says 'Yes', that is the price fixed by the Bengal government. That will be even more interesting. Rs 38 is the price of mustard oil per maund fixed by the Government of India and the Government of India itself – I have seen the order with my own eyes – wants to purchase mustard oil at the rate of Rs 50 per maund. Who creates black market? Who creates profiteering? Mr Suhrawardy says, 'That is right'; 'that has been done'. (Laughter). What is the scheme and how are the starving millions of Bengal going to be saved from the oppression of the Bengal ministry on the one hand and of the department under the control of the Government of India on the other?

Sir, we are utterly dissatisfied with the system of distribution now operating in Bengal. Even if food grains do arrive, as indeed we are told they have been arriving from different parts of India during the last few weeks, we have no confidence in the ability, integrity and honesty of the present government so as to be able to say that a fair, just and equitable distribution will take place among all sections of the people. There can be only one solution to save Bengal and that is hundred per cent control over supply prices and distribution to be carried on by an agency enjoying hundred per cent confidence of the people at large.

Nawabzada K Nasarullah:[9] That is yourself.

Syama Prasad Mookerjee:That is not yourself this much I know: whether it is myself or not, it remains to be seen. This means that the traders and the public must be called upon to make sacrifice for the common good of all, and they must have implicit faith in the government of the day. Corruption and

[9] Nawabzada K Nasrullah, a member of Muslim League in the Bengal Legislative Assembly and parliamentary secretary. He had earlier campaigned against the Huq-led Progressive Coalition ministry and mobilised public opinion in favour of Muslim League.

jobbery must be ruthlessly suppressed, whether among officials, traders or the public. Mere threats of punitive acts will be useless if the machinery of governmental administration itself which it is supposed to detect, and crush corruption leaves the backdoor open for the encouragement of the social vices which it says it is out to crush.

Without the fullest cooperation among all the units, it is impossible to save the chaotic situation into which the province has been thrown. The unplanned and ill-executed administration of the government has been indeed of a shocking character. Let me say with a full sense of responsibility that the activities of the government seem to suggest that whatever food grains may be available will be kept in greater Calcutta area and the rest of the province will be left to its own tragic fate. The utter callousness of [the] government in respect of equitable distribution will be evident from the fact that though acute distress prevails in the mofussil, rice is still being purchased from those areas, irrespective of local needs. Hoarded stocks are still lying there [in the mofussil areas] although people in the very localities are dying for want of food. Unless public opinion in Bengal is [a]roused, we shall find ourselves caught in a deep-rooted conspiracy to starve millions of Bengal's rural population.

It is indeed amazing that the government has bungled throughout. I am at a loss to understand what the policy of the government is. Does Mr Amery still hold the view that the people of Bengal are suffering because of over-feeding or of deliberate hoarding, specially by greedy agriculturists? Why are food grains not being rushed to Bengal from Australia and other parts of the world outside India?

There has been no planning for increasing the production of food grains within the province, and if the present deplorable policy of drift continues regarding the handling of the aman paddy, Bengal will be doomed beyond remedy. Even if a mere fraction of the people who have actually died of hunger and disease in Bengal had met the same fate in the streets of London, Oxford and Edinburgh, the people of England would have risen to a man and the government of the country would have been thrown out of office. Here news is gagged, motives are imputed, jail gates are thrown wide open if governmental incompetence is disclosed and criticised. Again, we are accustomed to transfer much of our miseries to the vagaries of fate. I have been attacked by men far and near as I have been supposed to make food a matter of political controversy. Some of the critics, members of the government party and the European Party, themselves combined only six months ago to throw out the previous ministry as it failed to solve the food problem. At that time, they claimed to act in public interest and for the goods of the community as a whole.

We ask, Sir, for no charity. Indeed, the gravest problem before us today is how Bengal can be saved from being turned into a province of beggars. People have to be fed and saved immediately no doubt. But no government worth its salt can allow a day to be wasted for discovering the means of re-stabilising Bengal's economic life and discovering means of saving generations of our people from ruin and disaster.

Let us make our position abundantly clear. We do not want food to be made the plaything of politics, but while we shall do everything possible to give and secure relief according to our means we have got to criticise government and its policy if we consider that such policy is responsible for the dangerous situation that exists today. After all, it is our political bondage that is responsible for our economic ruin. It is not nature's hand alone that has given or is giving Bengal a deathblow. Political mal-administration lies at the root of the present economic catastrophe and no lasting solution can come until India is economically and politically free. If there had been a truly national government, enjoying full power…

(Cries of 'Ah, Ah' from the **European Benches**.)

Syama Prasad Mookerjee: … there cannot be any national government so long as you people are here. I am not talking of the national government under the Constitution Act of 1935.

(**Khwaja Shahabuddin**:[10] You were supposed to be there for 16 months.)

And I learnt a lesson which I shall never forget in my life.

Now, Sir, if there had been a truly national and responsible government enjoying full power at the head of the country and also of the province instead of it being ruled by the iron hand of oppressors and exploiters, the food problem of Bengal and India would have been solved without much difficulty. But we do not want to raise the bigger issues just now. We do not want to raise any controversy relating to party politics just now merely for the fun of it. If a party government is in power today, it is not our fault. If parts of the bureaucratic machinery and some of the real representatives of British rulers are soaked in partisanship callous to the needs of the common people, it is not our fault.

We assert without fear of contradiction that [the] Government has forfeited its right to rule over the province because of its failure to control the food situation in this province. How can [the] government complain, I ask, that the Opposition has merely criticised when the fact remains that

---

[10] He was a member of the Dhaka Nawab family. He was the Minister of Commerce, Labour and Industry in Khwaja Nazimuddin's government from 1943 to 1945.

our constructive advice at every step has been flouted until we have reached a stage when government finds itself caught in its intricate net of its own misguided policy and acts? As regards the future, the Opposition offers in a genuine spirit of goodwill and service, its hand of fullest cooperation. Let the policy of the Government be determined and carried out in a manner which will be acceptable to all parties and sections, and we shall be prepared to do everything possible to save the situation.

On the other hand, if [the] government chooses to carry on its present policy of exclusiveness and decides on its schemes and measures on its own responsibility, we shall, as now, co-operate when we consider such cooperation is justified and we shall ruthlessly oppose when we consider such opposition to be paramount.The supreme need of the hour is unity and oneness of mind. We are prepared to keep all controversies in the background and work jointly for mobilising both men and resources of the province in a true spirit of comradeship, provided the proper atmosphere is created by those who are in power today and the real masters and rulers of the country demonstrate by the deeds and not by their words that for the time being at any rate, the interests of [the] government and the people have merged together in saving this great province whose contribution to the building up of the national life of India will ever remain a proud record in the history of India's struggle for freedom.

(Loud applause from the Opposition Benches.)

Ways to Resolve Crisis

15 October 1943

Editor's note: *By mid-October 1943, epidemics started to pose greater threat to lives of people. Need for food, cloth and medicine were pervasive. Lower middle-class people, dissuaded by sense of dignity from thronging at the Langarkhanas, were particularly vulnerable. Private relief efforts were scant in comparison of the enormity of the necessity. Without full-scale government involvement, there was little hope of saving the victims.*

The League ministry, characterised by its insensitivity, ineptitude and communal agenda continued to fail in reaching the people of Bengal food, medicine and other relief. After irresponsible handling of such a grave crisis which included stubborn rejection of the Opposition demand in the Legislative Assembly to apply the famine code[1] *to the province, the civil supplies minister Suhrawardy admitted on 10 October that Bengal was in the grip of an unprecedented famine. However, that seemed to be a compulsion rather than any change of heart. The ministry, with a stony heart, was simultaneously busy in bringing an ordinance to throw the famine victims out of Calcutta and other big towns.*

In such a trying time, Syama Prasad remained steadfast in the service of the distressed humanity across caste and creed. On one hand, his commitment to relief operations grew more determined. On the other hand, he gave some pragmatic suggestions to the government. He urged the provincial government to shed its partisan approach, secure trust of all classes of people and assume responsibility for supply and distribution of food stuff. Time showed that though not the League ministry, the new Viceroy, Wavell adopted several of these measures Syama Prasad suggested in this article and as a result food supply situation began to improve perceptibly.

---

[1] In order to address the issues of famine in India, the colonial rulers created an Indian Famine Commission to devicee ways to prevent and avoid future famines in India. So in 1880, the Secretary of the Commission wrote a draft of the Indian Famine Code.

More famine codes were created after the Indian Famine Code, and they addressed similar ideas that the Indian one did. The Indian Famine Code was the foundation of multiple famine codes/scales. Famine codes and scales measure the intensity and magnitude of the in the famine land.

The Famine Code defined three levels of food insecurity: near-scarcity, scarcity, and famine. 'Scarcity' was defined as three successive years of crop failure, crop yields of one-third or one-half normal, and large populations in distress. 'Famine' further included a rise in food prices to above 140 per cent of 'normal', the movement of people in search of food, and widespread mortality.

The Indian Code was one of the first attempts to predict famine, and by predicting it, prevent it. It was the first modern reaction to the famines in India. The codes classified food scarcity and had steps that governments were required to take to mitigate the risk of famine.

Syama Prasad wrote this article titled, 'Pratikarer Upay', in Bengali which in English means 'Ways To Resolve' on 15 October 1943 and it was part of his book, Panchasher Manwantar. The following is its English translation.

The bad days engulfing Bengal are unprecedented in India's modern history. Due to nearly two centuries long subordination, the people of India spend days amidst poverty and partial starvation even during the normal times. [Now] Clouds of greater peril are gathering over Bengal – that of war and a grave political misfortune.

The 'fifty's famine' has not been caused by a divine accident of fate. True that food grain yield in a few districts did suffer on account of flood and cyclone, but there are other reasons for the ghastliness that has engulfed entire Bengal. The purpose of this article is not to criticise or censure. The British government continues to claim the lordship of India. I want that a Royal Commission be constituted at their initiative. Judicious and impartial persons be its members and [let] Them investigate into the root cause of the famine. [Only] Then shall [it be] revealed how colossal has been the scale of lapses, corruption, and incompetence underlying the bureaucratic governance system. [Simultaneously] The sheer irresponsibility on the part of the representatives of British government, in whose hands vests the real power, will come to light. The hollowness of the phantom of 'provincial autonomy' shall also be exposed. At one end there is a council of ministers encumbered with huge responsibility but devoid of power. At the other end there is the Governor and his bureaucracy – they are 'all powerful' but without any accountability. Arguments and mutual recriminations have been endless. If truth is to be found, the responsibility for investigation has to be entrusted to people who command respect and in whom the people of the land have full trust.

We had issued appeals to save Bengal. That evoked unprecedented response from every part of India. Spontaneous help has been streaming in from all sections of people. It has deeply touched the heart of the Bengalis. But I have been repeatedly stressing that this crisis cannot be solved by the efforts of the people alone. The foremost task of the government is to provide food to the residents of the land. The government must be compelled to discharge this duty.

At least two things have happened due to our endeavours. First, public opinion has been built [not only] in Bengal and other provinces but even outside India. Enough efforts were made to suppress news and dilute the gravity of the situation. But the truth did not remain hidden. The gaze of the entire civilised world today has been riveted on Bengal. Bitter criticism has been underway in and outside the country on the effects and impacts of British rule in India.

Second, the governmental efforts were bare minimum up till now. We had been hearing only one rhetoric [all along] – that abundant food grains have been clandestinely stored in households. After the non-governmental organisations have come forward to render help, the tune of the ministry has changed. It will no longer be possible to get away by shifting the blame to 'greedy businessmen' and 'thrifty householders'. The government's eyes have been opened to the fact that the duty to save the lives of people of the country is essentially its very own. [Still] Not enough has been done on behalf of the government till today. But the benefit is that the authorities have been made to continuously explain their actions to the entire world. Those who claim themselves as the ruler of the land can never escape from the responsibility to protect the lives of the common people.

The situation in Bengal is very dreadful. It cannot be resolved merely by opening Langarkhanas. Foodstuffs are altogether unavailable in rural areas. Driven by hunger and misery, people are leaving villages in droves and heading to towns hoping to get food there. Numbers of people, dead and dying, are rising by the day. Lakhs and lakhs of men and women have reached the outer limits of their life force. They include dignified middle-class families too. Unless [the situation is] remedied immediately, they will be wiped out.

People have been out, abandoning [their] homes. Wandering aimlessly, they are scattering away without any trace. The ties of community are tearing asunder. The social and economic structures of Bengal are rapidly breaking down.

The sick 'skin and bone' children have raised apprehensions about the future of Bengal. The non-governmental organisations are lining up help as fast as possible. They have also evoked inspiration in the local populace. But all efforts are being hindered due to the want of foodstuff. Again, if [some] food is somehow procured, reaching them to proper destinations has become utterly difficult for want of transport.

It does not seem the arrangement planned by the government will be of much use. There is no mechanism [in the Government] to coordinate the working of different agencies. The consequences of a desperate policy – that rice must be bought whatever be the price – has been disastrous. There is a significant shortage of food grains in Bengal. In such a case, the government has to take full responsibility for both the supply and the distribution. These two issues are to be managed in such a manner that no section of people starves for want of food. But for that purpose, a government is needed in which all classes of people in the country have trust. Also, such a policy for national welfare can become successful only when the interest of the government and the people of the country become identical.

I have already presented before the government and the people of the country my scheme to get rid of the frightening situation. Only seven per cent of the total population of Bengal resides in Calcutta and adjoining industrial areas. There are nearly one lakh villages in Bengal divided under 5,000 union boards. Other than that, there are nearly one thousand municipalities. Today the vast rural area has become totally emptied of rice. Villagers are embracing death bit by bit. If Bengal is to be saved, then rice, wheat and other foodstuffs will have to be sent to these 5,000 union boards and 1,000 municipal centres without delay. Let the government immediately start the work by sending at least 1,000 maunds [of food grains] on an average to each centre (it will be necessary to send more quantities in a few big towns). This arrangement will require to be strengthened with whatever help comes forth – locally and from outside. There shall be provision for supply of additional [foodstuffs], depending on need. Unless such extensive help is organised immediately through the combined efforts of the state and the public, the aman produce that is due to be harvested in the month of *paush*[2] too will not be of use to the people of the land. Mismanagement will continue to afflict its procurement and distribution. [And] Famine will become permanent in the land.

There should be a government warehouse in every centre. A responsible government official will supervise it. Without

---

[2] The name of a calendar month as per the Bengali calendar which roughly corresponded to the English months December – January.

giving any consideration to communal and party interests, he will arrange the relief operations, in association with the local union or municipality and eminent persons. Such an arrangement can stop people leaving their homes in search of food. Even if the quantity of food grains in the proposed warehouses for the distressed villagers are not adequate to meet their requirements, such an arrangement will awaken the social consciousness of the public. They will become self-motivated to foster the storehouse. The famine has thrown the traditional lifestyle of Bengal out of gear. This is the only way for its possible reinstatement.

For Calcutta and a few other big towns, the granaries are to be constituted in completely different manners. It should never ever so happen that the villages are kept starving to save the towns.

Two objections might be raised on behalf of the government against this scheme of food procurement and distribution. First, where is the stock of food? Second, what are the means of transportation? The public is never informed about how much quantity of food grains lie in the hands of the government. Lots of goods have been imported into Bengal over the last two months but, then what? This information remains shrouded in mystery. Whatever be the means, we must have food grains! Let the government forthwith arrange to import them from different provinces and even from outside of India. Several organisations have been allowed to store foodstuff for five to six months [of consumption]. Let the cooperation of the railway company, port trust, owners of factories and defence authorities be invoked – let them save the life of the nation by lending some portions of their stocked food temporarily. The warehouses can be replenished with food grains [later], but the lives once lost, will never return. This loan shall be repaid as soon as the new crop is harvested. The Government of India will assume this responsibility. Over the last eight months, we have been insisting on importing foodstuff from abroad. That proposal has been rejected. The responsibility for this [inaction] needs to be fixed.

Through newspapers and media, people are made to hear that the 'Allied Nations' have maintained a huge stockpile of foodstuff. Once freed, the unfortunate nations presently under the axis power will be helped by this stock. But us, supposedly fortunate to be living under the British rule, are dying in thousands today! Why isn't a part of this huge food store being given to us?

Through a telegram sent by the Reuters from Canberra on 28 September 1943, we came to know:

> The minister of agriculture and commerce Sir William Jones Skale has said Australia alone can supply wheat to meet the entire requirement of the [famine] distressed India, provided the United Kingdom makes available necessary ships. The wheat is ready for dispatch, the wait is only for the ship. There is no response to this on behalf of the United Kingdom. Australia is all set to send the consignment. There are an estimated 80 to 100 million bushels of wheat in Australia while new crop will be harvested in a few months. It means there is enough stock of wheat for sending to India.

Few weeks ago, Mr Skale had said, fifty thousand tons of wheat have been sent to India, more will be sent upon availability of ships.

Therefore, it is apparent that Australia has a stock of nearly two and a half crore maunds of wheat. They are eager to send wheat to India, but ships are not being arranged. British

Government can resolve this crisis in Bengal, if it only desires to do that. Where there is a will, there's a way.

A second objection can be raised against my proposal. There is a dearth of transport – how can the foodstuffs be reached across villages? But this objection is completely baseless. If [the task is] treated as absolutely essential, there won't be shortage of transport. Let an extensive programme be adopted for a fortnight. Let railways, steamers, boats, motor vans, military and civil lorries and even bullock carts start carrying food, keeping all routine activities in abeyance. At the present juncture, what can be a more important duty than building up granaries for lakhs of starving people? Would we have stayed put for want of transport if Bengal were invaded by enemy today? Famine and epidemic are in no way less dangerous than the Japanese invasion. This matter too must be considered as a war-related emergency. Bengal has almost arrived on the verge of extinction. Even at this stage, if frank and sincere attempts are instituted to save her, people, cutting across classes, will never be miserly in extending help. Enterprise, far sight and indomitable will-power are the need [of the hour].

Every day – every moment is precious. Extremely frightening reports of misery, distress and scarcity are reaching from various parts of Bengal. In such perilous times the apathy and inefficiency of the bureaucracy to ensure public welfare has been matchless! We are blamed that we have dragged the issue of food crisis into the arena of politics. As a matter of fact, the present economic distress of India owes to her subordination to foreign rule and that has been the very reason that Bengal has reached the extremity of distress.

By no means we want to convert food into a plaything of politics. But when we see that the mistakes and stupidity of the rulers lie at the root of this famine, then has it been a terrible sin on our part as Indians to spell it out and demand changes in the erroneous policy [of the government]?

What would have happened if the English people were placed in this situation today in England? If driven by starvation, epidemic and death, vast masses were to wander in desperation from county to county and from town to town, if the main thoroughfares of London were to turn into a vast burial ground ringing with panic cries of skeletal naked children, if hundreds of corpses were to lie on excreta-soaked ground of Hyde park and Hampstead Heath, what would have been the plight of Downing Street? How long would have the [British] cabinet survived?

What is the condition of India today? Save the fortunate few connected to the war affairs, the plight of the rest has become miserable. The future of our nation is steeped in darkness. But none has the power to raise a finger to protest [against] this distress. Thousands of patriotic men and women are shut inside prisons. Above all, the eternal refrain of fatalism embedded into our whole being rules supreme. We hold unsurpassable destiny responsible for all our misery and distress. We tend to forget the brutal truth that it is 'man' who stands as a wall, depriving us of our birthrights. Today, India has to overcome all obstacles of political subordination, economic crisis, imbecility of mind, and intellectual inertia to get indoctrinated in a new life-giving mantra.

Pt H N Kunzru's Statement

15 October 1943
Observations on Bengal famine

Editor's note: *Pandit Hriday Nath Kunzru, a distinguished member of the Council of State and a respected public figure, was a leader hailing from Kashmir with all-India stature, known for his remarkable catholicity of outlook and an incisive mind ever dedicated to public welfare. He visited famine-affected areas in both parts of Bengal – West and East. He came to Calcutta on 4 October 1943 and visited various parts of Calcutta city, Diamond Harbour, parts of Burdwan district, as well as Contai and Tamluk subdivisions of Midnapore district in West Bengal over a period of ten days. At the end of the visit, he issued a statement and delivered a speech at the University Institute Hall in Calcutta.*[1]

[1] Ghosh, pp 146-8.
The *Council of State* was the upper house of the legislature for British India (the Imperial Legislative Council) created by the Government of India Act 1919.

It was clear from his speech and statement that he was overwhelmed by the terrible miseries wrought on people in 24 parganas, Midnapore and Burdwan districts by hunger and starvation. The spectre of women and children having been abandoned by their husbands and fathers because they were incapable of supporting their dear ones moved his heart. He gave a heartrending description of what he witnessed: 'I have seen women and children suffering uncomplainingly the agonies of starvation. I have seen little children, exhausted by want of food, laying their heads submissively to the ground never to raise them again.' In the midst of such hopelessness, he thought the doctors and medical staff were fighting manfully with whatever meagre facilities available. But the famine victims in hospitals were no better than corpses and Pt Kunzru had grave doubt, even if some of them managed to survive, what would be their condition!

He was struck by the condition of famine victims in Calcutta city as well. He thought they were like moving corpses. He described them as 'starving wretches rummaging the dustbins and heaps of garbage for a few food-grains'. But even such horrible experience paled into insignificance by what he saw in Contai and Tamluk. He found Contai a city of the dead. Wherever he went he came across dead bodies. The condition of women and children who were surviving was most pitiable. In Tamluk, which was supposed to have been better, he came across corpses in every village he visited. Humanity seemed to have been degraded to its lowest ebb with regard to the condition of the dying. Pt Kunzru was credibly informed that in both Contai and Tamluk sub-divisions 'jackals and dogs had been attacking people in whom life was not quite extinct'. Amidst such terrible conditions, the officials were resorting to inhuman methods to depict a multitude of deaths as that of professional beggars.

Pt Kunzru was critical of the League ministry of the province for both, mis-governance and communalisation of the food crisis. He also held the British regime, in particular Amery, the Secretary of State (SoS) and Linlithgow, the Viceroy, responsible for the colossal tragedy. He wondered how the British government would have behaved if similar crisis had struck the British people! He also made a poignant observation: 'Had the British Government realised its primary duty to save the lives of the people and not allow people to die indefinitely on the altar of Provincial Autonomy, the situation would have improved long ago....'

However, in the midst of such gloom and despair, Pt Kunzru felt that the non-official relief organisations were rendering invaluable service to alleviate the suffering of the distressed population. He concluded that, 'Perhaps it would be true to say that their example has compelled the Government of Bengal to move faster than it would otherwise have, either in Calcutta or in the mofussil'.

His second round of visits covered a few important places of East Bengal viz., Dacca, Narayanganj, Brahmanbaria and Chandpur. At the end of it he issued another statement on 22 October 1943. Syama Prasad gave the essence of this statement in Bengali in his book. The English translation of the same is furnished here.

Pt Kunzru observed that things were equally tragic in the eastern parts of Bengal. On the whole he witnessed indescribable sufferings of millions of famine victims andsensed how diabolical politics was behind the holocaust. The only glimmer of hope, he noted, was the role of the non-governmental organisations in serving the distressed humanity. His statement helped in convincing the rest of India that the opposition political parties in Bengal did not exaggerate the famine situation and rather, every letter of what they said was true. Incidentally, a US Senatorial Committee had also visited famine affected places in Bengal around this time and its observation also corroborated Kunzru's statements.[2]

Following is the essence of H N Kunzru's statement on the famine after his visit to East Bengal from the Bengali excerpt published in Panchasher Manwantar:

It is difficult to believe that adversity everywhere could be so menacing, unless one sees it with their own eyes. Starvation is the fate of the people both in towns and villages, but rural areas are more seriously affected than the urban ones. The sufferings of the villagers, particularly of women and children, bring tears to one's eyes. Incidents of parents abandoning their children and husbands deserting wives are rising by the day. Small cultivators and landless labourers are selling their land and houses in order to have a few rupees to buy food with. The scene of starving villagers dismantling their tin roofs and selling those away came to sight in Narayanganj.

The multitude of homeless people go to towns penniless and crowd the Langarkhanas. The allegation that the farmers have stocked rice has now been proved as complete falsehood. The villagers are dying of starvation. To bring allegation of hoarding against them is exceedingly cruel. I have seen very little quantities of rice being sold in the village markets. Nowhere has the price of such rice been less than 50 rupees per maund. The price is much higher in towns. Since the 'price control' orders have not brought results, withdrawing it, in my opinion, may result in making (at least) some quantities of rice available

2 On 20 October 1943 Senator Ralph A Brewster described the Bengal famine as terrible and said that the Committee saw dead people lying around the streets and women and children in the last stage of starvation. Ghosh, p105.

in the markets in the mofussil areas. In this regard I had the opportunity of meeting not only civic personnel but many government officials too. They told me even such measure will not help in making rice available in sufficient quantities.

In places like Dhaka, Chandpur and Narayanganj etc. shelters have been opened [for the homeless]. The people who are set to die lying on streets are being brought here. Emergency hospitals have been opened for starving people who are afflicted with malaria, dysentery, stomach related and other diseases. Still corpses and dying people can be seen lying by the roadside. The starving emaciated men and women on roads seem like moving corpses. If they somehow manage to survive [this onslaught] that would have to be considered providential. The same thing can as well be said about those accommodated in the shelters and emergency hospitals.

In the House of Commons, Mr Amery has bluntly denied the pervasiveness of the epidemic and scarcity in the supply of medicine. His statement is completely opposite to the facts on ground. There is an acute shortage of medicine. In a way it may be said that Quinine is [altogether] unavailable. Diseases have engulfed the race as men and women have lost their vital force.

The governmental and the non-governmental Langarkhanas are doing lots of relief work. But their numbers are very less. [Worse] Even they have to shut doors from time to time for want of foodstuff. Between two to two and a half *chatak*[3] of *khichdi* is given to each [destitute] in these free kitchens. Everywhere, the quantity of food being given is very meagre. Dhaka Central Relief Committee is managing the supply in Dhaka town. Session judge Mr Dey is the president of the

[3] It is a unit of measurement to quantify weight that was in use in Bengal. It corresponded to 60 grams. Khichdi: A cooked meal of lentils and rice.

committee. I have heard that the *Mohalla* committees[4] have given twelve chatak of rice and twenty chatak of wheat per person per month. There is scarcity not only of rice, but of every kind of foodstuff in all places. The low middle-class people have become the most endangered lot.

Before coming to Bengal, I had a notion that the political opponents are exaggerating the [situation] to unfairly attack the government of Bengal. But now I am realising that every word of what those leaders of Bengal have said is true. They have rendered great service to the country by revealing the true condition [of Bengal] to the people of India and Britain. The scarcity of cloth is comparable to that of food. Not only dhoti and saree,[5] now there are acute requirements for warm clothes as well.

Mr Amery has said that nearly one thousand people are dying every week. But my guess is that the death rate would be much higher. I was informed about one single block in which between seven hundred to one thousand people have been dying every week. The death rate in towns is exceedingly high too.

People have particular anxiety about what policy the government will adopt about the aman crop. They are of the opinion that if the government buys out the entire crop, the result will be grievous.

There is yet another allegation against the government– that they are busy in saving the lives of the residents of Calcutta and do not spare a thought about the mofussil areas.

Everyone should be aware of the gravity of the situation. In this regard the maximum responsibility vests in the central government. The future of Bengal depends on the effectiveness of Lord Wavell to a considerable extent.

---

4 Mohalla means neighbourhood.

5 Wraparounds used as clothing by men and women in India.

Syama Prasad's Statement

5 November 1943

Editor's note: *The new Viceroy, Archibald Wavell, took oath on 20 October 1943 and began to take measures to improve the food supply to Bengal. Slowly, food-grains started reaching Bengal from rest of India and overseas. But these initiatives hit roadblocks as the League ministry stuck to its old ways of communalisation of relief measures, corruption and inefficiency. There was lack of transparency in handling the 'import' and condemnable inefficiency in transporting them to the deficit areas. In the midst of the terrible famine, the League pushed ahead its political agenda.*[1] *Its heartlessness towards famine victims was stark and became obvious as it drove the hungry and the destitute out of Calcutta and other big towns by using the Vagrancy Ordinance.*

---

[1] This tendency was in evidence throughout the famine. Earlier, on 1 October Jinnah, in his Eid message from Bombay, complimented the Muslim League for their victories in various by-elections in Bengal and the NWFP. He added: 'It is obvious that today we stand more solid and united and stronger than ever before.' IAR, Vol 2, 1943, p 19.

In the process, family members began to be separated for the second time since the famine began. These hapless victims were acutely short of clothing even as winter set in. The government's ineptitude to tackle the scourge of epidemic caused greater threat to them at this juncture. Cholera, small-pox and malaria raged in various parts of the province.[2] *Medical care was shamefully scant. The government seemed indifferent to its basic responsibilities.*[3]

Syama Prasad drew the attention of the concerned authorities to several critical issues pertinent to alleviation of the distress through a statement that urged the Bengal government to undertake tasks which were essential and warning them against repeating earlier mistakes, e.g. like the government plan of buying aman paddy. Simultaneously, two relief agencies mentored by him were spiritedly fighting to protect human lives amidst extreme adversities while trying to ensure that beneficiaries had no feeling of loss of dignity. This statement reveals the depth of Syama Prasad's feelings for the victims, his spirit and enterprise, his pragmatic approach and his ever-readiness to help the government to overcome the crisis.

Syama Prasad issued the statement on 5 November 1943. It was included in his book Panchasher Manwantar in the chapter titled 'Collections'. The following is an English translation of the statement.

---

[2] Epidemic diseases were still in early stages. Because the government did not act promptly, they spread like wildfire across the province. Eighteen districts were declared under grip of smallpox and cholera in epidemic form by June 1944. Malaria was affecting nearly 80-90 per cent of their population. In a press conference on 6 June, 1944 Dr B C Roy, heading the Bengal Medical Relief Coordination Committee, disclosed that more than 2 crore people of the province stood affected by epidemic. IAR 1944, Vol I, p89.

[3] The Woodhead Commission observed: 'there was, in fact, almost a complete breakdown of health services, affecting both the centre and the periphery.' IAR 1944, Vol I, p89.

Text of the Statement

For more than last two-and-a-half months, we have been straining all our energies to alleviate the sufferings of the people of Bengal. I am taking this opportunity to acknowledge our gratitude to all those generous souls, both from and outside India, who extended help through money and [relief] materials.

Majority of the non-governmental organisations have been working in mutual cooperation. I am directly involved in the activities of the Bengal Relief Committee and the Bengal Provincial Hindu Mahasabha. Till today, the Bengal Relief Committee has collected twenty lakh rupees in the form of cash and kind, while the Bengal Provincial Hindu Mahasabha has collected nearly four lakh rupees. Every day the Bengal Relief Committee is rendering service to nearly three lakh men and women in 125 centres, spread across twenty districts. To many [destitute persons] cooked food is given free, while many others are given food grains either free or at low prices. Besides, help has been rendered by way of providing medicine and clothes. To be able to continue to work this way till December, the expenditure will far exceed rupees twenty lakh that has been received [so far].[4]

The Bengal Provincial Hindu Mahasabha is serving more than 60,000 people in 125 centres across twenty districts every day. Many temporary shelters and hospitals have been set up. Clothes and medicine are being distributed. We have paid special attention to develop cottage industry. The distressed

---

4 Lots of money was raised thereafter too. The accounts relating to the Bengal Relief Committee and Bengal Provincial Hindu Mahasabha have been furnished in the appendix.

persons are being encouraged by the relief centres to do some work in exchange, for the help they are receiving. We have so far spent over Rupees 40,000 to render help to distressed middle class families. The families of the political prisoners and pundits of Sanskrit toles[5] have [also] been rendered help from this money.

Considering the enormous scale of the programme that has been underway much more money is needed. We are making earnest appeals to the general public to render more financial help to Bengal Relief Committee and Bengal Provincial Hindu Mahasabha. Soon the detailed reports of the services rendered [by each] will be published separately and sent to each donor.

Many other non-governmental organisations and us are doing our best in the present crisis. But the problem is so humongous that to achieve a complete solution is beyond our capacity. We have been able to do little compared to the requirements. However, without a shred of doubt we can say that it is only due to our efforts that the attention of the entire India and outside world have been focussed on the plight of Bengal. It seems that the government has also finally realised their grave responsibility in this crisis. The famine of 'fifty' is a slur on the British rule in India. Time and again we have been demanding that the real causes behind it be found through [serious] inquiry. The ghastly story of misery and distress has already spread across the whole of India. I don't wish to say anything new. The death toll is rising very rapidly. Everyday, brings us numerous heart-rending stories.

Coordination must occur between the government and the non-government initiatives according to a well-regulated policy, keeping in view the welfare of lakhs of men and women

[5] School.

of Bengal. There is no other way to save lives. I am mentioning a few important issues with regard to which, the government and common people must pay attention without delay.

1. Arrangements have been made to evict penniless people from Calcutta, but great chaos is resulting as the classification has not been done familywise. Even force is being applied while removing persons. Those 'left out' are getting completely separated from their relatives. They have no means to find out where the rest of their family members were shifted. I have said it several times that [these] penniless people will have to be finally restored to their own homes and social life. For this reason, every such person [forcibly removed] should be taken to the relief centre which is as near to his native village as possible. In every [such] case, food and other essential goods must be supplied. It is essential that the country knows whether or not this necessity has been kept in view. The government must publish a detailed report in this regard. From time to time, non-governmental people should be allowed to inspect these relief centres. Things will grow much more complicated if the people who are being driven out of Calcutta die for want of food.
2. It must not be forgotten even for a split-second that these people had abandoned [their] homes and become beggars on the streets [only] for want of food. Many more like them, who had stayed back in villages and towns, are silently embracing death by starving. About a month ago I had proposed that one centre each will have to be set up for every few villages. [Further], There has to be a storehouse of food grains for each such centre. Similarly, [such] storehouses should be there for each

town. Food grains have to be distributed free of cost or at reasonable prices from these store houses. This has not happened. Today, the trust of the common people with regard to the government's capacity to supply food grains to meet their bare minimum needs has faltered. It is not possible to restore this trust by issuing a series of statements and releasing pamphlets.

In every area, food grains have to be stored and it must be made visible to the public eyes. Only that can bring about changes in their attitude and inspire them to put in all their might in protecting [lives of] people. The government account shows that over the last seven months (April-October) more than 475,000 tons of food grains have been imported into Bengal on behalf of the government. But it is a matter of regret that nowhere have these food grains been stored to meet local needs. The crisis is gradually escalating. It has to be borne in mind that this period of seven months we are talking about, has been under the tenure of the present ministry.

We want unambiguous answers from the government as to where and to whom have these food grains been sent? Where have the foodstuff been moving over the last three months? Merely citing the names of the districts will not suffice – we demand that the names of the block, the union, even the village be disclosed. Let people of every area come to know of the actual state of affairs. Foodstuff will have to be sent to different village centres in accordance with the policy of fair distribution. No purpose will be served if foodstuffs are sent to districts or blocks in an unplanned and chaotic manner. Shiploads of food grains are arriving at Calcutta but, the distribution policy is faulty from top to bottom.

Why are the food grains not being sent rapidly right from the port to the mofussil places through vehicles and steamers, in accordance with a well-thoughtout programme of actions? How many days did the clothes and the food grains lie in the steamers for want of clearance and for how many days did the government agents fail to take delivery of these goods? I am demanding a statement from the ministry on this matter. Often a special agent customarily unloads the goods, taking several days. Thereafter, these goods are consigned to hoarders patronised by the government. In consequence there has been unnecessary delay in these goods reaching the distressed areas. How does the government justify this? We know that these hoarders make profits of lakhs of rupees by way of commission. How much longer will such partiality and incompetence be indulged in, bringing ruin to the distressed people of the land? We are demanding that a plan be prepared immediately so that there is no delay for the clothes and food grains to reach the main relief centres (*Sahajya Kendras*). From these main centres, these [goods] must be distributed very rapidly amongst various branches in accordance with a definite policy. The full details of such operations will have to be published every week so that the public is kept informed and they can check it.

3. The next problem is to pool together whatever local resources are potentially available for the purpose of relief. If that were to happen, the government will have to give up its policy of indiscriminate buying [of food

grains] altogether. The lives of lakhs of men and women of Bengal are being destroyed during the present crisis. The policy of reckless buying [of food grains] is one of the chief reasons for creation of this crisis.

We are getting reports that the agents of the government are still actively engaged in buying [of food grains]. Wherever they have bought or attempted to buy, the prices of goods suddenly shot up. [Still], If the Government intends to buy, they must simultaneously assume the responsibility for distribution. No patchwork will do in this matter. In one distressed area in the Burdwan [district], the government had detained the goods of licensed businessmen, but did not allow distribution of these goods to the starving populace. Some days ago, an oral order of the government has reached these businessmen [asking them] to hand over the entire stock [they had purchased] on behalf of the government to Ispahani & Co. In the same way, the government agents have been buying rice from other distressed areas including even Medinipur and Bankura. The people are becoming extremely vulnerable.

4. Reports that the government has decided to buy aman paddy have been published. This purchase policy is loaded with serious implications. There has been decent production of aman crop this year, but that alone is not enough to save Bengal. Having said that, the miseries of people will certainly abate, provided its distribution is fair. We are specially warning the government not to pursue its present purchase-policy in respect of aman paddy. In course of patronising a few favourite businessmen, there was humongous loss in the past. Let this not be repeated.

The villagers themselves will have to keep watch so that the annual [consumption] need of food grains remains [stocked] in every village. Surplus, if any, alone can be taken away to meet others' needs. Let the people themselves handle this matter – so that the agents cannot indulge in reckless buying, nor can there begin a tug of war for the so-called surplus [stock of food grains]. Calcutta and its adjoining industrial belts are to be considered as a completely separate zone. The Government of India will take responsibility for supply to this area out of the food grains imported from outside Bengal. If separate arrangements are made for greater Calcutta and both the government and the speculative buyers retreat from the markets of the mofussil areas for some days, the crisis will disappear at once and normalcy will rapidly return in the country.

The government will have to keep keen watch and exercise due care regarding movement of goods across the country. The businessmen and the hoarders must be compelled to render proper accounts of the stock held by them. Attempts at profiteering and excessive hoarding will have to be curbed with iron hands. Even if [the consumption need of] greater Calcutta is excluded, it is difficult to say how many days the aman paddy will feed Bengal. Still, there will be some time to observe the situation and chalk out the longer-term food policy for full 1944 and beyond. This [respite] is not insubstantial.

5. Medical treatment-related help is one of the key requirements [today]. Cholera, dysentery and malaria have broken out in large scale. From both, the Bengal Relief Committee and the Bengal Hindu Mahasabha,

cholera vaccines have been administered to around one lakh people. But this is meagre compared to the need. There is lack of coordination between the governmental and non-governmental initiatives in this area too. This is really deplorable. The efforts of the government in this regard are exceptionally tardy and inadequate. Another important and essential goods is clothing. Winter has almost arrived. The need for clothing will be felt more acutely now. The condition of the children is heart rending. Planned arrangements are a must to save them. Shelter is an absolute necessity. Till normalcy returns, they will have to be stationed there, fed, clothed and brought up.

The situation is one of great despondency. Still, I am saying this and earnestly so, that this misfortune can be countered in such a manner as to rejuvenate the social and economic system of Bengal to acquire a new form. The condition of an average Bengali is usually very pathetic. The blow of this man-made famine has left the Bengalis crushed. We will have to constitute a network of cooperatives, one each covering a few villages. And we need to be specially educated about the following things:

a. Food grains will have to be procured both locally and from outside and distributed;
b. Movement to 'grow more food' needs to be initiated;
c. Matters relating to health, economic policy and education need to be (reviewed and) reconstructed.

After carefully preparing a full-fledged programme, the work must start as early as possible. This is imperative because Bengal is rapidly moving towards destruction. In the present moments of crisis, the (extant) governmental rules and provisions have totally failed. They will flounder yet again unless the government efforts are combined with the people's endeavour. It is not my objective to raise issues of party politics. But if Bengal is to be saved from 'ruin', party politics must be stopped altogether.

An environment will have to be created such that our unity efforts can take practical shape. The ministry has forfeited the respect and trust of the people because they betrayed ineptitude in discharging their duties. There is huge chasm between the common people and the government. How can this gap be removed? The representatives of the British government who are still clinging to power, who did not give up the policy of repression even in the times of (such) grave crisis, and who are unable to repose trust in people, alone will have to answer this question. What has been happening in Bengal is not only a blot on the British Government but on the 'Allied Power' nations too. It is because they claim to have united in order to uproot miseries and oppression from the face of the World!

Will the Famine Come Again?

24 January, 1944

Editor's note: *Right since November 1943, thousands of troops were delivering food grains to deficit areas of Bengal to tackle the food crisis.*[1] *In the last week of 1943, the government of India also agreed to take responsibility to feed Calcutta and adjoining industrial areas. It was also a matter of relief that there was good yield of aman crop in the province in the winter months. In consequence, the acute food crisis began to wane. However, it was a matter of concern that the price of rice was still way above what the average person could afford. The process of normalisation thus continued to be fragile. Wrong policy or repeating past errors could send the nascent rehabilitation process haywire.*

On 1 December 1943, the Bengal government announced its decision to introduce a rationing system in important urban areas besides Calcutta and its surroundings. Still, in some areas,

---

1 Claude Auchinleck, Commander In Chief of the Indian Army, in a press conference on 7 November 1943 said that several thousand troops, including a number of motorised units, were being employed to distribute food to deficit areas. IAR 1943 Vol 2 pp25-6.

it delayed its implementation for the reason that sufficient numbers of Muslim employees were not available to meet the criteria of 'community ratio rules'. Further, driven by communal consideration, it refused to make use of the ordinary channels of trade (owned by non-Muslims), though they were in a position to reach famine victims in farthest corners efficiently. The poor of both communities thus turned victims of the resultant delay.

On the day he wrote this article on the famine's return, Syama Prasad also said in a press conference in New Delhi that without a radical shift in the existing methods of administration in Bengal, a second famine in 1944 could not be avoided.[2] *In his article Syama Prasad made a comprehensive survey of the situation in the province and offered a range of suggestions for a holistic solution to prevent the scourge yet again.*

The 24 January article was titled 'Manwantar Ki Abar Ashibe?' meaning, 'Will The Famine Come Again'. It was incorporated in his book titled, Panchasher Manwantar. The following is an English translation of the article.

Many hold the view that Bengal has gotten over the crisis and is gradually returning to normalcy. Whatever the situation, if the manner in which the government is exerting its authority now is allowed to continue, there is apprehension for a repeat of the disaster. Special precautions are a must in this regard.

There is an urgent need for extensive medical facilities to save Bengal. Simultaneously, determined endeavours must begin to restore the social and economic institutions. Utmost care is to be taken so that food crisis of the sort [experienced] in the present year can never recur. Number of people who

---

[2] IAR 1944 Vol 1, p 30.

perished for want of food over the last six months is beyond imagination. Amongst those who somehow survived, lakhs have been gripped by diseases. As the life force in people has nearly extinguished, diseases have acquired menacing grip over them everywhere. Additionally, there is shortage of cloth. Medicine is unavailable and diets for the sick are absent altogether. There is no limit to the misery of the people.

Lakhs of families have lost their earning capacity. Even if the price of rice comes down to Rupees 10 or even 8, still people will not be able to maintain themselves. Heart-rending stories of grief and pain keep coming from all parts of the country. Many amongst the distressed people have lost their physical capacity. Again, several of them who are still able cannot find jobs. Such pathetic conditions afflict innumerable men and women of all ages and across all communities. There is another group consisting mostly of women and children floating across towns and villages after getting separated from their families. They have been gradually turning into full-fledged beggars. The economic foundation of the society has been pulverised. It is imperative that we dedicate ourselves to the task of social reconstruction without delay. There can be no stable solution to the problem by merely feeding the distressed or helping them with money and clothing. People are resorting to begging to fill their stomachs. Consequently, the sense of self-confidence and self-respect are on the verge of extinction from the entire race.

A fair scheme for the administration of relief must be drafted by enlisting the efforts and cooperation of all. This will be applied to various areas, keeping in view the [unique] local needs. One home shelter each, covering a few villages will have to be constructed for the poor. These shelters will provide food and cover to all those who are homeless and fully incapacitated.

For the rest, jobs will have to be found. They will be provided with food and money in exchange for rendering labour.

Craftsmen and the artists have become fully bankrupt. Simultaneously, efforts must be made to restore them to their respective professions. Even within the middle class, there are lakhs of families without or with meagre earnings, gradually succumbing to death. It is this middle class who contributed the most to the cultural and economic life of Bengal. The foremost duty of the government is to protect them.

If there is continued negligence in rescuing the economic institutions and restoring people to their social life, there are possibilities that the famine will manifest again. Those who have watched the sequence of events [leading to the famine], will say in one voice that incompetence, mismanagement and corruption of the government officials were at the root of the endless miseries that Bengal suffered in 1943 AD. Lots of attempts were made on behalf of the government to hide the truth. In distorting facts and misrepresentations none can match Mr Amery. The story of Bengal's distress has spread all over [the world] despite [his mischief]. The prestige of the government too has been severely dented in this regard.

At present, I do not wish to discuss the extent to which the present ministry is responsible for the loss of innumerable lives in Bengal. I am hoping there will be impartial investigation in this matter at some point of time. The full truth will be out then. But I am drawing everyone's attention to one matter. Whatever may have been the fault of Mr Fazlul Huq, his cabinet had, in March 1943 [itself], announced before the world that a terrible food crisis was about to strike Bengal and that it will be essential to import foodstuff to save its people. But his ministry was removed within the next few weeks by hatching conspiracies at the levels of certain high officials. Right since its inception and over the next few months, the [new] ministry of Sir Nazimuddin began to issue a series of untruthful statements conveying that Bengal did not have shortage of food, and that some people have stocked large amounts of food resulting in the crisis. In the month of June, the ministry began a 'food drive' with great pomp and show. That campaign became a dismal failure. The cabinet ministers have not yet gathered courage to publish the results of that campaign.

The cabinet encouraged their pet businessmen to buy rice. As a result, the rural belt became empty of rice. The normal price structure collapsed. People lost trust in the measures adopted by the government. At that time, Mr Amery, sitting in London, gave statements, one after another, that Bengal [food] situation was good and there were no issues. And [his] yes-men in Bengal and the rest of India began to recite and re-recite his sound bites.

My grievance against the present ministry is that right from April 1943, they made criminal waste of extremely precious time. Mr Fazlul Huq had emphatically declared about the shortage of rice in the month of March. Had they too followed the same line, such a dangerous situation would not have arisen in Bengal. Over the last two or three months, the military and the civic officials have demonstrated much activism with regard to procurement of food and distribution to the dying people. Why did not such industry start in April? [Instead] The new ministry was not only messing up things, they were also suppressing the warning by people who had sensed the impending crisis and were urging them to wake up.

[As a matter of fact], Unless non-governmental relief initiatives began, the outside world would not have come to know about the distress and miseries of Bengal for a much longer period. The government officials too would have come to their senses only after a much longer period.

There has been a good yield of aman paddy in the present season. Notwithstanding that, many are of the view that if the same kind of wretched administrative policies are continued, the famine will reappear in Bengal. [Now] the British government and the Government of India have taken full responsibility to ensure that the scandalous misfortune of 1943 does not recur. Therefore, Mr Amery will not be able to get away this time by citing the ruse of provincial autonomy.

Of course, the price of rice now is lower compared to what it was during the famine. But the price has again begun to rise throughout Bengal. Rice is being sold at much higher prices over the price band fixed by the government. The fact that the government is unable to maintain the price level within the control limits in the month of January in spite of abundant rice [yield], reveals deficiencies in the administrative machineries and the absolute incompetence of the council of ministers. The programme for procurement of food grains has been haphazard and insincere. It is not oriented towards public welfare nor is it being directed to inspire trust between the businessmen and the common people.

For the last four months I have been insisting that the government should open one storehouse each for every few villages, to create trust in the public psyche and to tackle the countrywide [food] crisis. The traditional business channels must be maintained as far as possible. Once the people see the stock of food grains for the rainy days in front of their eyes, they will regain confidence. This arrangement will have to be made covering all zones of Bengal. For this to happen, the Government must have full cooperation of the public. [Needless to say] Such a programme becomes successful only when interests of all [sections] are unified. But no such arrangement has been made till now. On the contrary, by allowing some favourite business houses to buy rice recklessly, the government has scuttled the prospect of such unity. Such [bias] has been generating jealousy in their fellow businessmen. There is no systematic supply arrangement to speedily respond to needs of the distressed areas. Such [kind of] arrangements cannot deliver solutions to the enormous crisis that has benumbed Bengal.

The Government of India has undertaken responsibility to feed over thirty lakh people in Calcutta and adjoining areas. [But] The Bengal cabinet has been fomenting trouble in setting up the requisite rationing system. Their objective is not to serve people but to strengthen the communal political party they have set up by taking advantage of the present misfortune. The motive of the ministry was to introduce the 'rationing' only through their favoured 'government shops' while completely ignoring the traditional shops. The Government of India has amended their irrational programme. I do not know on what logic the cabinet had repeatedly insisted on their demand, even though it was completely against the Gregory report.[3]

The Government of India has directed that on an average fifty-five per cent of the shops will remain under government control while forty five per cent will be at the hands of common businessmen. Yet, the directions of the Government of India have been circumvented by arranging to divert larger numbers of customers to the government shops. If even the rationing system is conducted not in accordance with a just policy but on the basis of party interests, then should we ask who is importing politics into the food issue?

---

[3] Report of the Foodgrains Policy Committee, 1943, headed by Sir Theodore Gregory.

Whether in Calcutta or the distant countryside, there is no communication between the Bengal government and the civil population. Government of India has assumed the responsibility to feed Calcutta and its adjacent industrial areas. In such a situation why should people still suffer while there has been much higher yield of food grains in the rest of Bengal compared to the [consumption] need? Why should there be apprehension of a food crisis in 1944 AD yet again? Still, if such a thing happens due to incompetence and corruption on the part of the [Bengal] ministry, the responsibility will vest upon the Government of India. Driven by communal considerations, this one-party ministry can never earn the trust of the wider society. The very ones against whom numerous serious allegations of injudiciousness have been made, can never be allowed to play truant with the lives of millions of people.

The people of Bengal do not ask for alms. They are only demanding the right that mankind has i.e., the right to live. [To provide] This is the foremost duty of any government that calls itself 'civilised'. Let Lord Wavell and Mr Casey[4] try to comprehend the crisis in Bengal dispassionately and impartially and create conditions such that between the government and the common people a tendency of cooperation rises spontaneously. Also, no consideration, whether political or communal, must be allowed to supersede the issue of public welfare. Only then Bengal will get rid of the crisis.

---

[4] Richard Gavin Gardiner Casey assumed charge as the Governor of Bengal in early 1944. He was to ensure implementation of the Wavell's plan to normalise situation in Bengal. However, the relief work in the province was impeded by the corrupt and communal agenda that was still being pursued by the Nazimuddin-led ministry. After loss of precious time, Bengal was put under Sec 93 in March 1945, whereupon Casey took over the reins of the province.

Unity is the Need

29 March 1944
Speech at Bengal Legislative Assembly

Editor's note: *The League ministry showed no signs of remorse even after a few million lives were lost to famine and epidemic. But for the measures, though much belated, initiated by Wavell since end of October 1943, which were carried forward by acting Governor Rutherford and later Richard Casey who took over charge as new Governor on 23 January, 1944, the crisis would certainly have taken much longer to abate. The overall relief operations were long drawn and all thorough. The League ministry showed incorrigible communal bias in reaching help to famine victims. It stuck to its corrupt, autocratic ways and tried to muzzle the press from criticising its policy.*[1] *The severe resentment in the opposition*

---

1 The issue of imposing restriction on writing of editorials in the *Amrita Bazar Patrika* continued to reverberate in the Bengal Legislative Assembly as late as 14 February 1944, when Khan Bahadur Mohammed Ali sought to justify the Ministry's action, saying that in the opinion of the government, two editorial articles of that newspaper were subversive in nature and contained veiled incitement to violence. IAR, 1944, Vol 1, p34.

parties against the ministry found an expression through several cut motions in the legislative assembly on 23 March 1944.[2]

As its various sins kept coming to light, the ministry showed a tendency to pass on the blame to others like governments of other provinces, Government of India, railway authorities etc. Its bluff was repeatedly called but it escaped dismissal, courtesy British Indian government. Due to its refusal to mend ways, the spectre of acute food crisis began to resurface in some places.[3] *Under the circumstance, considering both the communal mindset and its callousness, Syama Prasad gave a clarion call on famine relief allocations to all political parties in the Bengal Legislative Assembly on 29 March 1944.*

While participating in a discussion on the 'Demand for Grant' of Rs 2.61 crore for expenditure towards famine relief, he delivered the following speech, urging them to come together and form a united front by shedding their personal, communal and party interests in a bid to save Bengal. While participating in the discussion, Syama Prasad spoke at length in English.[4]

---

[2] On 23 March 1944, after a scathing criticism of the working of the civil supplies department in the Bengal Legislative Assembly, as many as 20 cut motions were moved. This followed a demand by premier Nazimuddin for grant of Rs 85, 057,000. IAR, 1944, Vol 1,p 43.

[3] On 28 February 1944, Fazlul Huq, taking part in the budget discussion, launched a vigorous attack on the ministry, questioning their loyalty to Bengal. He said: 'here Ministers were not responsible to the legislature but to Mr. Jinnah as the head of the Muslim League'. He also lamented that the Ministers were working the machine of provincial autonomy, not in accordance with the wishes of the people... but 'according to the dictates of a director utterly ignorant of the real feelings of the people.' IAR: 1944, Vol 1, p179.

[4] Source: Assembly Proceeding Official Record, Bengal Legislative Assembly, Eighteenth session, 1944. In his book, he gave the essence of that speech in Bengali with the heading viz., Aikya Chai, which in English means 'Unity is the Need'. Here, the original speech is reproduced in full under the latter heading. The speech is reproduced as delivered in March1944 except minimum editing to improve readability.

Syama Prasad Mookerjee: Sir, we are not here to discuss the relief operations of the non-official relief committees, but I shall refer to their activities in the course of my speech. We have met here to pass the budget estimates of the Bengal Government and not of the Bengal Relief Committee or of the Bengal Provincial Hindu Mahasabha Relief Fund.

Abdul Motaleb Malik: Provocation came from your side.

Syama Prasad Mookerjee: No, it did not. It came from your side. Sir, we are here to discuss today the question of Bengal famine not with reference to what happened in 1943, but to the conditions in 1944. I do not wish to discuss in details as to who has been responsible for the Bengal famine, except to say this that the part which has been played by the present Ministry has not helped to ease the situation; on the other hand it has aggravated the situation considerably.

(Cries of 'Question' from the **Coalition Party Benches.**)

Sir, today is 29th of March. This day last year, the resignation of Mr Fazlul Huq as Chief Minister was obtained by the then Governor. The House will recall that during the Budget discussion of 1943, the then Ministry made it abundantly clear that the situation then in existence was alarming, that there was a serious shortage of food grains in this province and that unless some radical steps were taken in the very near future, Bengal may be plunged into disaster. Sir, I do not wish to take the House through the remarks made by Minister after Minister after the assumption of office of the new Ministry in April 1943, stating that there was no food shortage at all, stating that everything was all right, stating that in the course of a few weeks…

Rai Harendranath Chaudhuri: In the course of a fortnight.

Syama Prasad Mookerjee: ...that was what the Finance Minister said – the prices would fall and that there would be peace and plenty throughout the province.

Now, Sir, the charge which we bring against the ministry is that if they had not lost valuable time during that period, the situation would not have worsened as it did worsen in the course of 1943.

Today, Sir, in 1944 what is the position? There is an exact repetition of the statements similar to what we heard in 1943. I have made here a tabular statement of what was said in 1943 and what is being said in 1944. There is the same assurance given without the adequate and required data behind such assurance. What is the charge that we bring against the government? Government did all it could to prevent the news of distress in Bengal spreading throughout the province and outside the province. What part did the non-official organisations play during those critical months?

The members of the House, if they analyse the situation dispassionately, will find that it was the non-official organisations which first thought it necessary to start relief operations and only after they had started work, the government started doing something. So far as call for help was concerned, appeals were issued by non-official bodies and individuals throughout Bengal and outside. Certain appeals and certain statements were tried to be suppressed under the orders of the Defence of India Rules, but had not public opinion been aroused throughout India through non-official efforts and through the efforts of some newspapers, specially *The Statesman* which does not occupy a place in the Opposition but which did invaluable service in letting out the truth and making it known throughout India and abroad, the Government of Bengal would never have been brought to its senses.

So far as non-official relief organisations, the two main organisations with which I have been connected, viz., The Bengal Relief Committee and The Hindu Mahasabha Relief Fund, are concerned, I can say without any fear of contradiction that there has been no distinction in respect of caste, creed or colour with regard to relief given by them. I have got before me the returns from various local relief organisations and from other places which go to show that we have served man [mankind] without any distinction of caste, creed or colour.

But what about the secret circular issued by the government to the District Officers that among Moslems, none but a Muslim Leaguer is to be appointed as a member of any relief committee? Mind you, Sir, that of these lakhs of rupees which have been raised by non-official organisations, 99 per cent has been raised by non-Muslims but according to instructions received and according to our own judgement, we decided that we should serve man [humanity] irrespective of any consideration.

On the other hand, whose money has the government of Bengal handled and mishandled? It is the money of the people of Bengal. It is not the money of the Muslim League Party sitting over there. It is not the money of the Hon'ble Ministers who have administered the funds; yet in every place distinction has been made both with regard to management and distribution. That is, however, not the main point we are discussing today.

The main point is how to prevent famine in 1944. I would say this with all the emphasis at my command that whatever we have said during the last few months is due only to our fear, based on reasoned facts that unless things are properly shaped, there may be a recurrence of famine. From one point of view, no question of recurrence arises. Has famine disappeared from Bengal? What was the price of rice before the famine days and what is the price of rice now? On the admission of the Government and its supporters, you cannot get rice at a price less than Rs 15 or 16. I ask you: does that not represent that famine conditions are still prevailing in various parts of the province?

But what has the Government done? What the Government has done is to gag public opinion. [The] Government has directed that there will be no criticism of the failure or inefficiency of the Government to be allowed to be published in any newspaper in Bengal. I ask you: is that the way in which the situation in Bengal is going to be tackled? It has been said right from the top to the bottom – everyone connected with government and outside has said – that unless and until you can restore public confidence, the conditions in Bengal can never alter; and how can confidence be restored if the ultimate responsibility for carrying on the food policy is left in the hands of the Ministry, which does not admittedly enjoy the confidence of large sections of the people of Bengal.

(Cries of 'No', 'no' from the **Government Benches.**)

Syama Prasad Mookerjee: It is no use your shouting 'no, no'. You know that in your heart of hearts you are a sectional ministry, that you are a ministry which commands the confidence of one section of the people and that there are large sections of the people who do not have any respect for your integrity, efficiency or honesty.

Now, Sir, only three days ago, the Associated Press issued this message from Bogra. It is dated 22 March. It runs thus: 'Batches of destitute are again pouring into the town in a very weak state of health. A body of a destitute was found lying on the Rangpur Road for some hours while another was seen being devoured by vultures and jackals on the Station approach road...'

(A voice from the **Government Benches**: 'Ah, ah'.)

Syama Prasad Mookerjee: Who is the gentleman who said, 'Ah, ah!'? This is an Associated Press message which has not been published except in one paper in Bengal.

Rasik Lal Biswas: It is false.

Syama Prasad Mookerjee: Mr Rasik Lal Biswas whose *rashikata*[5] knows no limits, says that the statement is false. [The] Associated Press representative has sent out a false message in order to tickle the vanity of Mr Rasik Lal Biswas. Now, Sir, I ask the Hon'ble Ministers: Can the Hon'ble Minister deny that it was only about 10 or 12 days ago [that] a report was sent by the Superintendent of Police, Bankura, who is not in league with the Opposition, addressed to the Deputy Inspector-General of Police, Burdwan Range, disclosing the serious state in Bankura and the anxious times which the officers were having.

These are the words: 'As regards rice and small coins'– I ask every member to pay close attention to it–'it appears that the situation is going to be a repetition of last year. Prices of rice and paddy are on the increase. Rice and paddy are disappearing from the market. The same is the case with small coins. There has been a continual complaint by the [police] force of extremely rotten supplies of rice coming from government stores. I have already brought this to the notice of the District Magistrate, but no practical solution has been reached.'

Now mark the comment on the administration of the Food Department: 'The supply consists of a mixture of four different kinds of rice with a liberal addition of stones and the users are mostly suffering from stomach troubles. I foresee a disabled force if this kind of supply continues.'

From Bankura you go to Chittagong. What is happening in Chittagong? In Chittagong, [the] government has arranged

---

[5] Humour

for the supply of food grains to about 15 per cent of the people through controlled shops and there also, the prevailing price is about Rs 16. There are thousands in that area who cannot afford to buy and live by purchasing rice at Rs 16. But that is only affecting 15 per cent of the people. Eighty-five per cent of the people in Chittagong are left to their own fate, which means that they cannot get rice at any reasonable price whatsoever, the prevailing price today being between Rs 22 and Rs 24 per maund.

Coming away from Chittagong to the *Calcutta Gazette*, take the *Calcutta Gazette* and read it every week. What are the facts which are disclosed here as regards the situation in Bengal, district by district and subdivision by subdivision? Take the figures given up to 8 March and published in the *Calcutta Gazette* of 16 March. Out of 89 districts and subdivisions, there are as many as 29 where on the government's own admission, black-market is prevalent or no information is available from the markets in those places. And those districts include Tippera,[6] Chittagong, Dacca and other places. What does it disclose? It discloses that something is rotten somewhere. In spite of the bumper crop which we have announced throughout India and throughout the world, the people of Bengal are suffering in March to this terrible extent.

You can throttle public opinion, you can gag the expression of free criticism but will that save millions of people? Did that save people in 1943? And why has the government lost the confidence of the people? Leave aside the party label of the Ministry. Take it on its merits. Why do we not trust the

6 It refers to Tippera district in British India, with HQ in Comilla. The princely State of Tripura was adjacent to it. Major parts of Tippera district formed part of East Pakistan after partition.

Government? Why did not the people trust the government? The reason is this: take some illustrations.

(At this stage there was loud noise from the **Coalition Benches.**)

Syama Prasad Mookerjee: It is no use shouting. Treat yourselves as human beings and be not the gramophone of the so-called leaders of your party.

Now, Sir, take the case of bad food. Mr Suhrawardy said repeatedly that the bad food, the bad quality of rice which was being supplied was the responsibility of the Central Government. He went on repeating that. I am not quoting him. I won't take the time of the House and quote them in detail. This was repeatedly said and the Government of India protested against it.

(Cries of 'who protested?', 'who protested?' from the **Coalition Benches.**)

Sir J P Srivastava protested.

(Cries of 'Oh!, Oh!' from the **Coalition Benches.**)

You shout 'Oh!', 'Oh!' because he is a Hindu: but Sir Azizul Huq protested and said it was the responsibility of the Bengal Government. Now who is this Sir Azizul Huq?

Abdul Motaleb Malik: He is a gramophone of the Government of India Secretariat there.

Syama Prasad Mookerjee: Then have the courage to repudiate the Government of India publicly and say that they have falsely replied. Then, Sir, it has been stated that the Orissa government was responsible for the bad quality of rice: Mr Suhrawardy, getting the rebuff from Delhi, ran to Orissa and said that it was the Orissa government which was responsible. But read the statement issued by the Orissa government on the 24 March which stated that the allegation was absolutely false and that the responsibility was not of the Orissa government. Whose responsibility then is it, I want to ask.

You have the right to ask, the members of the Government party have a right to ask, whose responsibility is it that the quality of rice has deteriorated? The point is that public confidence has [been] shaken because the Minister in charge of the Civil Supplies Department says one thing in Calcutta one day, throwing the responsibility on the Central Government and something else from another place on another day, throwing the responsibility on another provincial government; and when these are repudiated by the governments concerned, the result is that public confidence is completely shaken.

Take the next point. When we brought forward the charge that thousands of maunds of paddy had been allowed to remain in a state of wastage near Jessore railway station platform, up rose Mr Suhrawardy there and said, 'Oh! what could we do? We could not get the transport facilities'. Who gave the reply to this from Delhi? It was Sir Edward Benthal,[7] who is neither a Hindu nor a Muslim, nor in league with the Opposition members. What was his answer? His answer was, 'We gave the Bengal government transport faculties according to their programme and this Jessore stock was never included in the programme submitted by the government of Bengal'.

You are sitting there as dummies and dolls, giving your support to the Ministers because you think that your Muslim League Party will remain alive. It will not remain alive. Whether the Opposition wins or not is a matter of indifference. If you think you can play with the lives of millions of people of this province in this way, you are utterly mistaken.

---

7 Sir Edward Benthal was the Member, War Transport in the Executive Council of the Viceroy during the Famine in 1943.

Now, Sir, what about profiteering? I am quoting these instances only to show why is it that the people have lost confidence in the government. Why is it so? Look at your profiteering scheme. It was said by the Hon'ble Minister that there was no profiteering at all. Getting wheat from the rest of India at a low price, that wheat was sold at a higher price to the dying people of Bengal enabling the Bengal government to make a clean profit of 33-44 lakh of rupees. Mr Suhrawardy said that that was all over. But read Mr B R Sen's[8] speech in the Council of States on 21 February 1944. On 21 February 1944, Mr B R Sen says that the Bengal government has been going on making profit even during the last few months – a fact which was denied here by the Treasury Benches and Mr Suhrawardy. Does that help to restore confidence?

The point is, Sir, that we are genuinely anxious that there must not be a recurrence of the distress of 1943 in 1944. That is the point I want to emphasise upon today, and that cannot be done until confidence is completely restored in the *bona fides* of the government. I say this, Sir, that a lead has been given in the Central Assembly where the Muslim League has joined hands with other parties for defending the rights of the people. The point is, will the Bengal Muslim League Party have the courage and statesmanship to play the same role?

Rasik Lal Biswas: You want to come in!

Syama Prasad Mookerjee: You have no reason to be afraid of that. We have tested you from the Congress Party to the Muslim League Party. Treachery has its limit, but you have outstripped that limit of treachery, Mr Rasik Lal Biswas.

---

[8] Dr Binay Ranjan Sen was an ICS officer and a diplomat. He acted as the Relief Commissioner during this famine. After independence, he served as the Director General of United Nation's Food & Agriculture Organisation. He was widely known for his commitment to fight against 'hunger'.

Sir, so far as the future is concerned, I say this in all earnestness and seriousness that there is absolutely no hope for Bengal unless you and we can combine. There is absolutely no hope for the province unless we all sink our party differences and unite to solve the food problem. The other day, Mr Suhrawardy said – I was not present in the House at that time – that I had gone to ask for the support of the European Party. The talk which I and two other friends had with the European Party I need not disclose, but I can say this without any breach of confidence, that there was no question of our asking for their support for any party interest. The point which we put to them and which we put to them today in public is that the Bengal Legislative Assembly, taking the Indian members, is divided into two sharp groups; we have 100 Hindus and Muslims in the Opposition and add to them the 10 members who are behind the prison bars which will give you 110; and on the government side you have about 110 or 115 Hindus and Muslims and 30 others who are neither Hindus nor Muslims but something else sitting over there to hold the balance. What we appeal to them is this: at this crisis when the offer from the Opposition is that we must present a united front to solve the food problem with which the country is faced, you should do nothing which will place Bengal under the heels of sordid party-politics and prevent that united front which alone can make any scheme of rehabilitation and food scheme successful.

What about the judgement delivered by the Chief Justice of Bengal? That shows how things are moving on. The Chief Justice is not a member of the Opposition, and we have no control over the Chief Justice's expression of views. We have no control over the Chief Justice's pen and views. The Chief Justice said two days ago…

(A member from the **Coalition Benches**: Is it Pollard?)

It is not Pollard. It is another MLA, an MLA who belonged to the Opposition against whom certain criminal proceedings were pending. He was made to go to the Government party and the bait was given to him that the proceedings would be withdrawn. The Chief Justice's judgement makes it clear…

(Voices from **Coalition Benches**: It is a lie.)

If you say it is a lie, you call the Chief Justice of Bengal a liar. Go and say that to him. Do not say that to me. He had before him the letters and documents and he had made it abundantly clear that the Secretary of a particular department was desired by – the name was not mentioned and the Chief Justice went on asking by whom he was desired – to approach the District Magistrate to give a long adjournment in respect of this case.

Sir, what I say is this. This is only one illustration. There are other illustrations of this sort where force and coercion are being brought to bear on members of the legislature in order to keep the government party somehow alive but, Sir, the point is that it will have a direct effect on the morale of the province. What we want is that there must be a strong and united government representing all parties who are willing to work the constitution and then it will be...

Fazlur Rahman: You are dividing the Muslims.

Syama Prasad Mookerjee: We do not wish to divide the Muslims. We want that all of us should unite and you say we are dividing the Muslims. It is you who are dividing the Muslims and not we. If we can unite it is only then that we can hope to solve the food problem. I offer the hand of cooperation in full earnestness and I hope, Sir, that the response will come from the party that now controls the destiny of the Ministry. On the other hand, if you go on as you are going on, you can keep your ministry for some days, but now, with the food situation being what it is, with the lack of confidence in the mind of the people as we witness in every part of the province and the war situation taking the turn that it has taken, it will be the greatest mistake that can ever be committed by any government.

I hope, Sir, that we shall be able to rise equal to the occasion and prove to posterity that although we might have fought and fought hard in the course of the last few years, when a real crisis came we stood up like men and we took up the great task and responsibility for saving the province which is the beloved motherland of Hindus, Muslims, Christians, and every one who can subordinate personal, party and communal interests to the supreme considerations of national welfare.

Syama Prasad on Woodhead Commission Report

Sudip Kar Purkayastha

Syama Prasad strongly insisted on a Royal Commission on this famine. Fazlul Huq also raised a similar demand. Eventually, faced with rising public outcry, the Government of India constituted the Famine Inquiry Commission in 1944 through an Ordinance, Ordinance No. XXVIII. Sir John Woodhead headed it. The broad terms of reference were to investigate and report to the Central Government on the causes of food shortage and subsequent epidemics in India and, in particular, in Bengal in 1943 and to make recommendations to prevent their recurrence. Its first report titled 'Report on Bengal' was published in May 1945.

Syama Prasad's observations on the report of the Commission find place in the later edition of his book *Panchasher Manwantar*. A gist of his observations is presented in this chapter under two parts. Part A lists the causes of the famine which were both identified by the Commission and cited by Syama Prasad with brief comments in some cases. Part

B highlights some areas where Syama Prasad found important inconsistencies between the Report and actual facts. On the basis of his examination of the Report, Syama Prasad made a couple of critical observations. These are mentioned at the end of this chapter.

Part A

Syama Prasad noted the readiness of the Commission to listen to and consider views of a very large numbers of representatives across a wide spectrum. Even if some of them were considered by the incumbent Nazimuddin Ministry, Syama Prasad believed this famine could certainly be averted! For the sake of better understanding, Syama Prasad arranged the long list of causes of the famine as identified by the Commission in a sequence. These are recounted here briefly without burdening the readers with associated data.

1. Natural calamities like flood, cyclone, and pest attack;
2. Stoppage of rice import from Burma;
3. Prevalence of war condition and need for procurement of military supplies;
4. Shifting railways-tracks, engines, wagons and officials to other countries;
5. Limitations of shipping sector to carry the load;
6. Priorities of war supply impairing transportation of food & other items of daily consumptions;
7. Threat of Japanese bombing and invasion creating a general fear psychosis;
8. Impact of Denial policy resulting in the removal of boat and rice etc;
9. Forcible acquisition of private land, especially farmland for military use including for building airstrips;

10. Distortion in market prices of rice due to the impact of contemporary developments;
11. Continued export of rice from Bengal;
12. Burden of refugees from Burma;
13. Political unrest in the country engaging the government's attention;
14. Bulk procurement of rice by large factories, corporations, government departments etc.;
15. Mismanagement of rice inventory in Calcutta and other places through wastage and by not directing them to proper destinations;
16. Government's 'no shortage' theory was misleading; people kept dying due to starvation;
17. Not applying 'famine code' to Bengal;
18. Delay in introducing 'rationing' in Calcutta and its suburbs;
19. Communal bias in selecting 'controlled price' shops for vending grains etc. resulting in inordinate delay in reaching the needy;
20. Fudging the reasons for death that hid the gravity of the situation;
21. Grossly inadequate public health infrastructure;
22. Dysfunctional tube-wells in countryside that led to problems of drinking water;
23. Government not providing adequate relief to famine victims and its reluctance to spend money for relief;
24. Inter party politics on the eve of famine that saw installation of League-led ministry;
25. Intensely communal politics by Muslim League and its unwillingness to accept any non-League Muslim as a Minister;

The Commission was satisfied that there were several opportunities available to the Bengal government to avert the famine through appropriate strategy changes. The Commission also criticised the Government of India for the kind of policy regime it applied which contributed to the horrendous famine. It cited delay in creating the food department, frequent transfer of its officials, erratic changes in rules relating to 'free trade' among provinces, indecisiveness on the issue of price control, encouragement of the 'denial policy', failure to meet its obligation to Bengal under basic plan, not coming forward to shoulder the responsibility for food supply to Calcutta and its suburbs etc. The Commission also observed that *the Government of India did not do enough to tackle the famine.*

Significantly, having considered myriads of factors, the Commission came to the conclusion that the rice situation was not so bad to warrant this famine. It hailed Wavell, the new Viceroy, who was able to address the food crisis in rather a short time through policy re-jig using available supply of food grains. Had timely actions been initiated by the governments, many lives could have been saved.

The Commission expressed its sympathy for people of Bengal who have been generally undernourished and emaciated and how they had succumbed to the double whammy of famine and epidemic.

Syama Prasad perused the report keenly. Having been intensely involved in serving the distressed population and fighting the nexus of ruling regimes, he was probably most qualified to study its worth. His response may be classified into two categories:

1. First, he recognised the relevance of the causes that were listed, though he thought in some cases, the Commission did not have adequate information while in some other cases, he felt the Commission probably underestimated the implications of destabilising the Huq ministry on the eve of the famine.

By way of example, Syama Prasad contended that the scale of forcible acquisition of farmland was much bigger than reported which resulted in the eviction of a larger population from their land, making them famine victims. Again, he thought, the Commission did not have full information about the extent of damage the 'denial policy' caused like impairing paddy cultivation in *delta* lands. Another case related to the scale of military consumption of food grains and procurement by large factories and organisations. Those, he reckoned, were much larger than what the Commission thought. On the question of the number of deaths, he was sure they were much under-estimated. The actual numbers were far more than the 1.5 million to 2 million estimated by the Commission.

Syama Prasad suggested that the 'unfair substitution of the Huq ministry by the League ministry' contributed to the famine in more profound ways than what the Commission thought and submitted in its report.

2. Though the Commission's list contained valid causes, it was not exhaustive. This was intriguing. Syama Prasad noticed many omissions, some of them vital, and also the 'manner' in which the causes in the report were presented. Syama Prasad pointed these out, calling them as 'inconsistencies'. These are summed up in the next part of this chapter.

The causes cited by the Commission were too numerous to convince any reasonable person that they were coincidences. This, coupled with the Commission's unequivocal assertion that the situation was not bad enough to invite this famine strongly suggested a nexus behind the creation of the famine. *Report of no other past famine commission showed that a disaster struck a land solely due to the lapse of its Government, as happened in the case of 1943's famine in Bengal.*

Right from the start of the famine, as he fought against myriads of manmade adversities to save its victims, Syama Prasad was never in doubt about the role played by the Nazimuddin-led ministry in causing this distress. It was lamentable and yet significant that the Nazimuddin ministry continued to be in the seat of governance even after a massive loss of lives! After the Commission went into great depth of records and evidences and its conclusion that this famine could well be averted, validated his assumptions with facts. Syama Prasad was certain that this famine disguised a vast massacre which deserved an open trial of the guilty and award of appropriate punishments for the conspirators and colluders.

Part B

Syama Prasad had reservations about the omission of certain issues of importance in the Report of the Woodhead Commission and also in their manner of presentation. As a matter of fact, he felt, they could be construed to be 'inconsistent with some truth'. He dealt with some specific issues of both types.

As regards omission of key issues: The thing that struck him most was that the Commission discussed the lapses at length but there was a marked unwillingness on the part of the Commission to hold the guilty officials accountable. It was crystal clear that the three top British officials involved in governing India played key roles in creating and exacerbating this famine, which need not have occurred at all. Syama Prasad identified Leo Amery, the British Secretary of State, John Herbert, the then Governor of Bengal and Lord Linlithgow who was the Viceroy of India at the time, as primarily responsible for letting the famine happen.

Amery, according to Syama Prasad, kept misleading the British Parliament and its people as long as he could on every vital issue, whether stock of food grains, scale and causes of death etc., through suppression and distortion of facts, thus preventing the much-needed help from reaching Bengal from the rest of India and the world at large. He acted hand-in-glove with Suhrawardy, Bengal's supplies minister, in hiding the Bengal government's misdeeds as well as the facts on the ground, as a result of which several million people lost their lives. This was tragic and avoidable.

Herbert, the Governor of Bengal, was obsessed with collecting applauses from his countrymen. Lives of people of Bengal did not matter at all. Though he was flooded with the ominous tidings of the famine from every corner of the land – from officials, the legislature, the press and many others – he turned a deaf ear to them. He dismissed the advice of the Huq cabinet even on critical issues such as the denial policy, taking rice inventories and carried out his policies through his English officials. These functionaries, under indulgence from him, undermined the instructions of the Huq cabinet.

Viceroy Linlithgow, being the ruler of the whole country, was, according to Syama Prasad, guiltier than the other two. Syama Prasad saw him as an embodiment of heartlessness. Millions died but he just did not bother. For a few months, he personally held the Food portfolio but did grave injustice to Bengal. All the lapses that the Commission attributed to the Government of India essentially belonged to him. As a matter of fact, the situation could have been countered with food, resources and equipment that were readily available. Only the Government policy warranted changes. This was accomplished by his successor, Lord Wavell in a few months and exposed thoroughly. The Commission did not name Linlithgow.

The fourth and a very important omission by the Commission was its lack of adequate condemnation of the flagrant misuse of the Defence of India Rules. As a matter of fact, the DIR was used in a tyrannical manner before and during the 1943 famine. The freedom of the press was brutally suppressed to keep the famine-struck province behind an iron curtain. Even within Bengal, the true state of affairs could not be published.

On the issue of the questionable style of presentation by the Commission, Syama Prasad cited two specific instances where it unfairly passed the blame on the Huq government. One was in regard to the abolition of price control on food grains in March 1943. The Commission held the Huq ministry responsible for that decision, which went on to aggravate the crisis. Syama Prasad clarified that the fact was, this decision was forcibly imposed on the Huq ministry by Governor Herbert at the instance of the Government of India.

Second, the Commission observed that on issues of food and general administration, the decisions taken by the Huq cabinet used to be accepted and implemented in the usual course. This, Syama Prasad asserted, was wholly untrue.

Another point that was wrongfully held against the Huq ministry was the question the Commission asked: If not allowed to function freely, why did the Huq ministry not resign? Syama Prasad, who was himself in that ministry, clarified this point as well. First, the cabinet had sensed that Bengal was in the throes of an impending food crisis and quitting at that juncture would have been an irresponsible act. Second, the Huq ministry was aware of the backroom intrigues between the Governor and the League that was in progress, to maneuver a League-led ministry to power in which case, the Huq Government feared, Bengal would lapse into a bigger crisis under League's communal mode of governance.

On the whole, the Commission, despite preparing an impressive list of numerous plausible causes of the famine, intriguingly refrained from identifying the real guilty, understated some vital facts, and interpreted some critical events in a questionable manner.

Syama Prasad understood these machinations. He was, however, hopeful that one day the full truth would be unveiled. When the entire government records would be available, Syama Prasad prophesied, it would transpire that there was no justification for this famine to have occurred at all. The world would also know that both the British and the Muslim League, worked in tandem and perpetrated a famine on Bengal.

As a matter of fact, truth has indeed come out with the passage of time. A major breakthrough followed the declassification of papers relating to British rule in India by the UK government. It revealed that, besides the three top British officials Syama Prasad indicted in his critique on the Commission Report, Sir Winston S Churchill, the then prime minister himself had played a key role with regard to this famine. Both Churchill and his schoolmate at Harrow and lifelong friend, Leopold Amery, the SoS, were united in their indifference and heartlessness to Indian lives in general and Bengalis in particular.

That gives us a better understanding of how a manageable situation of food crisis was allowed to degenerate into a horrendous famine. Today, we have additional evidence relating to domestic and international events and their underlying political dynamics which are relevant for the present purpose. My final chapter examines Syama Prasad's assessments of the real causes of the Bengal Famine of 1943 and those guilty of bringing it about, by juxtaposing his book with several new evidences that has come into the public domain since.

The Fifty's Famine
A Genocide

The Permanent Scar it left on Bengal's Psyche

Sudip Kar Purkayastha

In his book, first published in 1944, Syama Prasad expressed his views on the causes of the Bengal famine of 1943 and warned about its potential impact on individuals, families and society. He had upset vested political interests then. Wielding influence over mainstream media, post-Independence governments have so long been obfuscating the true reasons.However, with the passage of time, what actually happened in between 1942-44 has become clearer. After several vital documents relating to the British India rule during the war years were placed in the public domain by the UK authorities as part of their disclosure policies, government communication on the Bengal famine became available to researchers, as a result of which, the world is getting to know the actual reasons for the mass distress and these correspond in large measure to what Syama Prasad said and wrote in the 1940s.

In this concluding chapter, we examine additional evidence, juxtapose them with the contents of Syama Prasad's book and present our assessment of the causes of the famine and by way of enhancement, examine the impact of this holocaust on the social fabric of Bengal.

Our assessment is categorised under five major sections. Each of them has been discussed at length thereafter.

First, we seek to point out that the range of perceptions as to the real causes for the famine of 1943 has changed over time and these various perceptions need to be studied afresh without bias. In his book, *Panchasher Manwantar*, Syama Prasad viewed the 1943 famine as manmade, driven by politics of imperialism and communalism. Successive ruling regimes of the land took pains to describe it as an 'outcome of natural disaster' and economic causes.

Consequent upon declassification of some vital documents relating to British rule in India in the first decade of the present century, attention has returned to the political factors and the colonial government's policies vis-a-vis India. However, it appears that the role of the contemporary provincial government in contributing to the famine has not yet been adequately investigated. Finding out the complete truth through due research in this regard remains an undischarged responsibility of the academia.

Second is the issue of governance. This famine was possible only because of the questionable actions and attitudes of the three levels of government – the provincial government, the centre or the Government of British India and His Majesty's Government in England; and all three acted in a concerted manner to cause the 1943 famine. The functioning of the triad during that period vis-a-vis the food crisis warrants particular and individual scrutiny.

Third, the abrupt manner in which the famine ended was a confirmation of its nature that it was essentially manmade and a political creation. This area also remains insufficiently investigated.

Fourth, one important reason that helped obscure the political causes behind the famine was the common disbelief that any civilised government would kill its people wantonly. The only way to make sense of why they engaged in such a course of inhuman actions would be to study and understand the political motives of both the British and Muslim League regimes ruling at the time in an objective manner without any preconceived notion.

Fifth is about the social impact on the victims. Studies done by the Indian Statistical Institute, University of Calcutta and others on the impact of the famine of 1943 on individual, family and social relations predominantly examined the immediate repercussions. As regards the long-term impact of 1943's famine, such studies may have at best extended to issues such as potential breaking down of the joint family system. But they did not encompass soft psychological quotients like love, sacrifice, trust, etc., which are the edifice of a healthy society. On the whole, the long-lasting impact of the famine on the wider society in Bengal in terms of erosion of these values has not been investigated adequately till today. This is a key fact generally ignored by both the wider society and the nation.

Long-time society-watchers, however, see the lingering impact of the now-distant famine in current social behaviour in a divided Bengal. A variety of incidents of heartlessness, suspicion, and violent behaviour vis-a-vis fellow members of society as recently as in 2020, under the shadow of the Covid-19 pandemic, as reported in the media, seem to be driven by the sole motive of self-preservation and suggest that the wound inflicted by Bengal famine continues to fester.

We dwell in greater detail on each of these five sections in the same sequence:

Real Cause of Famine – Changes in Perception

Syama Prasad, an important politician of the time, crusaded to save countless innocent human lives from starvation and epidemic. He was convinced that the massive death toll was brought about by the three governments.[1] In a later edition of his book, while discussing the inconsistencies in the 'Woodhead Commission Report', he had written[2] people were entitled to demand open trial of all those actually guilty of perpetrating such mass murder. Subsequently, declassification of government papers related to the British rule threw open the question whether deaths of millions of people in Bengal could actually have been a genocide? Let us examine few other important views as well.

Views of Leaders of the Time & Media

To begin with, it may be relevant to visit how some of his contemporary politicians of distinctions and political organisations of importance thought about the issue.

K C Neogy, an important Bengali politician, categorically held the British regime and the provincial government conniving with it responsible for the disaster. Speaking in

---

1 The Oxford English Dictionary describes the word 'genocide' as: The deliberate killing of a large group of people, especially those of a particular nation or ethnic group. In the Bengali original, Syama Prasad used the words ব্যাপক নরহত্যা, meaning killing of people on a massive scale.

2 Rashtrasangram p79

the Central Legislative Assembly[3] he bemoaned that while starvation, death, pestilence have been customarily associated with victorious tyrants overrunning foreign territory, they were ironically taking place in Bengal under the much-vaunted British rule which was nearly two century old.

Neogy said, 'In the present instance, however, this gigantic tragedy is being enacted while a well-established Government is functioning in the country.' Considering the whole gamut of actions by the government to prevent the outbreak of this famine, he waged a more scathing and direct attack on the Imperial regime, saying, *'We cannot help thinking that this famine is primarily a state industry, and to my mind, in certain of its aspects it bears the hall-mark of a genuine British manufacture.'*

After pointing out how energetically and in unison the central and the provincial governments in British India always acted in implementing policies of repression, so much so that a press of the button in New Delhi sets the whole country ablaze at an instant, he noted the conspicuous absence of any coordination while it came to tackling the Bengal famine: *'If, however, it is a question of preserving human life and providing food for the people, well, then comes the rub.'*

Another distinguished member, Dr Deshmukh, in his speech in the Central Assembly on 17 December 1943 observed that the famine has been '*brought about according to plan*'.[4]

The 24th session of the National Liberal Federation of India was also critical about the role of all three levels of governments viz., the HMG, the centre and the provincial government. In a resolution passed at Bombay in December

---

[3] Speech of K C Neogy in Central Assembly on 15 November 1943 : Ghosh p 171-2.

[4] Ibid, p 69.

1943, the Conference observed,[5] 'The Federation is strongly of opinion that both the Central and Provincial Governments as well as His Majesty's Government are largely responsible for the serious maladministration which has led to the calamity by lack of provision and effective planning and the shortage of food which should have been foreseen and prevented....' It drew attention to the significant fact that of all the countries within the British Commonwealth, in India alone has such a tragedy taken place.

H N Kunzru who had visited several famine and epidemic-affected areas in both eastern and western parts of Bengal during October 1943 made some critical observations[6] on the role of the Government of India and the British Government. He noted how the two of them let millions of people die by refusing to intervene, citing 'provincial autonomy'. While noting that the Bengal Government bore heavy responsibility for the catastrophe, he said: 'the primary responsibility for the catastrophe which has overwhelmed Bengal and the sufferings of the people in some other parts of India is that of the British Government and the Government of India....'

He held Viceroy Lord Linlithgow and Secretary of State for India Amery primarily responsible for the deterioration in the food situation. On the issue of how the British government was shirking its basic responsibility by using the League government as a shield, his anger burst forth, 'Had the British Government realised its primary duty to save the lives of the people and not to allow people to die indefinitely on the altar of Provincial Autonomy, the situation would have improved long ago....' He lamented that if only the British government had become conscious of its responsibility a few months earlier, 'Bengal

---

5 IAR, 1943, Vol 2, pp 315-6.
6 Ghosh, p 147-8.

would not have been in the grip of a famine for which there is no parallel in recent history.'

Kunzru noted that it was ironical that the same British regime had repeatedly intervened in the working of the previous secular coalition government of Bengal led by Fazlul Huq, had set aside all its suggestions and attempts to avert the food crisis, and had finally ousted it by deceit just on the eve of the famine.

Even *The Statesman* newspaper, perceived as a mouthpeice of the British in India, could not help expressing its apprehension about the political nature of the famine, so vicious became its manifestation in the city of Calcutta. By July 1943, the city was flooded with tens of thousands of rural destitute. Private charities, coupled with a limited-scale official relief operation, were clearly inadequate to feed the surging population. Consequently, dead bodies of the starving lay scattered on the city's streets. Evidence of official apathy was apparent all around. In September 1943, the paper, in an editorial, categorically opined that unlike all past famines which were due to calamities of nature, the present one was different and occurred despite the fact that rainfall had been plentiful. Without any hesitation it accused the ruling regimes and concluded, 'This sickening catastrophe is manmade...'[7]

Mainstream View

The mainstream media across the world, however, seemed to ignore the primacy of political factors and highlighted the economic and other causes. For example, the *Sydney Morning Herald* of Australia in its website even today seeks to ignore the political causes. It describes the Bengal famine as a 'consequence

---

[7] Ibid, p187: On 23 September 1943, *The Statesman* wrote an editorial titled 'Reflections on Disaster'.

of crop failure, wrong policies of export and import relating to food grains and administrative ineptitude'. Thus, while recognising and listing it amongst the 'ten worst famines in the world in the twentieth century', the paper continues to give a brief description of Bengal Famine thus:

> Between 2.1 and three million people died as a result of crop failure, the exporting of foods by India's British administration to Allied soldiers fighting in World War Two, the end of rice imports from Burma following Japanese invasion and a lack of food price controls by the British administration.[8]

Woodhead Commission Report

Historically speaking, the foundation of the above genre of 'world view' about Bengal famine was probably laid down by the Woodhead Commission Report (1945).

Its observations suited those in power. The Commission did a clever job of diverting focus from the 'true causes' by giving a long list of reasons, important and trivial. The serious ones were: absence of policy, policy mistakes, policy blunder, administrative chaos and bungling, official complacency and so on. There was a tendency to show the government lapses as 'involuntary' human lapses. There was a modification of the Woodhead line of thought subsequently, which began to call the famine as 'manmade' because these lapses were attributable to human beings. Interestingly, however, no attempt was made to identify the guilty, discover their real intention, and fix accountability.

The Woodhead Report was silent on why the ruling regimes did not tackle the 'reasons' that it listed. Both, the

---

[8] Date of the report 15 Aug 2011. https://www.smh.com.au/world/ten-worst-famines-of-the-20th-century-20110815-1iu2w.html<29.9.18>

preventive and remedial measures, were within their means, but the Governments did not act and instead, allowed these impediments to develop into a full-blown crisis. The inherent bias in the Woodhead Report in favour of ignoring the 'political factors' as causes for the famine undoubtedly influenced the way the world looked at the 1943 famine and also the attitude of subsequent researchers about this issue.

Out of several studies undertaken on the Bengal famine since the Woodhead days, few deserve mention for introducing fresh perspectives although they essentially rest on framework of 'economics'. Noble Laureate, Prof Amartya Sen saw the famine primarily as a manifestation of 'entitlement' economics and 'market failure'. Incidentally, Sen's analysis includes inter alia a critical examination of data relating to overall food availability in 1943, an important aspect to which we shall revert later. A different perspective was brought by Madhusree Mukerjee through her book (2010).

'U' Turn – Impact of De-classification of British Documents

A radical change in the direction of research came about following the de-classification of government papers relating to British rule in India during the famine.

Madhusree Mukerjee's well researched book, *Churchill's Secret War: The British Empire and the Ravaging of India during World War II* (2010), gave a new insight into the causes of the Bengal famine and showed that the then British prime minister, Winston Churchill, had played a key part in it.

Based on extensive research of military records, private papers of British leaders and oral accounts of survivors of the famine era, Mukherjee's work brought to light several hitherto unknown immoral political decisions by Churchill and his cabinet.[9] For example, India was not permitted to use its own sterling reserves or indeed, its own ships to import food. Further, foodstuffs were diverted from starving Indians to already well-supplied British soldiers and stockpiles in Britain and elsewhere in Europe. It was by Churchill's order or influence over the War Cabinet that Australian wheat sailed past Indian cities 'to depots in the Mediterranean and the Balkans' while dead bodies of famine victims littered the streets in Bengal.

Her work brought to light how the poor in rural Bengal were facing the threat of certain extinction as the rice went into the warehouses of big stockists, hoarders and profiteers. The latter were waiting to make windfall gains out of the food crisis. Their vicious scheme would have collapsed at the sight of shiploads of food aids approaching Indian ports! Churchill could have easily made them disgorge their hoards simply by arranging to send wheat or rice and that too, not in enormous quantities. But he refused offers of help for famine victims from other countries on various pretexts.

Mukerjee's book began to make a powerful impact on world view about Bengal Famine, essentially because of authenticity of source and rigorous analysis of facts.

More academicians are now trying to come out of the shackles of the stereotypical thinking and waking up to the role played by the British regime in that famine. For example, Prof Cormac O'Grada, Emeritus Professor at University College of Dublin, in his book, *Eating People is Wrong, And Other Essays on Famine: Its Past and Its Future* (2015), differed not only from the mainstream traditional view but also from the new insight

---

9 https://openthemagazine.com/essay/hero-or-war-criminal-churchill-in-retrospect/ *<22.6.19>*

offered by Amartya Sen's 'entitlement' theory, and observed a key role played by Churchill and his government behind the famine.

In his book Prof O'Grada said, though the 1943 famine has become paradigmatic as 'entitlements famine', whereby speculation born of greed and panic produced an artificial shortage of rice, the staple food of people, it was the *lack of political will to divert foodstuffs* from the war effort rather than *speculation* – in the sense outlined – that was mainly responsible for the famine.[10]

But the 'lack of political will' by the British does not seem to explain the famine fully. Was it the consequence of far deeper politics of connivance, involving both *racial hatred* and *communal agenda*? What was the role of the Provincial government during the famine? Clearly, there is need to cover more ground to explain that terrible disaster.

Prime Minister Winston Churchill, then heading the British government, was known for his disdain of Indians in general and Bengalis in particular. He had famously described Indians as a 'beastly people' with a 'beastly religion'.[11] He had wanted shiploads of food to go to feed the 'sturdy Greeks' instead of the 'anyhow underfed Bengalis'.[12] It was probable that Bengali people in particular attracted special wrath and disdain of the Empire for their revolutionary activities against the Raj. But was there more to that famine? Was the political tentacle longer and more vicious?

---

[10] https://core.ac.uk/download/pdf/6492793.pdf<22.6.19>

[11] https://www.independent.co.uk/news/uk/politics/not-his-finest-hour-the-dark-side-of-winston-churchill-2118317.html

[12] To justify diverting ships loaded with food grains to Europe, he had famously said this replete with racial hatred: "the starvation of anyhow underfed Bengalis is less serious than sturdy Greeks': https://winstonchurchill.hillsdale.edu/did-churchill-cause-the-bengal-famine/

The full truth is not known conclusively as yet. But the fact that the *political factors* behind the Bengal Famine 1943 have begun to be investigated as the *prime reason* may help humanity to know it more comprehensively and accurately sooner or later. It seems that international research has, for now, stopped at the door of the British government. But there is compelling evidence to suggest that the communal politics of the incumbent Bengal ministry also shared responsibility for the famine. The role of the then Muslim League ministry and its political allies warrants rigorous examination alongside that of the Government of India and His Majesty's Government to get hold of the complete truth.

Roles Played by Governments and Pro-poor Forces

Before we begin to delve into the roles of three levels of government, including the provincial one, it may be useful to look at the actual situation of Bengal in terms of food availability.

Food Availability in 1943: Facts and Fiction

Bengal, as a province of British India, was traditionally deficient in rice and depended on import although it was a rice-growing land. Neighbouring Burma was a key exporter. This source dried up in 1942 in the aftermath of Japanese occupation of that country. There were also cyclone, flood and pest attack in 1942-43 winter in the coastal areas of the province, reducing the quantity of rice coming to Bengal's market and driving up prices.

But how serious was its role? In hindsight, the natural disaster as a factor for the food crisis seemed to have been hyped to justify the famine by vested interests. What was the actual availability of food grains during the 1943 famine and did that justify such severity?

From Prof Amartya Sen's essays on Bengal Famine 1943, we get an analytical account of the food grain availability in 1943, in the backdrop of a broader canvas of 5 years from 1939 to 1944.

To start with, we may refer to his observation on the normal pattern of rice production and the actual production during the relevant period. Bengal cultivated three rice crops viz., Aman (Sowing period: May/June and Harvesting: November/December) known as the winter crop; *Aus* (Sowing period: April-August and Harvesting: September) known as the autumn crop; and *Boro* (Sowing period: November and Harvesting: February/March) known as the spring crop. Out of the above, *Aman* catered to 73 per cent, *Aus* 24 per cent and *Boro* 3 per cent respectively of Bengal's consumption need. Natural disasters like cyclone in 1942-43 winter had essentially impacted the Aman crop, i.e., the winter crop but only to the tune of 17 per cent. The crop loss in respect of *Aus* was only 3 per cent, Sen noted.

Next, the 'actual availability' of rice in 1943. Having examined the issue from various perspectives including carry over from previous year, skewed distribution of import of food grain e.g., bundling of it in the last quarter, etc., Prof Sen noted that 'the current supply for 1943 was only about 5 per cent lesser than the average of the preceding five years'. Still, it was 13 per cent higher than in 1941, and there was no famine in that year. *Mutatis mutandis* such observation held good in terms of 'per capita' food availability index which was about 9 per cent higher in 1943 over 1941. In any case, Sen wrote: 'While 1943 was not a very good year in terms of crop availability, it was not by any means a disastrous year either'.[13]

---

[13] Poverty and Famine: An Essay on Entitlement and Deprivation: Amartya Sen, p 58: Clarendon Press, Oxford University, London & others, 1981 (hereafter, Sen).

As a matter of fact, worse food situations had arisen in the past, but the deficit was managed by the government through appropriate policy regime, including inter alia adjustment of export and import. In 1943, the governments at all three levels took a series of wrong steps and omitted to do the right things as detailed hereafter, that turned the shortage into a grave crisis.

This had begun with the Governor repeatedly interfering in the working of the Syama-Huq ministry, which was popular with both Hindus and Muslims and enjoyed their confidence. He replaced it on the eve of the famine with an inept communal Muslim League led ministry. The British India Government did worse. The fervent plea by the outgoing ministry that an all-party cabinet be formed to protect the interest of the people was also rejected. Though this trigger for ruin was pulled by Herbert Anderson, the Governor of Bengal, the rein was held by His Majesty's Government in London. We start with its role.

His Majesty's Government: Ugly Discrimination

Britain, being in the vanguard of Allied nations during WWII, was sending troops and war supplies to various war theatres in Asia, Europe and Africa. Towards that end, it was exploiting India to the hilt by manufacturing war supplies and recruiting soldiers.[14] It even shifted railway tracks and engines together with their experienced operators out of India to facilitate

[14] At the peak level of the WWII, the British Indian army constituted of a staggering 2.5 million Indian soldiers who fought for the Allied side at various war theatres. As regards monetary burden, out of total expense incurred by British India on defence and supply services during 1939-40 to 1943-44, nearly Rs 800 crore were expected to be charged to Indian revenue, under the terms of the financial settlement. Significantly, that burden was assessed to be so heavy that it could retard India's economy for the next few decades. This was revealed in the reply given by CE Jones, Secretary, Finance Dept to a question on 21 Feb 1944 in the Council of States. Ghosh, p62.

military supplies in war-affected theatres. Incidentally, this impacted movement of food grains to the famine-affected areas.

Factories in India were forced, on a large scale, to make war supplies instead of producing peace-time goods. As a result, prices of essential goods kept soaring. Inflation broke the backbone of people. An inter-country comparison may drive home the point better.

The cost of living index in England remained practically stationary since April 1941, at not quite 30 per cent above its pre-war level due to proactive government policy of imposing ceilings and providing subsidies for many leading goods.[15] In contrast, the cost of food and essential goods in India rose by few hundred per cent. For example, the wholesale price of rice in Calcutta rose 3 to 4 times or even more over the period from early 1942 to June 1943. From Rs 6.25-6.50 per maund on16 January 1942, it shot up to Rs 31-32 per maund on 28 May 1943.[16] It kept soaring higher and reached Rs 37 per maund on 20 August 1943.[17] Large quantities of rice had entered into black market where the price was even higher. For example, in Dacca rice was sold at Rs 105 per maund in the middle of October, 1943.[18] The market price bore no correspondence with the 'control rate' fixed by the government. On 4 November 1943, Pethick Lawrence admitted in the British Parliament that 'large numbers of people in certain provinces in India, have not the purchasing power to enable them to buy such food grain as will keep them alive.'[19]

---

[15] Ibid, p46.

[16] Sen, p54 & Ghosh p41.

[17] Ghosh, p 41 giving rates quoted in Free Trade Journal.

[18] Ibid, p 41.

[19] https://api.parliament.uk/historic-hansard/commons/1943/nov/04/india-food-situation <22.6.19>.

Besides complete indifference to the miserable state of affairs in Bengal, His Majesty's Government all through this period, was encouraging continued procurement of food grains from the province of Bengal for military consumption.

Was HMG Unaware of Facts on the Ground?

It is true that the HMG was primarily dependent on the Government of India for information on what was happening on the ground. However, the SoS had elaborate mechanisms to explore alternative sources of information as well.

The Statesman, in its editorial titled 'The Death Roll' on 16 October 1943 exposed the mischief! It came down hard on the SoS, charitably calling him a seemingly 'strangely misinformed man', despite the fact that 'his great office ought to afford him ample means for discovery'. It expressed grave anxiety at the manner efforts were continuously appearing 'within India's Governmental machine, perhaps out here, perhaps in Whitehall, to play down, suppress, distort or muzzle the truth, about Bengal, which was 'dragging the fair name of the British Raj needlessly low'.

Colossal Apathy

Had His Majesty's Government had even reasonable concern and slight compassion, it could have ascertained what was happening on the ground in Bengal. Instead, the manner in which the SoS seemed keen to stick to the League ministry's statement that there was *no food crisis in Bengal* and the problem was one of maladministration and hoarding by private consumers and agriculturists, was unusual.

As a matter of fact, the severe food crisis was due to hoarding by dishonest traders, excessive stocking by large factories, govt organisations, and the military but the HMG did not bother to intervene in any way to change this state of affairs.

The ugly face of the 'civilised' HMG was further exposed in the manner the British parliamentarians showed their insensitivity to the food crisis in Bengal, India. In November 1943, when famine and epidemic were devouring hundreds of thousands of lives in Bengal, over ninety per cent of the members of the House of Commons showed little interest in a session of the House convened to discuss the issue of food crisis. The attitude of prime minister Churchill on the issue was most significant. Despite being the head of the cabinet, he did not find time to attend it. This was revealed in a report by MR Jayakar[20] on what was happening in the British Parliament at the time.

On 10 November 1943, MR Jayakar wrote that '... for few newspapers have reported it, that at the last debate held in the House of Commons on the Indian food question, the attendance of Members varied from 35 to 53 out of the total of 600 and odd.'[21]

Malicious Intention

Not only abdicating on His Majesty's Government's basic duty in feeding its people, Churchill rejected humanitarian offers of food aid from countries like Canada and Australia. He also blacked out the unconditional offer of help of 100,000 tons of rice for the hungry people of Bengal from Subhas Chandra Bose, president of the Indian Independence League, based in Singapore. This help could have arrived in Bengal in the shortest possible time and saved numerous famine victims.

---

[20] MR Jayakar was an eminent lawyer, scholar, politician and above all a freedom fighter of distinction. He was also the first Vice Chancellor of Pune University.

[21] Calcutta: The City Revealed: Geoffrey Moorhouse: p 126.

Bose categorically mentioned, the 100,000 tons was the first tranche of his offer and more would follow.

The HMG chose to remain indifferent even though people were dying in hundreds of thousands due to hunger. As late as in October 1943, its professed position before the British parliament was against any kind of intervention by the Government of India in the functioning of the League ministry in Bengal to maintain the sanctity of a so-called 'provincial autonomy'.[22] From deliberations in British parliament it was clear that HMG's only concern was the 'war supply'. As long as it was not affected under the League ministry, millions of human lives in the province meant nothing to it.

The vile attitude of the HMG was undiminished even after Churchill decided to diffuse the food crisis as part of his war strategy in October 1943. Thus, in March 1944, when agreeing to send 250,000 tons of wheat to India in response to the repeated demand of one million tons by India, SoS Amery asked Viceroy Wavell to export 150,000 tons of rice in exchange of 150,000 tons of wheat. He also wanted Wavell to announce import of 400,000 tons of wheat and conceal export of 150,000 tons of rice. This attitude seemingly repulsed even the British Viceroy who referred to it in his journal: 'I shall certainly do nothing so dishonest or stupid....'[23]

---

[22] IAR Vol 2, 1943, p 363: On October 20, 1943 Undersecretary Munster made clear the HMG's position in a Debate on India – that HMG was not in favour of such intervention unless a 'province failed to cooperate in handling the food problem to such an extent that the war effort was seriously affected'. Excepting such situation, he made it clear: 'I think... that it would be an unhappy development if the Government of India were to exert these powers and brush aside responsible democratically based Governments whenever an ugly situation threatened or developed in a particular province'.

[23] The Viceroy's Journal: entry dated 24 March, 1944, p61.

As more information keep coming into the public domain, the role of Churchill and his cabinet in creating and sustaining the famine is becoming increasingly apparent. One thing can certainly be said without fear of contradiction. What they did or failed to do was certainly much more than that of negligence. It smacked of an evil 'intent'.

Government of India

From the start, the Government of India made it clear that as the HMG's protégé, it was eager to squeeze India in various ways to help Britain in carrying out the war. It also became a willing purveyor of Churchill's scheme to starve Bengal. Instead of attempting to save sixty million people of the province who were the subjects of the Empire from the food crisis, it, in utmost apathy and gross dereliction of its basic duty of governance, employed a policy framework[24] that rapidly turned the situation into a horrendous famine.

Aware of Ground Situation

In a way, the introduction of 'denial policy' in a knee-jerk fashion, providing for inter alia paddy removal and boat control in coastal areas disregarding viewpoints of the Huq ministry on the issue was largely responsible for the soaring rice price in Bengal. The Government of India was very insensitive to the advice by the Huq ministry in this regard. It also refused to consider the ministry's requests for help, save that, in the face of repeated demands by the latter for

---

[24] Quoting Famine Commission Report, the IAR wrote that the government of India betokened an uncertain, restless attitude that kept changing from one plan to another like basic plan, unrestricted free trade, modified free trade, control, de-control, etc. IAR, Vol 1, p 83.

additional quota of rice and other cereals,[25] it committed to send a few lakh tons of additional food grains under the Centre's 'basic quota' scheme, but did not carry out even that undertaking.

Going Back on Commitments

Instead, the Government of India began to reap advantages that flowed from the Governor's act of throwing out the Huq ministry and bringing into power a new ministry led by the Muslim League, which was ready to toe the British line at the cost of hungry millions of Bengal. It went back on its commitments though it was keenly aware that the starved masses of the province were already reeling under the 'denial policy' and no import from Burma. Neither did it take any initiative to stop export of rice, nor did it make any alternative arrangement for rice import from elsewhere. It also looked the other way as government, semi government, big undertakings and factories resorted to large-scale procurements of rice from Bengal for their employees. That was not the end. Over-enthusiastic to extend support to British war effort, it reportedly backed the *diversion of huge tracts of paddy-growing field to producing* jute, ostensibly to augment manufacture of jute sandbags for war purposes. The area under rice cultivation in Bengal during 1942-43 was reportedly reduced by seven lakh acres from what it was in the year 1941-42.[26]

---

[25] In his speech delivered on 15 Nov 1943 at a Muslim League Conference, then Bengal premier Nazimuddin said that, when his ministry took over, there was a standing commitment by the central government to give 793,000 tons of food grains to Bengal under its Basic Plan: Ghosh, p17.

[26] Ibid, p174: Speech of K C Neogy , 15 Nov 1943.

Insensitivity that Questions its Intention

The Viceroy ruled over Indian provinces with an iron hand through the British Governors. The latter, in turn, wielded over-riding power over the elected governments in provinces under the provisions of the Government of India Act, 1935. During this period, the Governors even usurped many of the routine administrative authority of the elected governments in the name of special war-time powers. Besides, the presence of strong intelligence network across the country meant that, it was unlikely that the terrible state of affairs in Bengal was unknown to the then Viceroy and his executive council. Still the Central Government chose to stick to the version of the League Government that there was 'no food shortage in Bengal'.

It was certainly not unaware of how rice from rural pockets were redirected to the warehouses of the dishonest hoarders and traders, how price of rice had flared up and black markets flourished in Bengal under the nose of the League ministry. But it remained deaf and dumb as the famine kept engulfing the poor.

Few more actions on the part of the Government of India strengthens the doubt about its intention. The most notable amongst them was with regard to its not taking due initiative in organising supply of food from remaining ten British Indian provinces as well as hundreds of native states in the sub-continent. The Viceroy could have dictated or at least persuaded any of them to send help. On the contrary, the general policy of the Central Government during the famine was 'ban' on trading of rice between provinces. A window of 'free trade'[27] in

---

[27] As a matter of fact, imposition of barrier by provinces on such trade itself was questionable. Maharaja S C Nandy of Cossimbazar in a booklet titled 'Rational of Food Crisis' argued that raising such trade barriers violated a Section of Government of India Act, 1935.The Centre quietly acquiesced to this unconstitutional action of the units and let the chaos in food prices assume dangerous proportions. MR LXXIV No 5 Whole No 443 November 1943 P 331.

eastern provinces was opened in May but closed quickly in July 1943.

Out of several of its misdeeds, the action that plumbed to the lowest depth of moral depravity was probably its participating, alongside the provincial League-led Government, in the trading of food grains, through agencies, with a view to earning profit at the cost of lives of common people. The food grains procured from Punjab and elsewhere were sold at hefty prices in Bengal. In several instances, these grains were further adulterated by agencies to add to the profit margin. There was little difference in the moral characters of these governments with the dishonest businessmen. If the latter were resorting to black-marketing, the government agencies were robbing people openly.

Cruel Viceroy?

The lion's share of the blame arising out of acts of commission and omission could be attributed to Viceroy Linlithgow. Syama Prasad found him an embodiment of heartlessness, who took the suffering and rising death toll of such a vast humanity, who were the subjects of the British empire, with striking indifference. For example, his insincerity reflected in the rapid manner in which he kept changing the Food Member in his cabinet.[28] For quite some time, he himself held the portfolio but did grave injustice to the responsibility that was inherent with the post. Again, incredible though it may sound, despite being the all-powerful ruler of the country, he did not pay

---

[28] Instead of any well deliberated move, committees and boards were appointed one after another. In April 1943, Regional Food Commissioners were brought into existence and three Food Members were appointed in quick succession to supervise the whole show. For some time, Viceroy himself held the portfolio: Ghosh, p15.

a single visit[29] to famine-struck Bengal – one of the most populous and politically important provinces of British India, where hungry men, women and children were courting death in millions.

Provincial Government led by Muslim League

The philosophy and political goals of the Muslim League-led ministry in Bengal were briefly mentioned in the 'Introduction' section. Here we look at those aspects in further details to get more insight into its action during the famine.

Denying Food Shortage in Bengal

Upon being re-installed at the seat of power by Governor Herbert, the League's first significant action was the proclamation denying food shortage in Bengal. Its civil supplies department issued a press note that any 'deficit' can certainly be met by the carry-over of the 1941-42 crop, rationalising consumption and popularising use of substitute food grains. Its position was essentially that there was no food shortage in Bengal and the problem was one of hoarding and maldistribution. Whether or not this was a fact, the ministry did not have any reliable data that warranted taking this stance. Its action thus seemed like quid pro quo, to its British benefactor! Such a 'stance' helped the Government of India to ignore its earlier commitments to the Huq ministry,

[29] A hurt Bengal did not fail to notice such heartlessness. The Indian Annual Report wrote: 'Lord Linlithgow's refusal to visit Bengal symbolised something, some defect in the character of the Anglo-Indian bureaucracy that the future historians only can rightly analyse. We are too near the event to judge it properly.' It surmised that this famine in Bengal was allowed to have such a free run, because, in the eyes of the British: 'the value of Indian lives was next to nil...' : IAR 1944, Vol 1, p86

of additional food grains and gave the HMG justification not to take Bengal's food situation seriously. Worse, the British did not have any moral guilt in continuing to plunder the province through procurement of rice for war purpose!

Driving Panic and Pushing Rice to Hoarders

If the crisis was due to hoarding and maldistribution, as the League government had contended, the common folk was to be blamed for it instead of hoarders and speculators! The League government effectively sided with the latter. Making a mockery of the 'food drive', it left out Calcutta and Howrah, the two key abodes of the big hoarders and speculators from the ambit of that exercise! Amidst the increasing unavailability of rice in the market and its soaring price, the League government carried out a 'house to house' search to detect excess rice holdings by the common man and agriculturists. This search, constituting the nefarious 'food drive', was done after infusing fear in the minds of the common people about penal measures that would follow, should excesses be detected. The civil supplies minister had threatened that he would himself search under the taktaposh in households to unearth the allegedly hoarded foodgrains. In panic, the common people sold away whatever meagre rice they held for their own consumption in the forthcoming days of hardships. Those were lapped up by unscrupulous traders and agencies with alacrity. The government programme proved a coercive measure against the vulnerable. As the price of rice shot through the roof, the poor never got any opportunity to buy even a fraction of what they had sold during the 'food drive'. While the masses were terrorised, the Government abused the Defence of India Rules to gag the press.

Blinded by Communal Politics

The League ministry in Bengal indulged in a kind of politics, which was rabidly communal and simultaneously driven by jealousy for non-League Muslim political parties. The normal response for any province faced with food crisis and starvation death would have been to seek immediate help from neighbouring provinces, in a brotherly spirit. That the League ministry did not do so was intriguing. Probably driven by the hidden agenda of annexing Muslim-majority Bengal in its entirety to its coveted homeland of Pakistan, the League considered help from the surrounding Hindu-majority provinces as politically harmful. Interestingly, it even failed to gather optimum help from Punjab, though distant but again, a Muslim-majority province with considerably surplus stock of food grains, but ruled by the Unionist Party, a Muslim-dominated but non-Muslim League and comparatively secular political outfit. Both Muslim League and the Unionist Party were competing with each other for Muslim votes in Punjab at the time.

In Bengal, the League ministry put communally driven political interests above the welfare of the distressed people. Efficient, quick procurement of rice from every available source in a financially transparent manner was the key need of the hour. It, however, appointed Ispahani & Co, a large business house, as its sole buying agent. Ispahani was close to both Muslim League and Jinnah. Driven by profit motive, the company acted against the interest of common people of Bengal. Seeing the prospect of making enormous private profit, the company insisted on its right to do trading on its own account, simultaneous with procurement of food grains on behalf of the Bengal government. This procurement has been discussed in some detail in earlier chapters. Whatever food grains were procured did not reach the poor they were meant for, because those were sold at high prices in Bengal. This not only secured the profit of the agents, the tragedy was that the government of Bengal too reaped large immoral profit by trading in these illegally procured food grains.

Corruption and Ineptitude

The Muslim League-led ministry betrayed exemplary ineptitude in tackling the famine. Its first duty, in fact, was to prevent the random 'wandering' of hungry people and convince them to stay put in their homes, because rendering of relief at the villages of the victims, would have surely reduced the scope for misuse and corruption. Nothing of that sort was thought of. Even after hungry masses were on road searching for food and family members were getting separated, the Government did not care. Though the capital city of Calcutta and several big towns across the provinces were overwhelmed by the rising number of the hungry, the Government did not provide adequate relief. Rice was sold in the black market in various places under the nose of the Government. It took no effective steps against the hoarders and profiteers. In many places the hungry died on the streets while the warehouses in the same locality lay locked, full of grain. There were also several instances of stockpiles of food stuff lying in ports and cities, but not being sent to deficit areas, citing non-availability of transport.

As a matter of fact, the severity of the famine was commensurate with the level of corruption. Nothing could perhaps better describe its vicious grip than how Fazlul Huq described it in a public meeting in Calcutta. Launching a scathing attack on the government, he said[30] that 'disgraceful corruption' permeated it from 'top to bottom' and was present in settling shops, granting permits, selecting agents, in requisition and distribution of food stuffs, in appointments 'and in hundred other ways too numerous to mention....' The Rowlands Committee[31] also exposed the ugly face of the administration from its inside. It observed that corruption became so widespread and the attitude towards it became so defeatist that the most drastic steps were necessary to stamp out the evil 'which has corrupted the public service and public morals'.

Inhuman Approach in Dealing with Famine Victims

Even in the matter of administering relief, that too grossly inadequate, the League ministry resorted to corruption, communalisation and politicisation. There was a tendency to obstructing relief work.[32] An extreme manifestation of its approach was in deferring relief works in some places as adequate numbers of Muslim relief-personnel were not available to meet the prescribed 'community ratio rules' between the two religious communities. This was, as if, hunger was community specific. This absurd rule was extended even to the domain of trade

---

[30] MR LXXIV No 5 Whole No 443 November 1943 P 327.

[31] It was appointed by the Governor of Bengal in December 1944 to suggest recommendations for the 'improvement of the administration' and presided over by Sir Archibald Rowlands: IAR 1944, Vol 1, p94.

[32] This was witnessed by dignitaries from other parts of India visiting famine-affected areas of Bengal. For example, Mrs Rajan Nehru, Secretary, AIWC, touring Midnapore told United Press how non-official relief organisations had to face colossal difficulties and that 'they have to conform to the most incredible restrictions and regulations.' Mrs Vijaylakshmi Pandit who also toured famine-affected areas extensively observed that 'Government persistently hampers non-official effort. ..' She added: 'Reasons are seldom given and they are not considered necessary. MR LXXIV No 5 Whole No 443 November 1943 P 326.

and commerce, including retail shops. Reflecting lamentable short-sightedness, the delay cost lives of the poor of both communities. Another example was the ministry's reported reluctance in giving an advance to the Calcutta Corporation, which was burdened with the influx of a large body of destitute into this city, as it was a Hindu-dominated body. Such discrimination arising out of communally driven attitude had, according to many, impaired the relief efforts in the city.

By July 1943, a large number of rural destitutes congregated in Calcutta. Initially, they thrived solely on private charity. The government moved in with an official relief policy only in August, rather under the moral pressure exerted by private enterprise. But its relief efforts were at best symbolic, devoid of earnestness. By October 1943, the numbers of rural destitute went up to nearly one hundred thousand. Due to the relief measures being grossly inadequate, hungry people were dying on the streets of the city, but no proper arrangement was made for disposal of the dead bodies. To hide its failings in preventing starvation death, the League ministry manipulated statistics of death and claimed that many of these victims had died due to 'chronic diseases' instead of 'starvation'.

The League government's cruelty to the famine victims was also manifested in its framing of the Bengal Vagrancy Ordinance 1943 on 30 July,1943. It was followed by the Bengal Destitute Persons (Repatriation and Relief) Ordinance, passed on 28 October 1943. The regime applied the weapon of Ordinances to tens of thousands of hapless destitute and threw them out of Calcutta and other big towns because these poor people, it said, 'were posing health hazards to the citizens' of Calcutta. Many famine victims got separated from their families in the process. This had happened once at the start of the famine – when myriads of villagers had hit the roads. It was now *deja vu* – a repeat performance of that terrible tragedy of separation of family members.

The Acid Test

It needs reiteration that NOTHING – not even death, diseases and distress of millions of hapless people cutting across communities – could make the incumbent Bengal Government and the Government of India apply the then existing 'famine relief code' to Bengal. The former steadfastly rejected the demand of the opposition parties in this regard. That measure could have made the governments at various levels more accountable and compelled them to give semblance of relief to the huge destitute population. Clearly, that hurt its political agenda and that consideration prevailed over millions of human lives.

How Pro-poor Political Forces Failed The Masses

The Case of the Communist Party

Having examined the role of the three levels of governments, it may be pertinent to look atthe role played by pro-poor political forces at this dark hour in Bengal, when hundreds of thousands of common people were staring at certain death for no fault of their own but due to Government policies and actions.

In this regard, the case of members of the Scheduled Caste Federation who considered their economic and educational backwardness more identical with Muslim common masses (than caste Hindus) and hoped for a better deal from a League-led ministry warrants mention. Around 21 members of this Scheduled Caste group[33] supported the Nazimuddin ministry.

---

[33] Scheduled Caste is a colonial government Census listing of certain communities in India.

Three of this group, including Jogendra Nath Mandal, joined the cabinet. Time showed the futility of this strategy. Vast multitudes of the poor, belonging to the scheduled castes, fell victims to the famine and pestilence though this group impassively continued to support the Nazimuddin government.

Next, let us look at another important political organisation that represented the oppressed people across caste and creed. The Communist Party of India had both the moral obligation and the potential to bring pressure on the Government of India to review its food policies and make it provide bare minimum of food grains to Bengal's people.

Bringing Pressure on the British Regime – Was it Feasible?

Some facts need to be considered at the outset. The British dependence on India's industrial base, comprising inter alia steel, cement, jute, cotton, matches, vanaspati,[34] sugar and various types of engineering products during wartime was critical. This diverse industrial infrastructure was used to the hilt by the regime by repurposing many factories to make war supplies, and also by introducing shifts, extending working hours etc.

Notably, a sizeable chunk of the country's industries producing war supplies was situated in Calcutta and its industrial suburbs. The Communist Party of India had direct or indirect influence over large sections of unionised workers in Bengal through the Bengal Provincial Trade Union Congress (BPTUC). Its influence extended to essential services providers in the city like Calcutta Tramways, Calcutta Electric Supply Corporation, Calcutta Port, Calcutta Corporation and Oriental Gas.

It may be reckoned that well ahead of World War II, the trade unions in the country had gathered considerable

---

[34] Hydrogenated vegetable oils.

experience in using 'strike' work as an instrument of collective bargaining. For example, during the year 1920 alone, nearly 2,500,000 workers across India were involved in going on strikes on a range of issues and in many cases, these ended in bloodshed.[35] Closer to the war period, during the 1937-39, important instances of strikes, for e.g, by the textile workers in Bombay, oil field workers in Digboi, glass bangles workers in UP, and by the BN Railway workers were reported.

According to some reports, nearly 60 per cent of all strikes in the country during 1936-37 were in Bengal. In 1937, the engineering industry witnessed eight major strikes.[36] In the first calendar quarter of 1937, a massive strike hit the jute factories involving tens of thousands of workers and it lasted till May 1937.[37] Bengal witnessed strikes even during the war period. For instance, in 1940, several thousands of workers of the Calcutta Municipal Corporation had participated in a strike.

It must be noted that in all cases, these 'strikes' were used to protect or enhance the interests of the workers who constituted a section of the society. Though this was natural for trade unions to do, yet at a juncture of time when the entire poor population faced existential challenges, not considering a 'strike' demanding food for the poor or, at least, a 'threat' to go on strike as a weapon to make the government review its policy has to be seen as 'myopic' as well as 'socially insensitive'. The party could have widened its perspective against the regressive government policies and held up the cudgel to protect the lives of the Bengali people. Instead, it seemed to have been obsessed

---

35 https://www.marxists.org/history/international/comintern/sections/britain/periodicals/communist_review/1922/05/indian_labour_mvt.htm.

36 http://sanhati.com/articles/347/.

37 https://shodhganga.inflibnet.ac.in/bitstream/10603/21131/13/13_chapter%206.pdf <22.6.19>

with just the interests of its own union members alone – ration for factory workers – and not look at the peasants, especially the poor peasants, starving across the countryside in a land that produced rice in abundance.

It may be argued that the threat of any major trade union action in factories – which could potentially put obstacles to production of war supplies – would have made the British anxious and persuaded them into changing their policy of starving millions of people. In any case, there was no contradiction between keeping the factories running and ensuring basic food supply to the poor and economically weak population. Moreover, with its branches present across India, the Communist Party was acutely aware that such severe scarcity was not present in any other parts of British India and it was feasible to arrange supplies to Bengal from other provinces.

Trying to bring pressure upon the ruling regime was probably the historic duty for a party that was widely perceived to be the sentinel of the interests of the working class, poor and downtrodden. But it failed. Unfortunately, not much material is available in the public domain on the party's inhouse deliberation on the 1943 Bengal famine and its policy regarding the famine. This leaves us with the option of looking at its publicly visible actions. These suggest that either the party genuinely lacked understanding of the politics behind the famine or it did not try to understand the Muslim League-British policy, due to its ideological bias.

Failure in Organising a Mass Movement

Since the governments at various levels were doing all the wrong things and not doing things that ought to have been done with urgency to save poor people's lives, it was only to be expected from the Communist Party that it would organise mass movements against the ruling governments at both the Centre and the Province.[38] Instead, it was seen in proximity with both.There was no report of any significant political mobilisation by any political organisation, including the Communists.The Communist Party was seen to be endorsing the British regime and standing close to the League-led regime, generally supportive of that dispensation rather than coming forward to save the lives of the poor starving masses.

The poor died silently and meekly. Quite unlike what hungry masses do when they stare at 'death', there was practically no violent movement in Bengal against the dishonest hoarders or the government officials. There were some reports of paddy looting in 1942, when the Huq ministry was in office and it was actually struggling to prevent the onset of the famine. As Greenough observed in his book,[39] that during the famine no political party tried to awaken the revolutionary spirit in the people. This reflected on the Communist Party more than any others. If at all, there were reports of two attempts of demonstration before the Assembly House by the hungry masses in September 1943, but the Government held that Syama Prasad Mookerjee and Fazlul Huq were behind them.

It may be of interest to look at how this issue was being seen outside of Bengal. Pandit H N Kunzru expressed his mind in a speech in the Council of State. He said that if there was a famine in the 'martial' Punjab, the government would have given it direct and immediate attention. Though he thought Bengalis were in comparison quiet and submissive, 'Had they

---

[38] In contrast, the Communist-led left parties waged a 'food movement' in mid 1960s against the provincial government in West Bengal just because rice was not available in adequate quantity though there were supply of alternate cereals e.g., wheat.

[39] Paul R Greenough, *Prosperity and Misery in Modern Bengal, The Famine of 1943-44* (first published in 1983).

asserted their will to live, I am sure, their troubles would have been attended to earlier', Pt Kunzru said.[40] It is interesting to look at Kunzru's assessment of the people of Bengal. Through the first three decades of the twentieth century, the people of Bengal were in the vanguard of the revolutionary movement against the British, ready to lay down their lives for the sake of the motherland. They were neither timid nor submissive. But yes, there was a marked change in their spirit since the beginning of the communalisation Governance of the province under the League in 1937. Probably that explained an uncharacteristic meekness that was on display during the famine. They were rendered completely helpless. It was evident that the ruling political regime and its supporters failed them.

Trying to Decipher the Communist Stand

The left party's soft approach towards the British in the course of the World War hinged on the position the USSR adopted in relation to the two combative blocks of nations. Following Germany's invasion of USSR in June 1941, there was a 'U' turn by the Communist Party of India from its anti-British position at the start of the war. Britain became a Soviet ally and ready to tinker its policy vis-a-vis the Communists. In India, the distance between the Government and the Communist Party began to narrow after 1941. Almost a year later, i.e. in July 1942, the Government of India lifted the ban on the CPI and that resulted in the party coming closer to the British, ostensibly to help the allies fight the 'People's War' against the fascists across the world. The party which in 1940 gave a call to

[40] H N Kunzru's speech at the Council of State on19 November 1943: IAR Vol 2, 1943, p83.

rise in revolt against the British was now committed to stand by Britain, the ally of USSR, under all circumstances. While PC Joshi, General Secretary of the CPI, went to meet Reginald Maxwell, Home Member, Government of India in the last month of 1942 to cement relations, party leaders even at the ground level were careful to ensure that labour movements did not in any way embarrass the British war efforts![41]

Misplaced Bias in Favour of the League Ministry

As indicated earlier in the book, the CPI had positive bias in favour of the Muslim League Government.This attitude impacted poor people through the famine. The party's closeness to Muslim League arose from two key factors. First, one of its own ideological constructs postulated that India was a 'family of multiple nations' (Muslims being a prime example), each of which was entitled to self-determination. The League's 'two-nation' theory fitted into this framework. Second, the party found a common subset of population – who were poor Muslims coming under the rising influence of the League – who could be converted into its own members.

The Communist Party pledged its support for the demand of Pakistan and actively participated in meetings, conferences etc, some of which were jointly organised by its various wings and that of the League. One of its top leaders, in fact, took pride in the fact that his party fought for and suffered for the cause of a separate home land for Muslims, no less than any other Muslim in that section of the freedom struggle to which the latter had no access due to the deeply divided polity in the country.[42] This may explain why the Indian communists of

---

[41] *The Sickle & The Crescent*, Sunanda Sanyal, Soumya Basu (hereafter, Sanyal), p23.

[42] Sanyal, p 35.

that time had favoured the ouster of the Huq ministry, followed by installation of the Muslim League ministry in April 1943, though a famine was looming on Bengal's horizon. It seemingly held that the League-led ministry was more representative of people than the earlier one. Unseating a stable government at that time was clearly fraught with risk and uncertainty. The Communist Party had reportedly also organised some hunger marches when the Huq-led coalition government was striving to ward off the impending famine, but it showed little zeal to organise any concrete agitational programmes, let alone any mass movement, after the League ministry took over and the famine actually ravaged the land. As the enormity of loss of lives in the province under the League ministry proved, there was lack of political sagacity in the Left party's stand in India.

Too Naive to Understand Happenings on the Ground?

To give the Communist Party the benefit of doubt, its approach towards and the League could be described simply as naive. Even if it had failed to read into their real intentions, the evil consequences of their actions on ground ought to have alerted it and prompted it to undertake a mid-term review and course correction. As a matter of fact, the situation on the ground was a typical replay of what Karl Marx had observed in relation to the famine of 1769-70 AD in Bengal. 'Between 1769 and 1770, the English manufactured a famine by buying up all the rice and refusing to sell it again, except at fabulous prices'.[43] The difference in 1943 was that both the British and the League governments had joined hands in snatching the stock of rice from common people through their agencies, and thereafter, began profiteering by trading in food grains while black

[43] https://www.marxists.org/archive/marx/works/1867-c1/ch31.htm.

marketing thrived and poor people starved to death because they could not afford to buy foodstuffs at high prices.

Errors of Judgement?

Be it due to its political compulsions to favour the Allied nations fighting the Fascists or any other cause, the CPI fought shy of pursuing a reasoned policy against the British. As far as the Muslim League was concerned, its judgement was influenced by its petty politics. Thus, its policies vis-a-vis both the British regime and the League ministry were, on the whole soft and supportive. It tended to believe that the League-led ministry was more representative of people than the earlier one and the food crisis was driven largely by hoarding and the ruling regimes were anti-hoarders.

The party also favoured directing of food grains from rural to urban areas, which the League government did through its 'food drive' campaign. But in both cases, its stand proved wrong. For, the League government was never serious about stopping hoarding, nor was there surplus food in the rural pockets. The food drive, therefore, aggravated the crisis and hit the villages hardest. Further, though monumental misdeeds of the authorised buying agencies in matters of procurement of food grains led to widescale starvation death, the Communist Party again supported the League government's plan of force-buying the autumn and the winter paddy from the farmers. That had sent shivers down the spine of the poor cultivators. If the above policies had aggravated the crisis, the CPI failed to do what was really the need of the hour. The party was extremely reticent about increasing pressure on the British to import food grains.

Interestingly, during this period between 1942 and 1945, the party was in a cosy relationship with both the League government in the province and Government of India. This helped it spread its wing in Bengal by launching several para-affiliation groups in the form of cultural outfits in the urban and rural belts involving women, youth, students and farmers. Its membership grew over six times over this period. It began to reach much larger audiences through its publications in more regional languages.[44]

This may explain why – instead of undertaking political mobilisation and using its hold over trade unions to force the governments to ensure food-grains supply to the poor at affordable prices – the party seemed busy in rationalising its inaction on the famine front. It seemed busy in searching for class enemies within. It sought to simplify the problem by taking the view that the famine was due to 'hoarding', which could be addressed by enhancing public awareness through platforms such as Artists and Writers Forum, Krishak Sabhas, Ward Committees etc. Its programmes and activities showed a predilection limited to using cultural platforms to raise public awareness about famine through cartoons, photographs, street plays etc.

It carried out some relief work with help from the League government. It also participated in spreading awareness in the society about malaria, once the epidemic broke out in the aftermath of the famine. Interestingly, the CPI was able to build up favourable public image through such activities and emerged as a beneficiary in the election of the Calcutta Corporation held in March 1944, when the party was able to open its account for the first time, securing two seats from the labour constituencies.[45]

---

[44] Sanyal, pp28-29

[45] https://shodhganga.inflibnet.ac.in/bitstream/10603/154909/13/13_chapter%208.pdf <22.7.20>

However, the party's success in terms of building a public image or its electoral success could not hide its failure in fighting the British and the League governments to save the lives of Bengal's famine victims. An academic question which history can throw at it is: whether its insensitivity to such a colossal tragedy in Bengal was influenced by the role played by Stalin with regard to the famine of Ukraine in the name of Communist ideology? We know that in 1932-33, a decade earlier, at least five million people had perished in Ukraine to pave the way for a 'higher goal', i.e., industrialisation of the USSR.Was the Communist Party in India obsessed in 1943 about fighting a 'People's War' across the world and saw the death of millions of its own countrymen as inevitable 'collateral damage'? Clearly, sufficient information is unavailable in the public domain to arrive at any conclusion. There is need to carry out more conclusive researches in this vital area.

Nature of the Famine – How it Came to a Sudden Halt

The severe food crisis began to show signs of abating rather abruptly in October end 1943. A new Viceroy, Lord Archibald Wavell, started rapid action to address the issue. Military and other large organisations were prevailed upon to release parts of their excess stock which then were sent to deficit areas in army vehicles on a mission mode. Though pervasive epidemic in the form of cholera, malaria and smallpox began to rage thereafter, and people kept dying in large numbers over the next few months, the starvation deaths began to decline from this point of time. A relevant question is, what made the British change their mind? The answer encompasses a whole range of plausible reasons – apparent and deep. We shall examine a few important ones.

Churchill's 'U' turn

Prima facie, the famine came to an end because the British PM, Winston Churchill, decided to do so. The same person who had disowned HMG's responsibility to feed famine victims and had repeatedly rejected humanitarian offers of food aids from other countries, in a volte-face, advised Viceroy Wavell in early October 1943 to ensure well-being of the masses and make every effort to deal with local shortages: 'Peace, order and a high condition of war-time well-being among the masses of the people constitute the essential foundation of the forward thrust against the enemy... The hard pressures of world war have for the first time, for many years brought conditions of scarcity, verging in some localities into actual famine, upon India. Every effort must be made, even by the diversion of shipping urgently needed for war purposes, to deal with local shortages.... Every effort should be made by you to assuage the strife between the Hindus and Moslems and to induce them to work together for the common good.'[46]

The change in Churchill's posture was stunning. The question, however, is whether it was voluntary or forced by external circumstances? Subsequent events prove that Churchill had not undergone any change of heart. Once the immediate military threat from across the eastern border was over, he and his cabinet repeatedly rejected a series of requests by Wavell to send India additional food grains from overseas. Though the severity of the food crisis began to be addressed since October 1943, it took a long time for normalcy to return. Churchill probably wanted merely to stop the starvation death. Thus, even in March 1944, despite Wavell's repeated demand of

---

46 https://winstonchurchill.hillsdale.edu/did-churchill-cause-the-bengal-famine/ quoting : Winston S Churchill to Members of the War Cabinet, 8 October 1943. (Churchill papers, 23/11).

one million tons of food grain for India, Churchill agreed to send only a quarter of it.[47]

Secret Behind British Decision to end the Famine – An Unstated Fact

Though, often not given attention in relation to the Bengal famine by academicians and researchers, it needs to be recognised that the above-mentioned change in Churchill's approach took place at a time when the threat of a joint expedition by the INA[48] and the Japanese army had become 'real' across Assam & East Bengal border. The Provisional Government of Free India was formed on 21 October 1943 and it almost immediately declared war against Britain and USA. As a matter of fact, as a part of the Japanese army's 'U Go', a plan for invasion of British India jointly with the INA, incursions and skirmishes were already going on between the two sides in the south-western areas of Burma, close to Chittagong in the southeast of Bengal around this period.

Also, as the British had rightly apprehended, the joint forces of the Japanese army and the INA launched a massive offensive at Imphal and Kohima in mainland India's eastern border within six months thereafter, i.e. in the March 1944. It would have been foolhardy to keep millions of people starving in Bengal while arch enemy of the British was knocking at the door. Local people form the first bastion against an invading enemy!

The prospective joint military invasion may be amongst factors that influenced Churchill to change track on famine. As stated earlier, it was under his instructions that Wavell got into action. He used his experience as the 'commander

---

[47] The Viceroy's journal, entry of March 24, 1944, P61.

[48] Subhas Bose's free Indian Army, known as the Indian National Army.

in chief' of the British troops in the eastern sector to use the army establishment and energise the relief operation and reach foodstuff to Bengal's starving population. Simultaneously, a few shiploads of foodstuff also began to arrive from donor countries, creating pressure on hoarders in the province to release their holding to the market.[49]

Two inferences can be made from the above discussion. First, no matter what the true reasons for Churchill's change of heart were, the famine began to abate when he decided to put an end to it. The second inference derives from the first i.e., it confirms the hypothesis that it was both manmade and political.

Political Dynamics of Relationship between the British and the Muslim League

From historical documents, it is clear that the British regime, starting from the HMG down to the Governor of Bengal, and the Muslim League-led ministry converted a situation of not-so-unusually-large food shortage into a severe famine. A question that is bound to arise is what exactly made the two work seemingly in sync to bring about this holocaust? Was there a nexus? Were they guided by any other consideration? Here we seek to understand the dynamics of their relationship by revisiting a few key facts mentioned earlier and importing into the canvas some new information.

Despite Resistane from Syama-Huq Ministry, British Re-install Muslim League

A group of pro-League academicians have endeavoured to pass on the blame for the famine on the Huq-Mookerjee ministry.

---

[49] The Storm of War: A New History of the Second World War by Andrew Roberts. Ref: English Speaking Peoples – The Role of the State: Why Churchill Changed His Mind.

A typical demonstration of this line of criticism came from Muslim League leader Hussain Imam in a debate on the food situation in Bengal in the Council of State.[50] He accused the Mookerjee-Huq ministry with a conspiracy of silence, with the collusion of the Governor and blamed the media in Bengal for not disclosing correct facts till the League ministry came to office. He tried to emphasise that the predecessor of the League ministry had 'mishandled' the situation. The facts demonstrate why such an attack was both unfair and malicious.

The Huq ministry had an extremely short span of life, i.e., of barely 16 months, during which it waged a spirited fight against the Governor's ill-conceived interferences on issues of critical public interest. Syama Prasad had resigned by the end of 11 months, protesting against the Governor's repeated meddling in the working of the provincial ministry. During its brief span, the Huq government achieved considerable success in removing the poison of communalism that was injected in the province for nearly four long years (1937-1940) by the League-led ministry during its earlier tenure. The sudden emergence of the Japanese threat in the eastern border and assumption of special war-time power by the Governor curtailed the operational freedom of the Huq ministry drastically, especially with regard to subjects of food and transport. To be fair to this ministry, it strongly protested against the colonial ruler's 'denial policy', imposed by the Governor without due consultation with the incumbent government at the time in Bengal.

When its views on this and related issues were unfairly brushed aside and the price of paddy began to soar, the Huq ministry, as a logical step in that scary scenario, wanted to take

[50] Hossain Imam, a prominent League politician from Bihar took part in a debate on 23 November 1943 in the Council of State: IAR, Vol 2, 1943, pp85-6.

census of available rice in the province. This was essential for the government to be able to frame any meaningful strategy to tackle the food crisis. Things were changing rapidly, and war-driven externalities were beyond its control. The Government's autonomy in dealing with the food situation was usurped by the Governor and the Huq government's proposal in this regard was rejected by him. In the given situation, the Huq ministry had, without the benefit of requisite information, shown some ambivalence with regard to its estimation about the actual availability of rice, which is unfairly held against it.

Finally, however, driven by anxiety for the people, it did succeed in bringing pressure on the Central Government and secure the latter's commitment to supply a few lakh tons of additional food grain to Bengal over the coming months. This must be treated as its success in a hostile environment.

The Huq ministry was a victim of circumstances but it repeatedly attempted to protect the people from the inhuman policies of the British regime. Deciding to hold an inquiry on the atrocities committed by the armed forces on flood victims of Midnapore was one of such important pro-people act of courage. It was a direct affront to the Governor as the Midnapore carnage was carried out under his watch.The Huq ministry's various stances and actions suggest that it would not have allowed the British a free run of the famine, had it continued to hold the reins of governance through 1943. That is why the ministry was changed by the higher authorities.

The fact that it went out of office rather than compromise on the issue of the people's interest also prove that it is unfair to blame the Huq administration for the 1943 famine. The Muslim League-led ministry that was brought in, entered through a back door, ready to sacrifice people's lives for the sake of power.

The British were singularly focussed on procuring food for war purposes without any hindrance. At the same time, the Governor was keen, as correspondence of that period suggests, in having in Calcutta a substitute indigenous government which would allow continued plundering of the province but save the British regime from corresponding ignominy. In such a situation, the Muslim League grabbed the chance of forming a government. It is evident that it had placed party interests and its communal agenda way above the life and death of the poor people of Bengal.

League Sealed Fate of Bengal from the Very Start

Ever since it took over the reins of the government, the League ministry played 'wall passes' as in soccer with the colonial master, snatching rice away from the poor. While a chunk of it went for war purposes, the bulk of the acquired grain entered the warehouses of the hoarders. These were facilitated by the League ministry's propagated theory of 'no food shortage in Bengal', with the British using it to say to the world that things were normal in the province. Whether or not there was really grave rice shortage in 1943, the unhindered export, stocking by large organisations and hoarding by dishonest businessmen had severely curtailed rice supply in the market, except at abnormally high prices. When the common man began to starve and hoarders flourished, both the governments at Calcutta and Delhi went out of the way to hide the enormity of the crisis from the rest of India.

Gagging the Press

The brutal suppression of the press in Bengal is exposed best through a comparison of how the press in other provinces and countries were viewing the famine. For example, the

Civil and Military Gazette of Lahore reported that foreign newspaper correspondents in India were not permitted to cable abroad even the bare facts of death and hospital admissions due to starvation – issued daily in Calcutta by the Director of Information to the Bengal Government. The Government of India gave the League government scope and opportunity to establish a vice-like grip over the press. *Modern Review*, reporting on the press gag, said, 'It is a censorship operating with the sole purpose of protecting the Government of India from the consequences of its own incapacity and folly'.[51]

The confirmation came from the American media. 'Nothing about the famine was cabled to American newspapers last September, when it had reached an acute stage in Bengal. Nothing trickled through to the American press in October, either.'[52]

Intriguingly, the League government, was equally agile in saving the Government of India from embarrassment. Thus, it banned publication of the joint statement[53] by opposition leaders in the Legislative Assembly that criticised the observations of R H Hutchinson, the Food Secretary of the Government of India, made with regard to the food situation in Bengal. The opposition thought Hutchinson betrayed an attitude of complacency and pious wishes that, in fact, had paved the way for 1943's famine.

---

[51] MR LXXIV No 5 Whole No 443 November 1943 P 329.

[52] Elsie Neil wrote in New York Monthly-Asia & America in February 1944: IAR, Vol 1, p 39.

[53] Hutchinson had made the observation on 22 February 1944. An adjournment motion was brought by the opposition in Bengal Legislative Assembly on 2 March 1944 to oppose the ban, but it was defeated as the treasury stood by the side of Hutchinson. IAR, 1944, Volume 1, p 179-80.

The period is replete with several such instances of excesses by the two regimes, with a view to strangulate the freedom of the press .

Debates were raging in the Council of State as well on what was happening in Bengal. H N Kunzru brought an adjournment motion in the Council of State in August 1943 on the issue of the Central Government banning Syama Prasad Mookerjee's press statement on the food situation in Bengal. He decried the tendency of the government to suppress publication of any news concerning the crisis in Bengal and charged that even in such repression, it was following a discriminatory approach in as far as *The Statesman* newspaper that had published some pictures of the Bengal distress 'which had created a deep impression on the minds of the Indian public'.[54] In course of the debate, the government admitted that the Chief Press Adviser had indeed advised newspapers not to publish Mookerjee's statement outside Bengal.

Three months later, Kunzru had to again lodge a strong protest against the draconian press gag. He lamented, 'if the truth had been told earlier, the situation would not have deteriorated to the extent it did. Whoever had controlled the news about Bengal, had done a very serious injustice to that province'.[55] A month later, again he repeated the charge against the provincial and Central Governments for their failure to keep the public informed of the reality of the Bengal situation for a long time.[56]

---

[54] Pt H N Kunzru said this while moving the adjournment motion on 31 Aug 1943: IAR,, V2, 1943, p 81.

[55] Ibid, p83: Pt H N Kunzru's speech at the Council of State on 19 November 1943.

[56] Ibid, p316: Pt H N Kunzru's speech at the Conference of the National Liberal Federation of India in December 1943.

Betraying People

It was incredible that the League, despite being a representative government of people of the province, was so indifferent to the immensity of their suffering. An important indicator of its callous attitude towards the famine victims reflected in its strange reluctance in the matter of applying the 'famine code' to Bengal, which could have given at least some relief to the distressed population. On the contrary, through its various acts of omission and commission, it strengthened the hands of the British and absolved them from the responsibility of feeding the hungry.

As suggested earlier, the famine continued for months because hoarders and profiteers were sitting on huge stock. It was possible to bring an end to it by importing a few shiploads of food grains. India's British rulers consciously did not do this. On its part, the League ministry was hand-in-glove with dishonest traders and did not take any meaningful step, compelling them to bring their hoards to the open market. Its undue patronage to Ispahani&Co, a League favourite and Jinnah-confidant, was irrational and invited bitter criticism from the opposition in the Legislative Assembly. Instead of taking action against hoarders across the board, the League communalised the matter and the Churchill Cabinet helped the League in this regard. It held the Hindu Marwari businessmen of Bengal responsible for hoarding rice and creating scarcity to embarrass the Muslim League government.[57]

Plumbing new depth of Ineptitude

Instead of relief, such lowly politics made the lives of famine victims miserable. H N Kunzru, in his speech at the Liberal

---

[57] https://winstonchurchill.hillsdale.edu/did-churchill-cause-the-bengal-famine/ referring to. War Cabinet Conclusion, 7 February, Cabinet papers, 65/41.

Conference in December 1943, wondered how such an inept government could be left at the steering wheel even after such colossal loss of lives. 'A government which has completely failed to discharge its elementary duties still claims to be the guardian of the masses and keeps all powers in its hands....'[58] Earlier in November 1943, in a debate in the Council of State on the role of the provincial government in handling the Bengal food crisis, he wanted to know if it was at all justified to leave the question of 'food to people' to the whims of provincial governments. 'We have thought too much of the independence of the provinces and too little of the welfare of the people', he said. Kunzru's anguish at the manner of handling the famine by the Bengal government made him suggest that 'food supply' should be tackled as a whole and no province ought to be free to deal with it as it likes.[59]

Another Council of State member, Sir Sobha Singh also criticised the tendency in the provinces of becoming insular in outlook regardless of the good of the country under the Government of India Act – and said this exposed a constitutional defect.[60]

But neither the Government of India nor the HMG was inclined to intervene in the working of the League ministry. As mentioned earlier, from what the Earl of Munster, Geoffrey Fitz Clarence, who was the the Under Secretary of State for India and Burma, at the time said in the British Parliament it was clear that Britain had no concern for the millions of famine victims in India and they had no intent of intervening in the matter of Bengal's so-called provincial 'autonomy', unless the working of the Provincial Government impinged on

---

[58] IAR Volume 2, 1943 p 316.

[59] Ibid, p83.

[60] Ibid, p 83.

the war supplies. Ironically, on this count, they had nothing to complain against the provincial government.

There are ample evidence that the colonial government threw its full weight behind the Nazimuddin-led League ministry in Bengal, notwithstanding the deaths happening on such massive scale due to famine and epidemic. Till the last days of Linlithgow as the Viceroy, the equations amongst all three levels of government were, therefore, harmonious. That went for small rejig after Viceroy Wavell took over the management of Britain's jewel in the crown. Being very upset at the manner of working of the Nazimuddin ministry, Wavell made out a case in early March 1944 for dismissing it and GOI taking over reins of Bengal under Section 93. However, the HMG remained steadfast in its support for the provincial ministry. Nazimuddin led ministry was the direct beneficiary of this policy largesse. Thus, despite its gross mishandling of the famine, his ministry survived till March 1945.

Politics Behind the Famine Inquiry Commission

On the whole, the colonial master and the League ministry operated in a seamless manner throughout the famine. The HMG's efforts to protect both the Government of India and the provincial government of Bengal from the attendant blemish continued even after the famine ended. This showed up in the matter of selecting the chairman of the Famine Inquiry Commission and framing its terms of reference.

Not only was there inordinate delay in appointing the inquiry commissioning due to dilly dally on the part of the HMG,[61] Amery, the SoS for India, who had a lion's share

[61] Majority members in the Council of State wanted immediate appointment of Inquiry Commission in January 1944: The Viceroy's Journal p48.

of responsibility for the food crisis, ensured that Sir John Woodhead, who enjoyed his trust, was appointed as its head. The fact that Woodhead had served as a top ICS officer in India and also had exposure as the Governor of Bengal probably justified his appointment. From the correspondence between the SoS and the Viceroy at that time, it is apparent that the SoS was keen that the terms of references for the Commission were framed with 'extreme circumspection'. In his communication with the Viceroy, Amery made it clear that the HMG was keen to extend the scope of inquiry beyond Bengal and to keep the 'political side of this business out of it'.[62]

Accordingly, the terms of reference were diluted in various manner to make light of the holocaust in Bengal. For example, the field of inquiry was to include (a) *food shortage and subsequent epidemic in India and in particular Bengal in 1943* and make recommendations *for prevention* of such recurrence; (b) *quality and yield* of food crops; (c) improving *system of administration with respect to supply and distribution* of food stuff; (d) providing *emergency medical relief* and *control of epidemic diseases* in famine conditions etc.

The significance of the report of Woodhead Commission may be better understood in the context of the above background. Catering to the expectations of the HMG, it did an impressive job of whitewashing politically motivated atrocities by couching them in milder terms such as absence of policy, policy mistakes, policy blunder, administrative chaos and bungling, official complacency etc. These jargons were often used presumably to hide political intents behind the famine.

If we re-examine the famine carefully vis-a-vis the report of the Commission, we cannot but recognise the fact that

---

62 *British Lion and Bengal Tiger*, p162.

not only did the British and the League regimes reap political dividends from the famine, they were also able to evade history's burden.

Mutual Political Benefits

Upon deep scrutiny, it is evident that the colonial regime made large gains in the form of securing war supplies by starving to death a few million people in Bengal. Their gain was immediate. A complex question is what was the 'benefit' to the Muslim League party from this exercise?

The plausible explanation is that the League was driven by mission Pakistan and it wanted whole of Bengal as part of it. Towards that end, it had to achieve two important goals. First, to vanquish other Muslim-dominated parties, especially the Progressive Coalition Party led by Fazlul Huq and it had to emerge as the sole representative of Muslims in the province. Second was to bulldoze the morale of the whole province of both – people and political parties – so that no opposition could come in the way of its Pakistan dream.

It may be seen that the bonhomie between the British and the League during the famine gave the latter an unprecedented opportunity to use the 'imperial power', thanks to the emergency nature of war situations and prevalence of Defence of India. The League used them to dominate over its colony, squash pro-independence voices, political rivals, gag the press and trample over its subjects. The manner in which the DIR Act and Rules were abused by the League ministry with complete connivence of the Government of India also spoke volumes on their nexus. In course of a discussion in the Central Legislative Assembly on misuse of the DIR Act & Rules by various governments, in which the League ministry excelled, Liaquat Ali Khan shifted the whole blame on the Government of India in a most shameless manner.[63] Despite such wild transgressions, Liaquat Ali and the League ministry believed they would continue to enjoy protection of the British regime.

Its tyrannical rule supported by the British helped the League not only in pushing other Muslim-dominated parties in Bengal to the edge but also strengthening its goal to emerge as sole representative of country's Muslims at the expense of few million lives! Nazimuddin, the League ministry's PM, having failed to save lives of such a vast number of people who were victims of British policy, should have resigned. That would have compelled the British to govern Bengal directly and provide food for survival. But he did not. The two political dispensations, it may be argued, cooperated with each other in a morally repugnant manner and sustained the famine.

That the League was successful to a considerable extent in demoralising and crippling the administration became evident in the findings of the Rowlands Committee.[64] Talking about how the League politicians had spread their stranglehold over the bureaucracy, it observed: 'there has been a marked deterioration in the morale of the services as a result of the impact of political forces on the framework of the permanent administration" The Committee said: 'This demoralisation became evident during 1943-44 when the policy carrying

[63] He simply denied any responsibility of the part of the League ministry in this regard, saying, if the Government of India felt that the provinces were incapable of applying Defence of India Act fairly and judiciously, their duty was to withdraw the Act. Then probably to a stunned audience he said: 'To say that the Central Government could not interfere with the Provincial Government even if the greatest injustice was committed under these Rules was like handing over a live cracker to a child and then expecting that child to be safe from disaster.'MR LXXV No 3 Whole No 447 March 1944 P 171.

[64] The Bengal Administration Enquiry (Rowlands) Committee 1944-45: Report 1945.

machinery in the Bengal Administration was found to be so morally inadequate.'[65] One probably notices that this situation, despite the pious avowal of the Governor, never improved. The same kind of inert administration, with its loyalty to the League regime continued even during the bloodshed on the eve of the partition in 1947.

Twin Conclusions

As to the question whether or not they brought about the disaster in nexus with each other, as if in accordance with an unwritten agreement, remains unknown and can be subject matter for further research. But two conclusions can surely be drawn, irrespective of if there was or wasn't a nexus. First, the sheer greed, corruption, and heartlessness on the part of these two ruling regimes make them party to a genocide, the perpetrators of which have managed to escape. Nearly 6 million Jews were killed by Nazis during World War II for which Hitler incurred eternal infamy and several of his accomplices were hanged. But all the guilty men of the 1943 Bengal famine which is said to have taken a toll of nearly 3.5 million lives, have escaped without any trial. Second, the British and the League regimes used each other to advance their respective political interests at the cost of millions of lives.

To reiterate, the British desperately needed the League to shield itself from international condemnation. This does not need elaboration. That the League was also looking at the British with some kind of 'use and throw' strategy was evident from time to time. A couple of examples follow. That the situation of Bengal was extremely miserable was recognised by Wavell who called the famine as 'one of the greatest disasters

---

[65] IAR, 1944, Vol1, p93.

befalling any people under British rule' and also by Richard Casey, the new Governor of Bengal who was reportedly 'aghast at the virulence and corruption of Bengal politics'.

Premier Nazimmuddin, on the other hand, had no hesitation in blaming the British and declaring that an independent Muslim country was the remedy to the kind of food crisis Bengal faced. He repeated this line in December 1943 in the Lahore session of the League. That he had no feelings for famine victims and that he was solely concerned about promoting political interests of his own ministry and party came to light on 8 January 1944 during his meeting with Wavell, when he told the anguished Viceroy that things would be all right if his ministry was given a chance and supported against his political enemies.[66]

How the Famine Impacted Bengali Society

Bengal famine is usually known for the death of millions of people. However, its more serious victim arguably was the very fabric of Bengali society. This aspect has been more or less ignored in various studies on the Bengal famine of 1943.

Need to Revise Some Established Notions

A popular perception exists that the famine of 1943 was essentially a rural phenomenon, mainly involving the rural poor. This viewpoint needs modification. It is true that the rural areas were denuded of rice by ill-conceived government policies and the people there were the worst affected. But runaway rise in price of rice affected the poor and the low middle-class people across the entire province. The city of Calcutta, with its industrial suburbs was given some protection, thanks to measures like ration shops, scheme of approved markets and food guarantee by

[66] The Viceroy's Journal, p 47.

large employers. Barring Calcutta and Chittagong to an extent, other towns including even Dacca, were badly affected.

The consciousness of the famine in Bengali society in terms of its expanse and severity was influenced by cultural expressions e.g., literature originating from Calcutta, which was the pivot of Bengal's cultural life. Notably, its citizens were relatively protected. Even their exposure to victims was of limited kind. Victims who thronged into the city did not represent even rural Bengal in its entirety. The victims were essentially from neighbouring districts like 24 Parganas and Midnapore, who clung to the city amidst extreme adversities for a few months before being evicted, starting from October 1943. Hundreds of thousands of remaining victims were spread across Bengal. They suffered and perished quietly without attracting attention and sympathy of the wider society.

Famine Rravaged One-fifth of Bengal's Population

Nearly 3.5 million people had died during the famine (according to estimates by the Dept of Anthropology, University of Calcutta). They constituted nearly 6 per cent of the total population of undivided Bengal at that time. Presuming each of them had, say, three family members on an average, who somehow managed to escape death, nearly 20 per cent of Bengal's surviving population may be presumed to have been affected by the disaster.

During this famine, separation from family members, selling teir own children, deserting the elderly and other relatives, resorting to mass prostitution for the sake of food, getting sucked into the vices of city life became a common practice for many of the survivors. Killing of babies due to the parents' inability to feed them and killing of sibling by the hungry were reported in newspapers. The only solace was probably that instances of cannibalism were not reported, unlike in the Bengal famine of 1770 AD. However, pangs of hunger had mercilessly assaulted the moral values of a sizeable chunk of the Bengali society in 1943. Unfortunately, before society could come out of that severe moral morass, Bengal was inflicted another terrible wound – partitioned in 1947, again evicting millions of people from their home and hearth and resulting in great destitution.

The Great Schism in Wider Society

What must have aggravated the survivors' grief and angst was the schism in the wider society. Employees of government departments, large organisations and factories were assured of guaranteed supply of rice and they lived in islands of safety. Rice was available in black market. The middle class managed to buy it by cutting down other expenses, while the rich flourished through the war economy and continued with their usual luxurious lifestyle. Posh hotels in Calcutta served a variety of dishes as usual. Food was wasted immorally in army establishments. There were places where food grains were stored in warehouses, but the poor were starving to death. Even the Assembly, where peoples' representatives congregated and deliberated the unprecedented food crisis, also turned a deaf ear to the proposal of declaring a 'famine' and refused to apply the 'famine code' in the province, which could have given the poor some relief.[67]

Such schism within society betrayed lack of compassion and lack of courage in standing united against the ruling regimes at

[67] On 20th September 1943 the Bengal Legislative Assembly rejected a cut motion brought by Rai HN Chaudhury of Bose Group of Congress to raise a discussion about the government's failure to declare 'famine code' in Bengal by 115 to 69 votes. It was an indication of lack of empathy for poor among majority numbers of people's representatives. IAR 1943, Vol 2, p 153-4.

Calcutta and Delhi. Such moral terpitude could be attributed to the political climate of communalism and opportunism that existed at the time. The League ministry was its architect. The British wrath against Bengalis, especially in the aftermath of the Quit India movement, gave opportunities to the League ministry to abuse power and spread tyranny amongst common people, Hindus or Muslims whosoever were its political rivals. There was pervasive fear in the rural masses about the ruling regimes. It probably explains why the remaining 75 to 80 per cent people did not come forward to save the unfortunate famine victims. Instead, they took the quiet path of self-preservation by availing quota allotments or buying rice from the black market. A careful perusal of the famine of 1943 show that if the dead left the world with loads of complaints against the heartlessness and cowardice of society, the survivors were probably left with still bitter feelings.

They were eyewitnesses to the ordeals of dear ones. Many were also witness to extreme indignities with which the corpses were dealt with. Many were rendered so destitute that they neither had the physical strength and financial means to perform the last rites for their dead relatives, nor did the government take proper steps for proper disposal of these bodies. Even in the city of Calcutta numerous dead bodies were stacked and subjected to mass funerals. In villages, bodies were thrown into canals and waterways or left in the fields to be devoured by jackals, dogs and vultures. Numerous cases were reported in newspapers of these animals dragging dying people, or beginning to bite their bodies even before the last breath left them.

Therefore, to the survivors constituting supposedly about one-fifth of the total population of Bengal society must have appeared as heartless as stone, and patently unjust. Large percentages of them were weakened due to prolonged starvation or illness, incapable of pursuing any productive means of livelihood. The abject selfishness of some sections of society tends to destroy the foundation of a healthy society by killing mutual trust, compassion and many other human values. The impact of the famine of 1943 on Bengalis must have been similar, though this aspect remains insufficiently investigated.

Damage to Bengal's Social Fabric

We can make a reasonable guess about the severity of damage done to Bengali society on the basis of perceptions of a couple of important persons. The admission by then Bengal Governor Richard Casey is significant in this regard. The IAR was critical of how the politicians of Muslim League in Bengal exploited their position as upholders of the Nazimuddin ministry to destroy 'administrative and social life' in the province. Significantly, it observed that 'It is not possible to have details of these nefarious activities recorded in official publications....'[68]

Casey ought to have been aware of the ignominious role played by the British regime in the whole episode. In the light of Churchill's turnaround and under Wavell's direction he was, obviously, trying to repair the damage done to Bengal. By this time, however, epidemic management posed a bigger threat than the food crisis. The situation with regard to tackling of diseases continued to deteriorate. In that still gloomy atmosphere, Casey, in his radio broadcast on 1 April 1944, observed how the enormity of the tragedy had 'darkened the minds of tens of millions of Bengalis who cannot help themselves' and admitted that the government had the moral responsibility to do its utmost for these poor millions.[69] Significantly, Casey stressed

[68] IAR 1944, Vol 1, p 93.

[69] Ghosh, p141.

upon the need for moral rehabilitation even more, saying in his address, 'What of those whose minds are still darkened by tragedy, who have lost confidence in themselves, in the future, and in our ability to prevent what is happening again?'

Then he sought to assure people: 'I look to the future with confidence and I appeal for confidence in the administration of which I am the head – for confidence in the determination and ability of [the] government to prevent another catastrophe...'[70].

Intriguingly, the League government which ought to have been more concerned about people of Bengal and through which, Casey should have been able to bring back the confidence in people, was still blinded by its communal goals. Viceroy Wavell raised the issue of bringing the province under Section 93[71] once or twice, but HMG was not interested. The League ministry was allowed to remain in office. This in fact impeded the task of moral rehabilitation in Bengal.

Kali Charan Ghosh, himself a Bengali, had intimate knowledge of the deadly blow the famine had delivered to Bengalis as a people. In his book, he wrote about the impact in these words: 'The famine of 1943 leaves its deepest and longest scar on human society. While the marks of every other form of injury will disappear with the passage of a few years, it will take many long decades to rehabilitate the social order that has been shaken to the very foundations.'

The Wound of Famine was Never Addressed

The legendary nineteenth century renaissance of Bengal had not only nourished Bengali society, helping it excel in

---

[70] Ibid, p141

[71] Under Section 93 of the Govt of India Act 1935, the Governor of a province could, under specified circumstances, assume and exercise any or all of the powers vested in or exercisable by any provisional body or authorities.

diverse fields of human attainments, but Bengal also acted as the beacon of light for the whole of India and motivated Indians in general in striving to rediscover their civilisational heritage. Statesman-politician G G Gokhale's much quoted statement says it all: 'What Bengal thinks today, India thinks tomorrow.'

It may be argued that the renaissance that started with Raja Rammohan Roy and continued with luminaries such as Bankim Chandra Chattopadhyay, Debendranath Tagore, Ishwar Chandra Vidyasagar, Keshab Chandra Sen, Ramakrishna Paramhamsa, Swami Vivekananda, Rabindranath Tagore, to name only some of them, stumbled during the famine of 1943.

Failure of Wider Society to do a Collective Catharsis

Was there any significant collective initiative to repair the damage suffered by the wider society in the post-famine Bengal? Does not seem so. The social behaviour of people during the famine had created several fault lines in Bengali society based on communal, occupational, economic and other factors. It was necessary for various erring sections of the society to admit their mistakes that contributed to the humongous suffering of the vulnerable section of society and try rapprochement. A collective catharsis led by social thinkers, litterateurs and other enlightened members was imperative. There is no evidence that enough was done towards this goal.

Instead, it is apparent that society continued to remain in a denial mode. Immediately following the famine, the attitude was as if society's progress would resume and remain unbroken if everyone pretended the Famine of 1943 was a 'non-event'. This was the outcome of both abject selfishness and short-sightedness.

Collective Amnesia about Famine – Political Mischief?

In this context, it may be instructive to contrast the Bengal famine of 1943 to the Ukraine famine in 1933-34. That famine was also manmade and the consequences of heartless politics by Stalinist USSR. However, unlike Bengal, it continues to be a raw wound in the collective psyche of the Ukrainian people till date. The entire Ukrainian people have consistently considered the '33-'34 famine as an act of 'genocide' and have been striving to persuade the UN to declare it as such. The Ukrainians commemorate last Friday of November each year to remember their innocent ancestors, who were victims of that Stalinist holocaust.

Such striking differences in approaches by two collectives of humanity with regard to two manmade famines in Ukraine and Bengal need study. Churchill alone could not have caused death to millions unless there was complicity on the part of the ruling regime in Bengal. In a nutshell, the famine of 1943 needs to be revisited, keeping in view the political angle.

The political factors in turn are to be studied holistically by juxtaposing British with domestic politics. It is only then that humanity in general and Bengalis in particular will be able to draw the right lessons from that terrible tragedy. *Future research in the 1943 Bengal famine must inquire more deeply into its political causes, including domestic politics.* If this famine, despite causing such massive annihilation of human lives and destroying the core fabrics of a glorious society, vanishes from the peoples' collective memory, it is reasonable to infer, this has happened due to political reasons and later-day political influences over thought-leaders, intellectuals, and academia.

Syama Prasad's book is probably a precious piece of political writing on the Bengal Famine of 1943 and an account indispensable to researchers and all those interested to get an insight into that famine.

Final Words

As we conclude this book, we examine the question whether the massive death toll in 1943-44 in Bengal can be called a 'genocide'. The killing by starvation and destitution of millions have rare precedents. Prima facie, the scale of destruction, massacre, and a substantial annihilation of an entire generation of Bengali society and value system evokes a sense of the event not being short of a genocide.

The Oxford English dictionary meaning of 'genocide' was earlier mentioned in a footnote. A more technical approach follows: According to Article II of Genocide Convention 1948 of the United Nations, the term 'genocide' encompasses a set of actions (any of them) committed with an intent to destroy, in whole or in part, a national, ethnic, racial or religious group. The actions include inter alia (a) killing members of the group; (b) causing serious bodily or mental harm to members of the group; (c) deliberately inflicting on the group conditions of life calculated to bring about its physical destructions in whole or in part; (d) imposing measures intended to prevent births within the group; (e) forcibly transferring children of the group to another group.

A careful examination of the course of events during 1943-44 reveals that conditions in the form of non-availability of food were imposed on millions of people deliberately, which resulted in massive starvation, death of millions from hunger and starvation-related diseases, causing physical debilities to a few more million, and sending tens of millions of survivours to the abyss of pessimism. More than a quarter of the entire population of Bengal either perished or turned victims of debilities, destitution and depression. There were also some reports of inter-group and inter-provincial transfer of orphan children by luring them with food. Further, these atrocities were imposed on the people of Bengal alone, while the rest of India remained unaffected.

It also needs to be added that the damages to Bengalis as a race were not confined to what have been listed above. The famine did them incalculable and long-lasting harm socially, economically, politically, and culturally. Hundreds of thousand of families were evicted from villages – their homestead since time immemorial that gave them livelihood, peace and stability. Communal divisions were sharpened and mistrust between rich and poor took firm roots. Over the next few years, the communal divide aggravated and brought about partition, ejecting millions of more families from their village roots permanently. The political importance of the race in the country's political sphere dwindled, and their leadership position in national life in the cultural and spiritual sphere (as was the case in the wake of the Bengal renaissance) was gradually lost. In summary, the onslaught began to reduce a glorious race and society to the periphery of national life. These long-term injuries which left a race bleeding and bruised constitute powerful collateral evidence.

Syama Prasad did not use the word 'genocide' in his book. Incidentally, the term was not in currency then. It was coined by a Polish lawyer R Lemkin in 1944 and began to be talked about widely after the UN convention on genocide in 1948. However, while commenting on the Woodhead Commission Report in a later edition of his book, Syama Prasad had observed the fact of 'bayapak narahatya (ব্যাপক নরহত্যা)', which may be translated as 'killings of people on a massive scale' or 'killing *en masse*. It may be argued that his apprehension of what was happening in Bengal during the famine was similar to what the term 'genocide' implied and described.

Reverting back to the technicalities of the term, another objection against using it in relation to the Bengal famine of 1943-44 may be raised on the ground that the element of 'intention' behind the holocaust cannot be proved. However, a chain of events between 1942-44 are powerful circumstantial evidence proving that *intention*. These include *inter alia* toppling of a popular ministry on the eve of the famine using unconstitutional means, confiscating boats, removal of rice from a wide stretch of land, food drive, atrocities on cyclone-affected famine victims of Midnapore and preventing relief agencies from providing them help, continuous export and procurement of rice for the armed forces, employees of the government and large factories far in excess of need from the rice-scarce province, repeatedly rejecting offers of food help from rest of the world, gagging of the media, throwing famine victims out of Calcutta by issuing an ordinance, and more. There are too many acts of commission to be dismissed as coincidences. On the contrary, these actions suggest a design and together they constitute a chain of evil deeds and lend credence to the existence of specific *intention*.

In addition to the above, de-classification of British government papers of the famine period has begun to provide documentary evidence of the presence of the element of 'intention' to a considerable extent. The task of finding more evidences rests on future researchers.

The Bengal famine of 1943 must, therefore, be revisited objectively and with the aid of additional facts. It can not only settle the question of genocide conclusively, but also encourage a new stream of research on his particular famine's social impact. With regard to the latter i.e., impact on society, the study may kindle interest in doing similar exercises with respect to other major manmade famines in other parts of the world as well. As a matter of fact, approaching and re-investigating manmade famines in terms of social impact can contribute to the body of knowledge in the realm of social science. Hopefully, Syama Prasad's book re-appearing before the global body of readers after nearly eight decades will not only help identify the guilty of the Bengal famine but also educate mankind in general.

Appendix I

Relief Work by Bengal Relief Committee

The committee has collected 2,742,363 taka[1] 0 anna[2] and 4 pie[3] and procured the following goods:

Food grains 54,447 *maunds*[4] and 5 *seer*[5]-

Genji[6] 4,526 dozens

Dhuti[7] & Saree[8] 8,737 pairs

Blouse 54 pcs

Markin[9] 200 *thans*[10]

---

1 Taka is the Bengali term for Rupee viz., the Indian currency of that time

2 An unit of currency equal to 1/16th of a Taka i.e.,1 'taka' consisted of 16 anaa.

3 One pie was one fourth of an anaa

4 Unit of measurement of weight equal to about 37 kgs

5 Unit of measurement of weight equal to 1/40th of one *maund*

6 Undervest

7 Dhuti or Dhoti is lower garment used by Indians

8 Upper garment used by female persons

9 Simple variety of cloth

10 A roller or hard boar around which a length of woven fabric is twined

Old cloth 200 *guite*[11]
Sujni[12] 7,178 pcs
Milk 1,632 pounds
Kambal[13] 3,450 pcs
Biscuit 13 *thalia*[14]

The committee has helped the distressed persons with the following goods:

Food grains 1,43,863 *mounds* and 5 *seer*
Old cloth 54 *guite*
Dhuti & *Saree* 1,54,804 pcs
Milk 1,632 pounds
Markin 1,770 pcs
Biscuit 13 *thalia*
Sujni 7,178 pcs
Milk 1,632 pounds
Gur[15] 2,213 *maunds* 11& 1/2 seer
Kambal 68,539 pcs

Half pants 2,760pcs
Genji 61,692 pcs
Kameez[16] 10,000 pcs
Blouse 4,754 pcs

The above account only relates to the food grains sent by the donors and quantities purchased in Calcutta. Other than

---

[11] A large bundle; a bale
[12] Bed sheet
[12] Warm sheet
[13] Blanket
[14] Bag
[15] Jaggery
[16] long shirt

the above the committee has purchased large quantities of food grains for distribution or sale at low prices at various mofussil centres. The accounts relating to the same has not yet been received.

The committee has incurred expenses under various heads as follows:

Distribution of food and sale of food grains at a loss, and distribution of milk 11,17,453/0/6 *pie.*

Help to Sanskrit Pundits and students (as per the wishes of the donors) 55,263*taka* 12 *annas*; Reconstruction plan 20,407 *taka* 12 *anna.*

Cloth 4,10,834 *taka* 10 *anna*

Tendering monetary help to some relief samitis 1,70,866 *taka* 3 *pie*

Treatment 1,19,406 *taka* 8 *anna*

Help to students 6,003 *taka* 8 *anna*

Home for children 36,105 *taka* 8 ½ *anna*

Transport fare, salary to people, publicity expenses, postal stamp, expenses for telegraph and telephone 12,694 *taka* 8 *anna*

Supply of seeds and fertilisers to farmers 5,122 *taka* 8 *anna* 6 *pie*

Student homes 18,461 *taka* 10 *anna* 6 *pie*

Balance 7,69,718 *taka* 5 *anna* 10 *pie*

Appendix II

Relief Work by Bengal Provincial Hindu Mahasabha Relief Committee

Till 29 February 1944, the Committee has collected a total of 761,035 *taka* 5 *anna* 9 *pie* and spent 638,136 *taka* 10 *anna* 4 *pie*. This money was spent on various heads as follows:

Purchase of food grains 2,99,612 *taka* 5 *anna*

Purchase of thread etc 9,440 *taka*

Purchase of cloth and *kambal* etc 64,247 *taka* 5 *anna* 10 *pie*

Interest and bank charges 907 *taka* 10 anna

Help rendered to teachers, pundits of toles[1] and middle classes 19,668 *taka*

Warehouse rent 250 *taka*

For inspection etc 2,500 *taka*

Personal assistance 7,650 *taka*

---

[1] Sanskrit school

Help to political prisoners 35,712 *taka* 8 *anna*

Assistance to various Seva-Samitis[2] 1,70,919 *taka* 6 *pie*

Till 31 March 1944 following quantities of food grains have been procured and spent:

Quantity bought 13,387 *maunds* (5139 gunny bags)

Quantity received by way of help 22,289 *maunds* (8891 gunny bags)

Total 35,676 *maunds*(14,030 gunny bags)

Quantity distributed 32,445 *maunds* (12,777 gunny bags)

Balance quantity 3,231 *maunds* (1,253 gunny bags)

---

2 Service Organizations

References

Panchasher Manwantar: Shri Shyamaprasad Mukhopadhyay: 2nd edition; 1944; Bengal Press: Calcutta.

Famines in Bengal 1770-1943: Kali Charan Ghosh: National Council of Education, Bengal: 2015.

The Viceroy's Journal: Edited by Penderel Moon: OUP: London: 1973.

Communism and Nationalism in Colonial India 1939-45, DN Gupta, Sage Publication India Pvt Ltd New Delhi, 2008.

Prosperity and Misery in Modern Bengal: The Famine of 1943-44: Paul Robert Greenough; Oxford University Press (2018).

Hungry Nation: Food, Famine, and the Making of Modern India: Benjamin Robert Siegel: Cambridge University Press (2018).

Eating People is Wrong, and other Essays on Famine, Its Past and its Future: Cormac O Grada; Princeton University Press (2015).

Hungry Bengal: War, Famine and the End of Empire: Janam Mukherjee; Oxford University Press (2015).

Rashtrasangram O Panchasher Manwantar: Shyamaprasad Mukhopadhyay: Mitra O Ghosh; 1st edition 1998, Reprint 2018.

Assembly Proceedings Official Report, Bengal Legislative Assembly, Sixteenth Session 1943: Bengal Government Press, Calcutta.

Assembly Proceedings Official Report, Bengal Legislative Assembly, Seventeenth Session 1943: Bengal Government Press, Calcutta.

Assembly Proceedings Official Report, Bengal Legislative Assembly, Eighteenth Session 1944: Bengal Government Press, Calcutta.

Selected Speeches in Bengal Legislative Assembly 1937-1947: Dr Syamaprasad Mookerjee: Ed. D. Reena Bhaduri: Asutosh Mookerjee Memorial Institute, Kolkata.

The Indian Annual Register: Volume I, Jan-June 1943: Ed: NN Mitra: The Annual Register Office, Calcutta.

The Indian Annual Register: Volume II, July-Dec 1943: Ed: NN Mitra: The Annual Register Office, Calcutta.

The Indian Annual Register: Volume I, Jan-June 1944: Ed: NN Mitra: The Annual Register Office, Calcutta.

Modern Review: Volume LXXIV No 5 Whole No 443 November 1943: The Modern Review Office, Calcutta: 1943.

Modern Review: Volume LXXV No 3 Whole No 447 March 1944: The Modern Review Office, Calcutta: 1944.

Churchill's Secret War: The British Empire and the Ravaging of India during World War II: Madhusree Mukerjee: Tranquebar.

Contemporary Famine Analysis: Olivier Rubin: Springer (2016).

Three Famines: Starvation and Politics: Thomas Keneally*:* *Public Affairs*(2011).

On the Impending Bengal Famine: Henry B Frere: Read Brooke Design (2010).

Bengal Tiger and British Lion: An Account of the Bengal Famine of 1943: Richard Stevenson: Geoffrey Moorhouse; Penguin: New Delhi: 1971.

The Political Economy of Hunger: Volume 1: Entitlement and Well-being: Jean D & Amartya Sen: Oxford University Press: (1989).

Communalism in Bengal: From Famine to Noakhali, 1943-47: Rakesh Batabyal: Sage Publications (2005).

Towards Independence: 1940-47:Memoirs of an Indian Civil Servant: Dr Asok Mitra: Popular Prakashan.

Poverty and Famine: An Essay on Entitlement and Deprivation: Amartya Sen: Oxford University Press (1981).

Bengal Famine of 1943: A manmade tragedy: J N Uppal: Atmaram (1984).

The Sickle and the Crescent: Communists, Muslim League and India's Partition: Sunanda Sanyal & Soumya Basu: Frontpage (2011).

The Bengal Famine and the New Viceroyalty, 15 June 1943-31, August 1944: The Transfer of Power 1942-7, Volume 4: India Office: HMSO (1970).

Bengal Famine of 1943: The American Response: MS Venkataramani: Vikas Publishing House Pvt Ltd (1973).

Bengal Famine (1943): As revealed in a Survey of the Destitutes in Calcutta: Tarak Chandra Das: University of Calcutta (1949).

archive.orghttp://www.historydiscussion.net/british-india/useful-notes-on-the-industrial-policy-of-british-in-india/646

http://sanhati.com/articles/347/

http://www.doccentre.org/docsweb/LABOURLAWS/labourhistory.htm

https://www.marxists.org/history/international/comintern/sections/britain/periodicals/communist_review/1922/05/indian_labour_mvt.htm

https://www.jagranjosh.com/general-knowledge/history-of-the-working-class-movement-in-british-india-1518007920-1

https://shodhganga.inflibnet.ac.in bitstream/10603/137004/5/05_chapter_02.pdf

http://cpiml.org/library/communist-movement-in-india/introduction-communist-movement-in-india/cpi-leads-workers-struggles/

https://ia801601.us.archive.org/31/items/in.ernet.dli.2015.32604/2015.32604.Bengal-Legislative-Assembly-Proceedings-1943-Vol65_text.pdf [Assembly Proceedings, Official Report, Bengal Legislative Assembly, Seventeenth Session, Vol. LXVI-No1].

https://ia601601.us.archive.org/31/items/in.ernet.dli.2015.32604/2015.32604.Bengal-Legislative-Assembly-Proceedings-1943-Vol65_text.pdf [Assembly Proceedings, Official Report, Bengal Legislative Assembly, Sixteenth Session, Vol. LXV].

https://ia801601.us.archive.org/8/items/in.ernet.dli.2015.32609/2015.32609.Bengal-Legislative-Assembly-Proceedings-

1944-Vol67-Pt3_text.pdf [Assembly Proceedings, Official Report, Bengal Legislative Assembly, Eighteenth Session, Vol. LXVII-No3].

https://shodhganga.inflibnet.ac.in/bitstream/10603/165661/

7/07_chapter%204.pdf

Internet Archive

The Indian Annual Register: January-June, 1943: Vol I: The Annual Register Office: Calcutta.

The Indian Annual Register: July-December, 1943: Vol II: The Annual Register Office: Calcutta.

The Indian Annual Register: January-June, 1944: Vol I: The Annual Register Office: Calcutta.

Translator–editor
Sudip Kar Purkayastha

Sudip Kar Purkayastha is an author and columnist. He is a Ph D (Arts) from Jadavpur University, Kolkata, and has an MBA & Post Graduate Diplomas in Journalism and Bank Management. A former banker, he held senior management responsibilities in a large public sector bank.

Purkayastha's last book, *On the Road to Freedom: Footprints on Indian History* was a two- volume work published by Vitasta that chronicled the pre-independence Indian history (1877-1947) with remarkable objectivity. Several of his articles on politics, history & finance have been published in leading dailies & magazines. Some of them, including his biographical piece *'Syama Prasad – Life and Times'*, are a part of Indian Parliamentary Documentation. Purkayastha was also the founder editor of a journal on 'bank marketing'.

His writings bear unmistakable marks of extensive research, deep analysis, scholarship and lucid presentation.